VISUAL QUICKSTART GUIDE

Premiere 5.1

for Macintosh and Windows

Antony Bolante

 Peachpit Press

Visual QuickStart Guide
Premiere 5.1 for Macintosh and Windows
Antony Bolante

Peachpit Press
1249 Eighth Street
Berkeley, CA 94710
(510) 524-2178
(800) 283-9444
(510) 542-2221 (fax)

Find us on the World Wide Web at
www.peachpit.com

Peachpit Press is a division of Addison Wesley Longman

Copyright © 1999 by Antony Bolante

Editor: Clifford Colby
Production Coordinator: Kate Reber
Copyeditor: Kathy Simpson
Compositor: Melanie Haage
Cover design: The Visual Group
Indexer: Rebecca Plunket

Notice of rights

Trademarks

Notice of liability

ISBN: 0-201-35475-6

9 8 7 6 5 4 3 2

Printed and bound in the United States of America

Dedication

To my parents, Gaspar and Marlene Bolante.

Thank You.

My family, whose love spans years and miles.

Atsuko Yamagishi, for her love, patience, and support.

Grant Balfour, for planting the tree.

Ying Sheng Lin, for helping with the Windows screen shots.

The folks at Video Arts, coworkers I can call friends.

Hannah Onstad Latham, for encouraging me to undertake this book.

Cliff Colby, Kathy Simpson, Kate Reber, Marjorie Baer, and all of the folks at Peachpit Press, who are the pit crew of the publishing world.

TABLE OF CONTENTS

	Introduction	**xiii**
Chapter 1:	**Premiere Basics**	**1**
Chapter 2:	**Starting a Project**	**5**
	Beginning New Projects	6
	Selecting Presets	7
	Specifying General Settings	8
	Specifying Video Settings	9
	Specifying Audio Settings	11
	Setting Keyframe and Rendering Options	12
	Saving and Loading Settings	14
	Using Suggested Project Settings	15
	Saving and Autosaving Projects	16
	Opening Existing Projects	18
	Locating Missing and Offline Files	19
	Importing Clips	22
	Importing Digital Audio	24
	Importing Still Images	26
	Organizing Clips	29
	Customizing the Project, Bin, and Library Windows	31
	Managing Clips	35
	Creating a Leader	37
	Customizing Premiere's Interface	39
	Using Palettes	40
	Using Shortcuts and the Commands Palette	42
	Correcting Mistakes	44
Chapter 3:	**Working with Clips**	**45**
	Understanding the Monitor Window	46
	Modifying the Monitor Window	48
	Viewing Clips	50
	Working with Still-Image Clip Windows	52
	Using Audio Clips	54
	Using Monitor Controllers	56
	Cueing Source and Program Views	58
	Using Markers	60

Working with In Points and Out Points 65

Using a Clip More Than Once in a Program 68

Working with Subclips 69

Using the Info Palette 72

Understanding Clip Properties 73

Chapter 4: Creating a Program   75

Drag and Drop Vs. Monitor Controls 76

Drag-and-Drop Editing 79

Editing with the Monitor Controls 82

Chapter 5: Editing in the Timeline   89

Customizing the Timeline's Appearance 90

Customizing the Time Ruler 92

Adding, Deleting, and Naming Tracks 93

Monitoring Tracks 95

Locking and Unlocking Tracks 96

Expanding and Collapsing Tracks 97

Displaying Shy Tracks 98

Opening a Clip in the Timeline 99

Getting Around the Timeline 100

Selecting Clips in the Timeline 103

Deleting Clips from the Timeline 104

Enabling and Disabling Clips 105

Locking and Unlocking Clips 106

Using Linked Clips 107

Moving Clips in the Timeline 108

Using Snap to Edges 111

Splitting a Clip 113

Cutting, Copying, and Pasting Clips 115

Chapter 6: Refining the Program   119

Using Timeline Trimming Vs. Trim View 120

Trimming in the Timeline 121

Making Ripple and Rolling Edits 123

Making Slip and Slide Edits 125

Using Trim View 127

Working with Links 132

Keeping Synch 135

Chapter 7: Transitions   137

Transitions Palette 138

A/B Roll vs. Single-Track Transitions 141

Expanded-Track Transitions 142

Collapsed-Track Transitions 144

Default Transitions 146

Transitions Settings 147
Special Transitions 150
Virtual Clips 151

Chapter 8: Previewing Transitions and Effects 153
Preview Effects 154
Previewing Files 156

Chapter 9: Mixing Audio 159
Adjusting Gain 160
Fading 162
Creating Cross-Fades 165
Cross-Fading Audio Linked to Video 166
Panning and Stereo 168
Audio Filters 170
Using Audio Filters 172

Chapter 10: Working with Filters 173
Keyframes 176
Filter Order 178
Filters and Image Size 179

Chapter 11: Creating Titles 181
The Title Window and Menus 182
Title-Window Options 184
Background Clips 187
Objects and Attributes 189
Draft Mode 190
Text Objects 191
Text Attributes 194
Kerning 198
Leading 199
Rolls and Crawls 200
Graphic Objects 202
Objects 208
Drop Shadows 211
Color, Opacity, and Gradients 212
The Color Picker 216

Chapter 12: Superimposing Clips 217
Track Hierarchy 218
Fading and Keying 219
The Fade Control 220
Keying 223
Keying Controls 224
Luminance-Based Keys 227

Chrominance Keys 229
Alpha Keys 231
Matte Keys 233
Garbage Mattes 236

Chapter 13: Motion Setting **237**
Using Motion Settings 238
Working with Keyframes (Again) 239
Setting Keyframes 241
Setting Keyframe Attributes 244
Using Other Motion-Setting Options 248
Saving and Loading Motion Settings 251

Chapter 14: Creating Output **253**
Exporting File Types 254
Creating a Movie 255
Using Special Processing Options 257
Working with GIF Sequences and
    Animated GIFs 261
Recording to Tape 263
Creating Clip Sequences 265
Exporting QuickTime Fast Start Movies 266
Exporting Still-Image Sequences 267
Exporting Filmstrip Files 269
Exporting Still Images 272
Exporting Edit Decision Lists 274

Chapter 15: Capture **275**
Preparation for Capture 276
The Digitizing Process 277
Scratch Disks 279
Capture Settings 280
Optional Settings 282
Hardware-Specific Settings 283
Basic Capture 284
Device Control 285
Capture with Device Control 286
Batch Lists 288
Batch-List Settings 292
Batch Capture 293
Manual Timecode Settings 295
Analog Audio Capture 297

Chapter 16: Premiere Online **299**
Unused Clips 300
Trimmed Projects 301

Manual Creation of Batch Lists
for Recapturing Clips 303
Replacing Clip References 305

Chapter 17: Video and Audio Settings   307
Choosing Settings 308

Index   327

INTRODUCTION

First, let me tell you what you already know. You already know something about Adobe Premiere, or you wouldn't be holding this book. You know that it's a powerful tool for editing digital video, audio, still images, and text on a desktop computer. You just don't know how to use it. Not yet, anyway.

You might even have used previous versions of Premiere but found the latest version to be unfamiliar. Premiere 5.x represents a major overhaul from Premiere 4.x, including not only new and improved features but also a very different interface.

Whether you've chosen Premiere to create video programs for the Internet, multimedia presentations, or video broadcasts, you've chosen this book because you're eager to get started.

The Premiere Visual QuickStart Guide distills this dense, multifaceted program by providing concise explanations and plenty of illustrations. The text avoids lengthy explanations or extraneous information but doesn't hesitate to give you helpful background information.

Chapters are organized to present topics as you encounter them in a typical editing project, but the task-oriented format and thumb tabs let you jump to the topic that you need. Tasks that require special video-capture hardware are reserved for Chapters 15 and 16. The final chapter explains video and audio settings in Premiere, and also serves as a kind of handbook for digital video.

This book draws on my experience as a Premiere user and as a video postproduction professional who is familiar with a wide range of tools and technologies.

In addition to working at a video-design and editorial studio in San Francisco, I edit and teach college courses in editing and postproduction. Long before I started teaching graduate students, I earned my own MFA in film and video.

Macintosh and Windows

Premiere is widely available for both the Macintosh and Windows systems, and it functions nearly the same way on both platforms. Except where noted, the information in this book applies to both versions.

Because the differences between the two versions are mostly cosmetic, this book includes screen shots from both platforms (**Figures i.1** and **i.2**).

Key commands are expressed with the Mac conventions but can be easily translated into their Windows counterparts. Simply substitute the Windows Control key for the Mac Command key, the Windows Alt key for the Mac Option key, and the Windows Enter key for the Mac Return key. Otherwise, the book assumes that you are familiar with your operating system and can use its conventions to make selections, access menu options, and manage files.

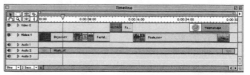

Figure i.1 A screen shot from a Macintosh system...

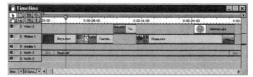

Figure i.2 ...and the same window on a Windows system.

System Requirements

Requirements for Macintosh

◆ PowerPC processor.

◆ Apple System 7.5.5 or later (or System 7.5.1, if you're using Radius Video Vision capture hardware).

◆ 16 MB of available RAM.

◆ 30 MB of hard disk space for installation.

Requirements for Windows

◆ Intel Pentium processor.

◆ Microsoft Windows 95 or later, or Windows NT 4.0

◆ 32 MB of RAM.

◆ 60 MB of hard disk space for installation (30 MB for application).

◆ 256-color video display adapter.

PREMIERE BASICS

Premiere is *digital nonlinear editing software*. A breakdown of this description can give you clues about the overall editing process.

Digital. Premiere manipulates digital media: digital video and audio, scanned images, and digitally created artwork and animation stored in several formats. Strictly speaking, Premiere doesn't convert analog video and audio to digital form, although it does contain controls that work in conjunction with built-in or add-on hardware.

Nonlinear. You can use Premiere to arrange the digital source files sequentially, add transitions and effects, and create graphics and 2-D animation. Editing in Premiere is described as being nonlinear because your media are not constrained to a linear medium such as videotape. In other words, you can instantly access any source clip without shuttling tape, and you can change the sequence of clips in the program without rerecording. Because Premiere works with graphical references to the source files, and not with the files themselves, digital editing is also called *nondestructive editing*.

Software. As a software-only package, Premiere can import and export digital files. To acquire and export material to and from videotape, however, Premiere relies on built-in or add-on hardware.

Workflow and Editing Strategy

A successful project depends on good planning. The editing strategy that you develop always proceeds from the same question: What is my output goal?

Often, you must reconcile your output goal with the capabilities and limitations of your system. These factors help determine your postproduction path as well as whether you perform offline editing or online editing (**Figure 1.1**).

Online editing results in the final video program. You can online-edit in Premiere if your system is capable of acquiring, processing, and delivering your program at final-output quality. The higher the image quality, however, the greater the system requirements. To achieve your output goal, you may need a fast processor; a high-end capture card; and large, fast hard drives. If your system doesn't meet your output requirements, use another system for the online edit and use Premiere for your offline edit.

Put simply, *offline editing* prepares projects for an online edit. In an offline edit, you edit with low-quality versions of the video. Rather than produce a final program at output quality, you produce an accurate draft version.

The completed offline edit can produce a kind of transcription of all your edits, known as an *edit decision list* (EDL). You can use the EDL and source tapes to re-create your program quickly and easily in a traditional tape-based online-editing suite. You could also use your offline edit to conform with a film edit.

Alternatively, you can offline- and online-edit on the same system. Because lower-quality clips are smaller, more of them fit on your hard drive, and your computer can process them faster. For the online edit, you can recapture only the clips that you used in the

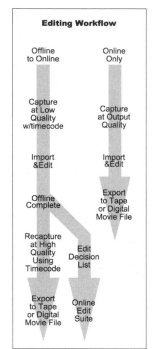

Figure 1.1 This flow chart outlines the typical online and offline editing strategies.

Figure 1.2 The Premiere interface at a glance.

program at the final-output quality. Premiere automatically uses the high-quality clips in your final program, and no reediting is required.

Before you can offline-edit, however, you must make sure that the clips in the program have timecode that matches the timecode of the source tapes. As explained in Chapter 17, timecode numbers identify each frame of video on a source tape. Premiere and other video equipment use timecode to track each edit in the offline edit and accurately re-create them in the online edit. Without timecode, an EDL would be meaningless, and recapturing clips would be impossible.

Interface at a Glance

Rather than take a window-by-window, button-by-button approach, this book addresses each window and tool as dictated by the editing process. Nevertheless, an overview of the interface can help orient you before you take a closer look (**Figure 1.2**):

◆ **Project and Bin windows**: list and organize the source clips that you want to use.

◆ **Monitor window:** displays the source clips in the left pane and the clips in the program in the right pane. It also contains playback and editing controls, and doubles as the trimming-mode window.

◆ **Timeline:** graphically represents your program as clips arranged in tracks.

◆ **Palettes**: (Information, Navigator, Transitions, and Commands) appear in tabbed windows and provide useful tool sets.

STARTING A PROJECT

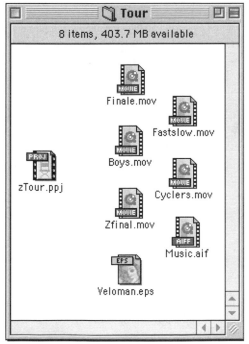

Figure 2.1 A Premiere project refers to files on the hard drive.

When you're editing with Adobe Premiere, you're creating a detailed set of instructions, called a *project* (**Figure 2.1**).

A project lists all the clips that you intend to use in your edited video program. It also contains all your editing decisions, including the arrangement of the clips, transitions, audio levels, filters, and other effects.

A project can be compared with a recipe or a musical score. Just as sheet music refers to instruments and indicates when they should play, the project refers to media files and when they should play. A project doesn't contain the files themselves—only references to those files, called *clips*. As a result, you never alter the source files directly.

Because it is simply a detailed set of instructions, a project is a small file, usually less than 1 MB. The source files, on the other hand, tend to take up a lot more drive space. Similarly, you can slip sheet music into your pocket, but the entire orchestra is considerably more bulky.

In this chapter, you learn to work with projects, import and organize clips, customize your work space, and correct (and avoid) mistakes.

Beginning New Projects

You can begin a new project when you start Premiere or while Premiere is already running. You can have only one project open at a time, however.

Figure 2.2 Double-click the Premiere icon or alias to launch Premiere.

To start a new project:

1. *Do one of the following:*

 ◆ Double-click the Premiere icon or its alias **(Figure 2.2)**.

 ◆ With Premiere running, choose File > New > Project **(Figure 2.3)**.

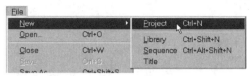

Figure 2.3 Choose File > New > Project to start a new project.

 If an unsaved project is open, you are prompted to save it.

2. Choose Project Presets, as discussed later in this chapter.

To launch Premiere without starting a new project:

1. Double-click the Premiere icon or its alias.

 The Project Settings window appears.

2. Click Cancel.

 Premiere starts without opening a project. From this point, you can open a new or existing project, or use one of Premiere's features that doesn't require an open project.

✔ Tip

 ■ You don't have to open a project to capture clips, open and view clips, get properties for a clip, use the Data Rate Analyzer, or batch-process clips.

Figure 2.4 The Settings pull-down menu allows you to choose options in any of five categories.

Selecting Presets

When you start a new project, Premiere immediately confronts you with a daunting number of settings. Some settings control the attributes of captured clips (see Chapter 15) and the final rendered movie (see Chapter 14). This chapter deals with the settings that determine how Premiere presents your program while you edit. These project settings do not affect the qualities of the source clips or the final movie.

At the top of the Project Settings dialog box is a pull-down menu that allows you to view the five categories of settings: General, Video, Audio, Keyframe and Rendering Options, and Capture (**Figure 2.4**). This chapter deals with the first four categories, leaving capture settings for Chapter 15.

Though this chapter outlines how to choose project settings, it doesn't attempt to fully explain each one. If you are new to digital video, look at Chapter 17 for a more detailed explanation of each setting. But even if you make a wrong choice or change your mind, you can change the settings at any time.

Generally, you want to specify project settings that allow you to edit and view your work quickly and easily, based partly on your computer's capability to process and play back video and audio. Often, you set the project to play back at a relatively low quality, so that your computer can process edits and effects faster. If you decide to record the program to videotape directly from the timeline, you specify settings that match the output quality you want.

Specifying General Settings

The general settings dictate the basic properties of the program, including the way that Premiere processes video, the timebase, the time count, and advanced settings provided by third-party manufacturers. The general settings also displays a summary of the current settings.

To specify general settings:

1. *Do one of the following:*

   ◆ In the Project Settings window, choose General from the top pull-down menu.

   ◆ Choose Project > Settings > General (**Figure 2.5**).

   The Project Settings window displays the general settings (**Figure 2.6**).

2. From the Editing Mode pull-down menu, choose a video format (or architecture).

3. From the Timebase pull-down menu, choose a timebase.

4. From the Time Display pull-down menu, choose a time count.

5. If you are using third-party hardware, such as a capture card, click the Advanced Settings button.

6. In the Current Settings window, view a summary of the current settings to determine whether you need to change other settings.

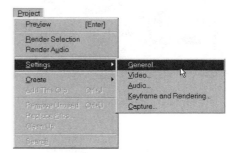

Figure 2.5 Use the Settings pull-down menu, or choose Project > Settings > General.

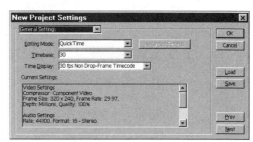

Figure 2.6 The general settings.

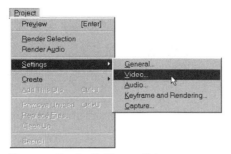

Figure 2.7 Use the Settings pull-down menu, or choose Project > Settings > Video.

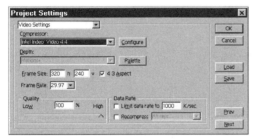

Figure 2.8 The video settings.

Specifying Video Settings

Video settings determine the compressor, picture quality, color depth, and frame size of the program that you play back.

To specify video settings:

1. *Do one of the following:*

   ◆ In the Project Settings window, choose Video Settings from the top pull-down menu.

   ◆ Choose Project > Settings > Video (**Figure 2.7**).

   The Project Settings window displays the video settings (**Figure 2.8**).

2. From the Compressor pull-down menu, choose a software codec.

   If you have a hardware capture card, consult the documentation included with the card to select a codec.

3. From the Depth pull-down menu, choose the color bit depth.

4. If you want to make or load a color palette, click Palette.

5. In the Frame Size fields, type the pixel height and width of the project video.

6. From the Frame Rate pull-down menu, choose the rate at which the project will play back, in frames per second.

7. *Do one of the following:*

   ◆ In the Quality field, type an image quality for the specified compressor.

   ◆ Use the quality slider to set the image quality.

8. If the option is available for the specified compressor, check the Limit Data Rate checkbox, and type the upper limit of

the rate of data transfer, expressed in kilobytes per second.

9. If you choose to limit the data rate, check Recompress to ensure that Premiere processes previews at or under the specified rate (**Figure 2.9**). From the pull-down menu, choose one of the following options:

◆ Always Maintain Data Rate.

◆ Always Recompress Frames, even if they are already under the specified limit.

◆ Maintain Data Rate recompresses only frames that are above the specified limit.

Figure 2.9 If you check Recompress, choose an option from the pull-down menu.

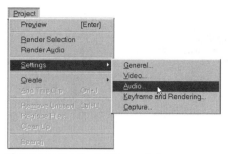

Figure 2.10 Use the Settings pull-down menu, or choose Project > Settings > Audio.

Figure 2.11 The audio settings.

Specifying Audio Settings

Audio settings control the attributes of the audio that the program plays back. When you choose Audio in the Project Settings dialog box, you can select a data rate, format, type of audio codec, audio interleave, and processing options.

To choose audio settings:

1. *Do one of the following:*

    ◆ In the Project Settings window, from the top pull-down menu, choose Audio Settings.

    ◆ Choose Project > Settings > Audio (**Figure 2.10**).

    The Project Settings window displays the audio settings (**Figure 2.11**).

2. From the Rate pull-down menu, choose a data rate for the project's audio playback.

3. From the Format pull-down menu, choose the bit depth of the audio, and specify whether it will be played back in stereo or mono.

4. From the Type pull-down menu, choose an audio codec.

5. From the Interleave pull-down menu, choose a method of inserting the audio information among video frames.

6. From the Enhanced Rate Conversion pull-down menu, choose an option that specifies how you want Premiere to convert the audio sample rate of the source to the sample rate that you specified in the project settings.

7. If you want to process audio gain levels by using a logarithmic scale, check the Logarithmic Audio Fades checkbox.

Setting Keyframe and Rendering Options

Keyframe and rendering options work in conjunction with the video settings to determine how frames of the program are processed and played back. These options become especially important when you begin previewing the program and rendering effects (covered in Chapter 8).

To choose keyframe and rendering options:

1. *Do one of the following:*

   ◆ In the Project Settings window, choose Keyframe and Rendering Options from the top pull-down menu.

   ◆ Choose Project > Settings > Keyframe and Rendering Options (**Figure 2.12**).

   The Settings window displays the keyframe and rendering options (**Figure 2.13**).

2. From the Field Settings pull-down, choose an option that specifies how Premiere should process video fields. (For more information on frames and fields, refer to Chapter 1.)

3. When you select Keyframe and Rendering Options, the Project Settings dialog box also offers you a few optional settings:

   ◆ If you want to play back program audio without the effects of applied filters, check the Ignore Audio Filters checkbox.

   ◆ To play back program video without the effects of applied filters, check the Ignore Video Filters checkbox.

Figure 2.12 Use the Settings pull-down menu, or choose Project > Settings > Keyframe and Rendering Options.

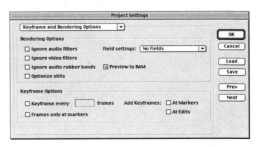

Figure 2.13 The keyframe and rendering options.

♦ To play back program audio without the effects of fading and panning, check the Ignore Audio Rubber Bands checkbox (see Chapter 9).

4. To allow Premiere to process still image files more efficiently, check the Optimize Stills checkbox. Uncheck this checkbox if exported video exhibits playback problems.

5. To set the interval of frames at which the codec inserts keyframes, check the Keyframe Every ... Frames checkbox, and enter a number. (For more information about compression and keyframes, refer to Chapter 1.)

6. To play back only frames that are located at markers in the timeline, check the Frames Only At Markers checkbox. (For more information about markers, see Chapter 3.) This option does not affect keyframes.

7. Optional: To create a keyframe for each marked frame, check the Add Keyframes At Markers checkbox. (For more information about markers, see Chapter 3.)

8. To create a keyframe for the first frame of each clip in the program, check the Add Keyframes At Edits checkbox.

SETTING KEYFRAME AND RENDERING OPTIONS

Saving and Loading Settings

Even if you're comfortable selecting project settings, making those choices still can be a chore. Fortunately, you can save different settings for different types of projects and load them as needed. Premiere also supplies several preselected settings for you to choose.

To save settings:

1. Display the Project Settings window, as described earlier in this chapter.

2. Click Save.

   The Save Project Settings dialog box appears.

3. Type a name for your settings, as well as an accurate description that summarizes your choices (**Figure 2.14**).

4. Click OK to close the Save dialog box.

5. Click OK to close the Project Settings window and start your project.

To load settings:

1. In the Project Settings window, click the Load button.

   The Load Project Settings dialog box appears (**Figure 2.15**).

2. Select the name of the settings that you want to load.

   The description saved for each setting appears in the description window.

3. Click OK to load the selected settings.

Figure 2.14 You can save your own preset settings.

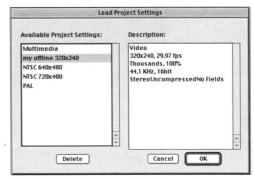

Figure 2.15 The Load Project Settings dialog box shows your settings.

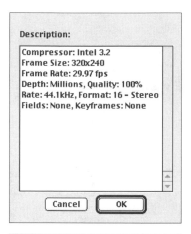

Description:

Compressor: Intel 3.2
Frame Size: 320x240
Frame Rate: 29.97 fps
Depth: Millions, Quality: 100%
Rate: 44.1kHz, Format: 16 - Stereo
Fields: None, Keyframes: None

[Cancel] [OK]

Description:

Compressor: Video
Frame Size: 320x240
Frame Rate: 29.97 fps
Depth: Thousands, Quality: 100%
Rate: 44.1kHz, Format: 16 - Stereo
Fields: None, Keyframes: None

[Cancel] [OK]

Figure 2.16 Suggested settings for a Pentium, top, and a PowerPC, bottom.

Using Suggested Project Settings

Previous versions of Adobe Premiere kindly suggested using a preset setting in case you were unsure which to choose. Although the current version provides several presets, it doesn't offer this comforting advice. Nevertheless, you may still be unsure which settings will work for you. **Figure 2.16** shows a few suggestions that work well for most systems. These suggestions should get you started until you become more at ease selecting your own settings.

Saving and Autosaving Projects

Because your project file embodies all your editing decisions, protecting it from possible mishaps is crucial. As with any important file, you should save your project often and keep backups. Premiere can help you protect your project by automatically saving it to the Project-Archive folder. In the event of a system crash or file corruption, you can retrieve one of the archived copies.

To save a project:

1. To save a project (**Figure 2.17**), *do one of the following*:

   ◆ Choose File > Save to save the project under the current name and location or to save the project for the first time.

   ◆ Choose File > Save As to save the project under a new name or location and continue working on the new copy of the project.

   ◆ Choose File > Save a Copy to save a copy of the current project and continue working on the current project.

2. If you are prompted to do so, name the project, and specify a destination (**Figure 2.18**).

3. Click OK.

To revert to the last saved version of a project:

1. Choose File > Revert (**Figure 2.19**). Premiere warns you that this operation can't be undone.

2. Click OK to confirm that you want to revert to the last saved version.

   The project returns to the state that it was in when you last saved it.

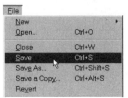

Figure 2.17 Choose Save, Save As, or Save a Copy from the File menu.

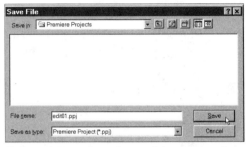

Figure 2.18 Name the project, and choose a location for it.

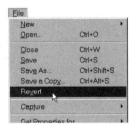

Figure 2.19 Choose Revert to go back to the last saved project.

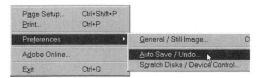

Figure 2.20 Choose File > Preferences > Auto Save/Undo.

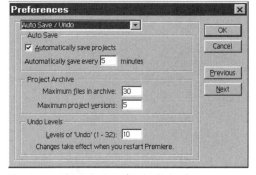

Figure 2.21 The Auto Save/Undo dialog box.

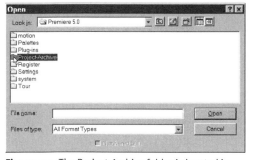

Figure 2.22 The Project-Archive folder is located in the Premiere application folder.

To set Auto Save:

1. Choose File > Preferences > Auto Save/Undo (**Figure 2.20**).

   The Auto Save/Undo dialog box opens (**Figure 2.21**).

2. Check the Automatically Save Projects checkbox, and type the time interval at which you want Premiere to save the current project.

3. In the Maximum Files to Archive field, type the number of copies of all projects that will be automatically saved in the Project-Archive folder.

   After Premiere saves the number of copies that you specified, it deletes the oldest project to make room for the newest copy.

4. In the Maximum Projects Versions field, type the number of versions of each project file that you want Premiere to auto save.

To open an archived project:

1. Choose File > Open.

   The Open dialog box appears.

2. Locate the Premiere folder, and open the Project-Archive folder (**Figure 2.22**).

3. Select the archived project that you want to use.

4. Click Open.

Opening Existing Projects

You can open projects created in Adobe Premiere 4.2 or later. You can even open Premiere projects that were created on other computer platforms, provided that you follow a few guidelines (outlined in your Adobe Premiere User Guide).

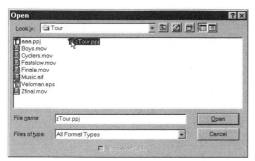

Figure 2.23 Open an existing project.

Locating Missing and Offline Files

As you learned at the beginning of this chapter, a project is simply a set of instructions that refer to files on a drive. When you open a project, Premiere looks for the files to which the project refers. If the source files have been moved or renamed since the project was last saved, Premiere may have trouble finding them. Premiere attempts to locate the missing clips and prompts you to confirm its choice. (Premiere also attempts to find missing preview files; see Chapter 8.)

Sometimes, the project refers to a file that is not currently available, or *offline*. Fortunately, you can tell Premiere to insert a blank placeholder, or *offline file*, to stand in for the clip. Although you can't view it, the project can still remember the name of the clip and recall how you used it in your program.

Just as Premiere can create placeholders for files that have been moved offline, you can create placeholders for files that you don't have but expect to use later.

When you make a source file available, you can connect the offline clip to it again, replacing the placeholder with the actual clip.

✔ Tip

■ In this chapter, the term *offline* means unavailable, or not on a drive. Don't confuse offline clips with the term offline editing (discussed in Chapter 1).

To open an existing project:

1. In Premiere, choose File > Open.

   The Open dialog box appears (**Figure 2.23**).

2. Select the project file that you want to open.

3. Click Open.

To open a project with missing files:

1. Open an existing project, as described earlier in this chapter.

   If files are missing, the Locate Files dialog box opens (**Figure 2.24**).

2. To find a file, *do one of the following:*

   ◆ Allow Premiere to automatically locate a file with the same name as the missing file.

   ◆ Manually locate the missing file or its replacement.

3. Select a file, and *do one of the following:*

   ◆ Click Select (Mac) or OK (Windows) to replace the missing file with the selected file.

   ◆ Click Offline to replace the missing file with an offline file.

   ◆ Click All Offline to replace all missing files with offline files, without prompting you for confirmation.

   ◆ Click Skip to remove the missing clip from the project. All instances of the clip disappear from the project, including the edited program.

   ◆ Click Skip All to remove all missing clips from the project, without prompting you for confirmation.

4. Save the project to update the status of the missing clips.

✔ Tip

■ Click Skip or Skip All only if you are sure that you want to remove the clip from the project.

Figure 2.24 If a file used in the project can't be found, the Locate File dialog box opens.

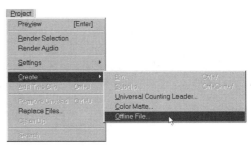

Figure 2.25 Create an offline file to act as a placeholder.

Figure 2.26 Enter information about the source clip in the Create Offline File dialog box.

Figure 2.27 Double-click the offline file that you want to replace with the source.

Figure 2.28 Choose Project > Replace Files.

Figure 2.29 The source file replaces the offline file, wherever it appears in the project.

To create an offline file:

1. Choose Project > Create > Offline File (**Figure 2.25**).

   The New Offline File dialog box appears (**Figure 2.26**).

2. Type a file name.

3. Enter a duration for the offline file.

4. Enter a timecode in point from the missing source file.

5. Type the name for the reel that contains the missing source file.

6. Choose a time format that corresponds to the missing source file.

7. From the Speed pop-up menu, choose a frame rate for the offline file.

8. If you want to use video from the missing source file, choose Has Video.

9. If you want to use audio from the missing source file, choose Has Audio.

To replace offline files in an open project:

1. In the Project, Bin, or Library window, double-click the offline file (**Figure 2.27**).

   The File Offline dialog box appears.

2. Click Locate or from the Project menu choose Replace Files to find the source file to replace the offline file (**Figure 2.28**).

   The Locate Files dialog box appears.

3. Select the source file.

4. Click OK.

   The file replaces the offline file (**Figure 2.29**).

5. Save the project to reflect the change.

Importing Clips

When you want to use a file in your project, you import the file as a clip.

Clips can be as big as 4,000 pixels tall by 4,000 pixels wide. By default, Premiere scales a clip to match the aspect ratio of your project settings (usually, a 4:3 aspect ratio). If you prefer, you can preserve the original aspect ratio of a still image (discussed later in this chapter) or a video clip (discussed in Chapter 5).

You can import one clip at a time, several clips in succession, or an entire folder of clips. You can even import another project into the current project.

Premiere can support a variety of video and audio formats. Over time, Adobe and other manufacturers undoubtedly will offer plug-in software modules to provide additional file-format support.

To import a clip into a project:

1. Choose File > Import > File (**Figure 2.30**).

   The Import File dialog box appears.

2. Locate the file (**Figure 2.31**).

   Double-click the name of the file, or click Open.

   The dialog box closes, and the clip appears in the selected Project, Bin, or Library window.

To import multiple clips (Mac):

1. Choose File > Import > Multiple (**Figure 2.30**).

   The Import Multiple dialog box appears.

2. Locate the file (**Figure 2.31**).

3. Double-click the name of the file, or click Open.

Figure 2.30 Choose File > Import > File or File > Import > Multiple.

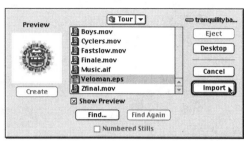

Figure 2.31 Select a file to import, and click Import.

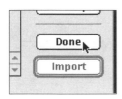

Figure 2.32 Click Done when you finish importing multiple clips.

4. Repeat steps 2 and 3 for each file that you want to import.

5. Click Done (**Figure 2.32**).

To import multiple clips (Windows):

1. Choose File > Import > File.

   The Import File dialog box appears.

2. *Do one of the following:*

   ◆ Hold down Ctrl as you click each file that you want to import.

   ◆ Hold down Shift to select the first and last files in a range of files.

3. Click Open.

Importing Digital Audio

If you're using the Mac OS, you can import all or part of a track from an audio CD. QuickTime converts the track on the CD to an .AIFF file. Because this process is digital-to-digital, it prevents the loss in quality associated with digital-to-analog-to-digital conversions.

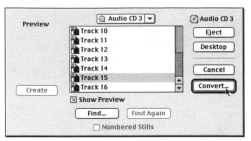

Figure 2.33 Select an audio track on the CD and click Convert.

To import an audio CD track (Mac OS only):

1. Choose File > Open.

   The Open dialog box appears.

2. Select the audio CD.

3. Click Open to view the audio tracks contained on the CD.

4. Select a track.

5. Click Convert (**Figure 2.33**).

   The Convert dialog box opens.

6. Enter a name and destination for the .AIFF file that you want to create and import (**Figure 2.34**).

7. Click the Options button to open the audio settings.

   The Audio CD Import Options dialog box appears (**Figure 2.35**).

8. From the Rate pull-down menu, choose a sample rate.

9. In the Size section, click a radio button to specify the bit depth.

10. In the Use section, click a radio button to specify mono or audio.

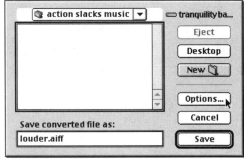

Figure 2.34 Choose a name and destination for the converted audio and click Options.

Figure 2.35 Choose audio options.

11. The dialog box offers you a couple of additional options:

To preview the track, click Play.

To select a portion of the audio track, enter the start and end times for the audio or drag the beginning and ending sliders.

12. Click OK to exit the Options dialog box and return to the Convert dialog box.

13. Click OK to convert the file.

14. Drag the audio clip from Source view to a Program, Bin, or Library window to import it.

IMPORTING DIGITAL AUDIO

Importing Still Images

Premiere lets you import still images or convert a sequence of numbered still images to a single clip. Although individual images are only single frames, you can set them to play back for any duration. Also, if the aspect ratio of the still doesn't match the project's aspect ratio (usually, 4:3), you must tell Premiere whether to maintain the still image's original proportions or resize it to fit the screen.

Illustrator Files

Premiere can rasterize Illustrator files, which converts the path-based (vector) art to Premiere's pixel-based (bitmapped) format. The program anti-aliases the art, so that edges appear smooth; it also interprets blank areas as an alpha channel premultiplied with white. In other words, the alpha channel appears as a white background.

You can import Illustrator art up to 2000 by 2000 pixels in size. Set crop marks in the Illustrator file to define the dimensions of the art that will be rasterized by Premiere (**Figures 2.36** and **2.37**).

Photoshop Files

Premiere can import files created in Photoshop 3.0 or later. You can even import a layer from a multiple-layer Photoshop file. Premiere also recognizes an alpha channel in the Photoshop file, so you can use it to define transparent areas (see Chapter 12).

✔ Tip

- The capability to open individual layers from Photoshop files can be a time-saver. When you create a graphical build sequence, for example, you don't have to create individual images for each part of the build. Instead, you can import each layer from a single Photoshop file (**Figure 2.38**).

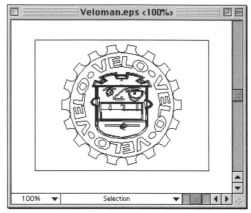

Figure 2.36 Path-based Illustrator art open in Illustrator.

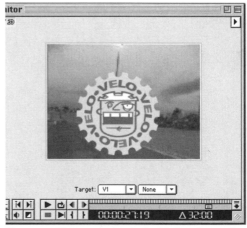

Figure 2.37 The same art rasterized in Premiere and superimposed over another clip.

Figure 2.38 Each element of this graph is added to the composition one at a time, in a series of builds.

Figure 2.39 Choose File > Preferences > General/Still Image.

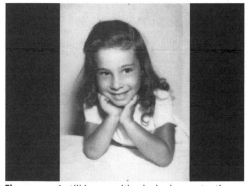

Figure 2.40 Enter the default duration for still images, and decide whether you want to lock the original aspect ratio.

Figure 2.41 A still image with a locked aspect ratio.

Figure 2.42 The same image resized to fit the project's aspect ratio.

To set the default duration for still images before you import them:

1. Choose File > Preferences > General/Still Image (**Figure 2.39**).

   The General / Still Image panel of Preferences dialog box appears.

2. In the Still Image section, type a default duration for still images (**Figure 2.40**).

   All still images imported into the project hereafter have the default duration. Still images that are already in the project or program remain unaffected. You can change the duration of a still-image clip at any time (see Chapter 3).

To lock the aspect ratios of still images before you import them:

1. Choose File > Preferences > General/Still Image.

   The General / Still Image panel of the Preferences dialog box appears.

2. In the Still Image section, check or uncheck the Lock Aspect checkbox.

   To keep the aspect ratio of the still image, check Lock Aspect.

   To resize still images to fit television's 4:3 aspect ratio, uncheck Lock Aspect.

   Unless the aspect ratio matches the project's, still images with a locked aspect may appear with a border and resized still images may appear distorted (**Figures 2.41** and **2.42**).

To import numbered still images as a single clip:

1. In Windows, confirm that each image in the numbered sequence has the correct extension and that the file names contain an equal number of digits at the end (for example, seq000.bmp, seq001.bmp, and seq003.bmp).

   In the Mac OS, confirm that each image in the sequence has the same file name, followed by and an equal number of digits (for example, seq.000, seq001, and seq002).

2. Choose File > Import > File.

   The Import File dialog box appears.

3. Select the first file in the numbered sequence.

4. Check Numbered Stills (**Figure 2.43**).

5. Click Open to import the numbered stills as a single file.

To import another project into the current project:

1. Choose File > Import > Project.

   The Import Project dialog box appears.

2. Select another project.

3. Click Import.

   The Import Project dialog box opens.

4. Click a radio button to determine where the imported project begins in the current project (**Figure 2.44**).

   You can insert the imported project at the beginning of the current project, at the current position of the edit line, or after the last clip of the current project.

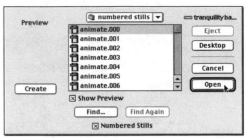

Figure 2.43 Select the first image in the numbered sequence, and check Numbered Stills.

Figure 2.44 Specify where the imported project begins in the current project.

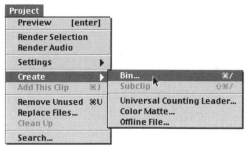

Figure 2.45 Choose Project > Create > Bin.

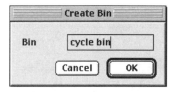

Figure 2.46
Name the bin,
and click OK.

Figure 2.47 The new
bin in List view.

Organizing Clips

Keeping organized is the key to having an efficient and successful editing project. In addition to the Project window, bins and libraries can help you manage your clips.

Bins

Premiere often employs a film-editing metaphor. Film editors literally use bins to store and organize their clips. The film dangles from hangers into a bin until the editor pulls a strip of film down and adds it to the sequence. Premiere's bins may be less tactile than film bins are, but they are also a lot less messy.

If you've never seen a film bin, you might compare clips stored in bins with files stored in folders on a drive. In fact, bins were called folders in previous versions of Premiere. If you import a folder of files, the folder appears in the project as a bin containing clips.

Unlike some other editing programs, Premiere saves bins as part of the project, not as separate files.

To create a bin:

1. Open the Project, Library, or Bin window in which you want to create a new bin.

2. Choose Project > Create > Bin (**Figure 2.45**).
   The Create Bin dialog box appears.

3. Name the bin.

4. Click OK (**Figure 2.46**).
   The new bin appears (**Figure 2.47**).

Libraries

Like a bin, a library simply lists clips that refer to files on the hard drive. Unlike bins, however, libraries can be saved as separate files, independent of a particular project. Libraries are primarily useful if you have clips that you want to use in several projects. You might use a library to store clips for the opening sequence of a series, for example. You can open one or more libraries while you're using a project. Clip attributes, such as edit marks, are saved with the clips in the library.

To create a library:

1. Choose File > New > Library (**Figure 2.48**).

   An untitled Library window appears.

2. Drag clips to the Library window to add them to the library.

3. Choose File > Save As.

   The Save dialog box appears.

4. Name the library and specify a destination.

5. Click Save (**Figure 2.49**).

Library files are saved separately from projects and can be opened in any project, as needed (**Figure 2.50**).

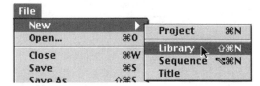

Figure 2.48 Choose File > New > Library.

Figure 2.49 Name and save the library as an independent file.

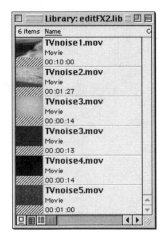

Figure 2.50 Libraries generally list clips that are used in different projects.

Figure 2.51 Use the view buttons at the bottom of a window to choose Icon view...

Figure 2.52 ...Thumbnail view...

Figure 2.53 ...or List view.

Figure 2.54 Choose window options for a project, bin, or library.

Customizing the Project, Bin, and Library Windows

Except for the names in the title bars, the Project, Bin, and Library windows look exactly the same. Each window can be displayed in three ways: Icon, Thumbnail, or List view. Furthermore, each view type has various display options. These choices allow you to customize each window for the task at hand.

To change a Project, Bin, or Library view:

At the bottom of the window, click the button that corresponds to the view that you want to use (**Figures 2.51** to **2.53**): Icon, Thumbnail, or List view.

To customize Icon, Thumbnail, or List views:

1. Select a project, bin, or library.

2. Choose Window > Project Window Options (or Bin Window Options or Library Window Options, depending on the open window) (**Figure 2.54**).

(continued on next page)

3. From the View pull-down menu, choose the type of view that you want to customize (**Figure 2.55**).

4. Choose options for the view (described in the following sections).

5. Click OK.

To choose Icon-view options:

1. Open the Icon View options for the Project, Bin, or Library window, as explained in the previous section (**Figure 2.56**).

2. Click the radio button for the icon size that you want the window to use.

3. Check the Snap to Grid checkbox to make the icons line up with an invisible grid.

4. Check the Draw Icons checkbox to make icons (the in-point frame of the clip) visible in the window, or uncheck the Draw Icons checkbox to prevent icon display.

✔ Tip

■ When Snap to Grid is off, clips in Icon view can look jumbled or even cover one another. To rearrange the clips neatly in Icon view, make Icon view active and then choose Project > Clean Up.

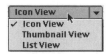

Figure 2.55 Use the pull-down menu to choose a view.

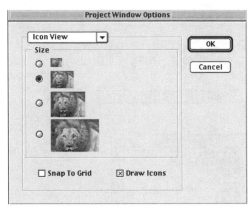

Figure 2.56 Icon-view options.

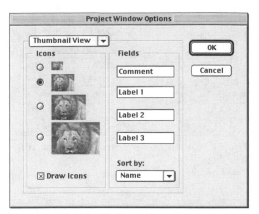

Figure 2.57 Thumbnail-view options.

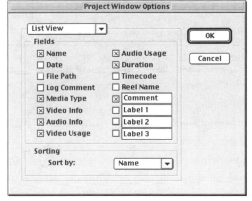

Figure 2.58 List-view options.

To choose Thumbnail-view options:

1. Open the Thumbnail View options for the Project, Bin, or Library window, as explained earlier in this chapter (**Figure 2.57**).

2. Click the radio button for the icon size that you want the window to use.

3. Check the Draw Icons checkbox to make icons (the in-point frame of the clip) visible in the window, or uncheck the Draw Icons checkbox to prevent icon display.

4. Type names for the four fields that you can define.

5. From the Sort pull-down menu, choose a heading on which to sort the clips in the window.

To choose List-view options:

1. Open the List View options for the Project, Bin, or Library window, as explained earlier in this chapter.

2. Check the headings for the type of information that you want to view in List view (**Figure 2.58**):

- **Name:** by default, the same as the file name. You can change the name that the clip uses in the project, however (see Chapter 3).

- **Date:** the most recent modification of the source file.

- **File Path:** the location of the source file on disk.

- **Log Comment:** if the clip was captured with Premiere, the text in the Comment field.

- **Media Type:** the kind of file (such as movie or still image).

(continued on next page)

PROJECT, BIN, AND LIBRARY WINDOWS

33

- **Video Info:** video attributes, such as the frame size.

- **Audio Info:** audio attributes, such as the sample rate.

- **Video Usage:** the number of times that the video track is used in the program.

- **Audio Usage:** the number of times that the audio track is used in the program.

- **Duration:** the length of the clip, expressed in the currently selected time display.

- **Timecode:** the timecode of the first frame, if timecode is present.

- **Reel Name:** if the clip was captured with Premiere, the name entered in the Reel field.

To rearrange headings in List view:

With List view active, drag a heading to the left or right to place it where you want (**Figure 2.59**).

To sort items in Thumbnail or List view:

You have several choices for sorting items in a Project, Bin, or Library when Thumbnail or List view is selected:

- Click a column heading to sort clips by that heading (**Figure 2.60**).

- Click the same column heading again to reverse the sort order.

- Open the window options of a Project, Bin, or Library window(as explained earlier in this chapter) and choose a category from the Sort pulldown menu to sort items according to that category.

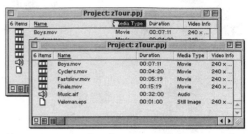

Figure 2.59 Drag a heading to move the column to the left or right.

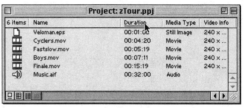

Figure 2.60 Click a heading to sort clips according to that heading. In List view, the heading appears underlined.

Figure 2.61 You can drag a marquee around clips in List view to select them.

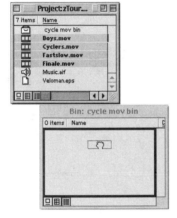

Figure 2.62 Simply drag clips to move them to a new location.

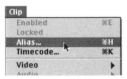

Figure 2.63 Choose Clip > Alias to rename a clip.

Figure 2.64 Enter a new name for the clip or click None to return to the original name.

Managing Clips

Premiere allows you to manage clips in the project in much the same way that you manage files on your computer's desktop.

To select and move clips:

1. To select a clip or clips, *do one of the following:*

   ◆ Click a clip.

   ◆ Shift+click several clips.

   ◆ Drag a marquee around clips (**Figure 2.61**).

2. Drag selected clips to another location, such as another bin (**Figure 2.62**).

To delete a clip:

1. Select a clip.

2. Press Delete.

   The clip is removed from the project, but the source file remains on the drive.

To copy and paste a clip:

1. Select a clip.

2. Choose Edit > Copy.

3. Select the destination project, bin, or library.

4. Choose Edit > Paste.

To rename a clip:

1. Select a clip.

2. Choose Clip > Alias (**Figure 2.63**). The Set Clip Name Alias dialog box appears.

3. Type the new name (**Figure 2.64**).

4. Click OK.

   The clip takes another name in the project. The source file on the drive, isn't renamed, however.

35

To restore the original file name of a renamed clip:

1. Select a renamed clip.

2. Choose Clip > Alias.
   The Set Clip Name Alias dialog box appears.

3. Click None to make the name of the clip match the source-file name.

To find a clip:

1. Select the Project or Library window that you want to search.

2. Choose Project > Search (**Figure 2.65**).
   The Search window opens (**Figure 2.66**).

3. In the Find pulldown menu, choose a category to search by.

4. In the next pulldown menu, choose a limiting option:
   Choose that contain, to find items in the selected category that contain the search content you specify.
   Choose that do not contain, to find items in the selected category that do not contain the search content you specify.

5. In the search field, enter search content.

6. To narrow the search more, add another search category, limiting option, and search content.

7. To search for clips in nested bins (bins inside bins), check the Find in Nested Bins checkbox.

8. Click Find to find an item that meets your search criteria, and click Find Next to find the next item that meets your criteria.

9. Click Done to close the Project/Library Search dialog box.

Figure 2.65 Choose Search from the Project menu.

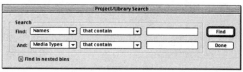

Figure 2.66 The Search window.

MANAGING CLIPS

Figure 2.67 Reference color bars and tone are located in the Goodies folder.

Creating a Leader

In addition to accepting a wide variety of source files, Premiere provides several useful clips of its own. Some of these clips are useful for creating a standard leader, which typically appears at the beginning of a master edited tape. Premiere not only supplies standard color bars and reference audio tone in the Goodies folder, but also offers a new feature that allows you to create a custom countdown. Originally, the visible countdown helped a film projectionist know when the program was about to start. It can serve a similar purpose for videotape operators. The standard countdown starts at 8, and ends at 2 (where there is usually a beep, or "2 pop," to test the sound).

To import bars and tone:

1. Choose Project > Import > Multiple.
   The Import Multiple dialog box opens.

2. In the Goodies folder of the Premiere folder, locate the SMPTE color bars (**Figure 2.67**).

3. Click Open.

4. In the Goodies folder of the Premiere folder, locate the 1KHz tone.

5. Click Select.

6. Click Done.

✔ Tip

■ To make a slate (which contains information such as Client, Producer, and Total Running Time), you can create a title card in Premiere, as explained in Chapter 11.

To create a countdown:

1. Choose Project > Create > Universal Counting Leader (**Figure 2.68**).

   The Universal Counting Leader Setup window opens (**Figure 2.69**).

2. Click a color swatch to open a color picker for each element of the countdown.

3. Choose a color for each element.

4. Click OK.

5. To display a small circle in the last frame of the leader, check the Cue Blip on Out checkbox.

6. To play a beep at the 2-second mark of the countdown, check the Cue Blip on 2 checkbox.

7. To play a beep at the beginning of every second of the countdown leader, check the Cue Blip At All Second Starts checkbox.

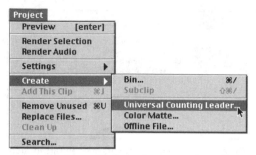

Figure 2.68 Choose Project > Create > Universal Counting Leader.

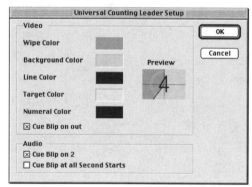

Figure 2.69 Customize the countdown in the Universal Counting Leader Setup window.

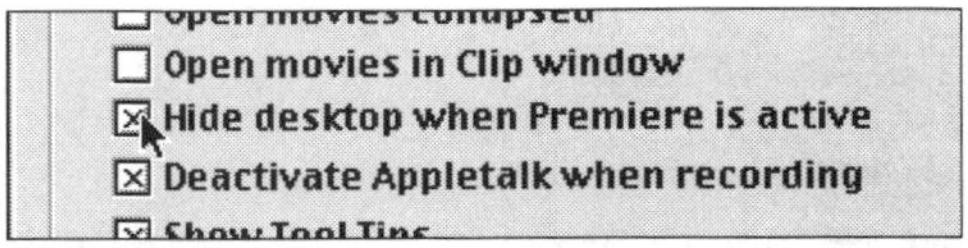

☐ open movies collapsed
☐ Open movies in Clip window
☒ Hide desktop when Premiere is active
☒ Deactivate Appletalk when recording
☒ Show Tool Tips

Figure 2.70 You can hide the desktop while Premiere is running.

Customizing Premiere's Interface

Now that you know how to create a Premiere project, make yourself comfortable. Customizing your work environment can help you maximize your efficiency. You can eliminate desktop clutter, take full advantage of the new palette windows, and create your own shortcuts.

To hide the desktop while working in Premiere:

1. Choose File > Preferences > General/Still Image.

   The General/Still Image panel of the Preferences dialog box appears.

2. Check Hide desktop when Premiere is active (**Figure 2.70**).

   This option conceals all icons and windows on the desktop. Uncheck this option to see the desktop in the background.

Using Palettes

In previous versions of Premiere, various controls were contained in a number of separate windows, which quickly consumed screen space. In the current version, the most important windows have been designed to use screen space more efficiently, and other windows now appear as *palettes*. Premiere's new palettes not only streamline the interface but also make it more consistent with other Adobe programs, like Photoshop, Illustrator, and AfterEffects. As in other Adobe programs, you can group palettes together, or dock them so that they're attached to one another.

Figure 2.71 Choose the name of the window that you want to open or close.

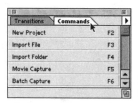

Figure 2.72 Click a tab to view the palette.

To display or hide windows and palettes:

◆ From the Window menu, and choose the name of the window or palette that you want to display or hide (**Figure 2.71**).

To display a palette in a group:

◆ In the palette group, click the palette tab to make the palette visible in front of other palettes in the group (**Figure 2.72**).

To move a palette to another group:

◆ Drag a palette tab to another group (**Figure 2.73**).

The palette tab appears in the same window as the group.

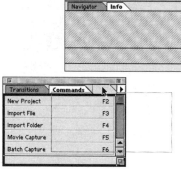

Figure 2.73 Drag a palette to add it to another group.

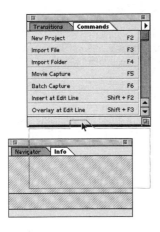

Figure 2.74 Drag one palette to the bottom of another...

To dock palettes:

1. Drag a palette tab to the bottom of another palette.

2. When the bottom of the destination palette is highlighted, release the mouse button (**Figure 2.74**).

   The two palettes connect (**Figure 2.75**).

To separate docked palettes:

◆ In a docked palette, drag a palette tab away from the other palettes.

   The palette separates from the others.

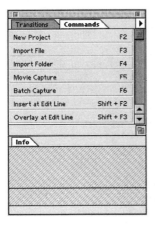

Figure 2.75 ... and the dragged palette docks to the other palette.

Using Shortcuts and the Commands Palette

Another way to increase your speed and efficiency is to take advantage of keyboard shortcuts and the Commands palette. Because a guide to keyboard shortcuts is available in Premiere, this book mentions only the most common ones. Similarly, this book rarely refers to the Commands palette. Although the Commands palette does have a default set of shortcuts, you undoubtedly will customize it according to your own tastes and needs.

To view the keyboard shortcuts:

1. Choose Help > Keyboard Shortcuts (**Figure 2.76**).

   Premiere opens Quickhelp (**Figure 2.77**).

   To find a keyboard shortcut, click a topic to view shortcuts in that category. or type a keyword to find a shortcut.

2. Quit to exit Quickhelp.

To use a command:

◆ Click a button in the Commands palette, or press the equivalent keyboard shortcut to perform the task (**Figure 2.78**).

To create a command button:

1. Choose Palette > Edit Command Set (**Figure 2.79**).

   The Commands Editor dialog box appears (**Figure 2.80**).

Figure 2.76 From the Help menu, choose Keyboard Shortcuts.

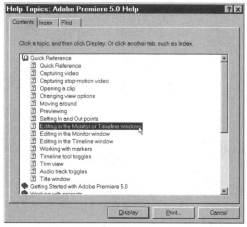

Figure 2.77 Use Quickhelp to find the shortcut that you want to use.

Figure 2.78 The default Commands palette.

Figure 2.79 Choose Palette > Edit Command Set.

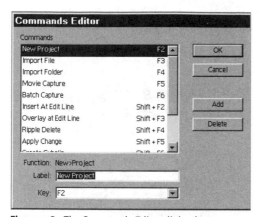

Figure 2.80 The Commands Editor dialog box.

2. Set the button for the command, as follows:

   To add a new button, click Add. A new button appears, labeled Undefined (Mac) or None (Windows).

   To edit the button, click an existing button.

3. Choose the command that you want to use from the menu bar (for example, File > Get Properties For).

4. If you want, type a label for the button.

5. If you want to choose a keyboard shortcut for the button, select one.

   The menu displays keys that are already assigned to other commands as dimmed (Mac) or not at all (Windows).

6. Click OK to exit the dialog box.

To delete a command button:

1. Choose Palette > Edit Command Set. The Commands Editor dialog box appears.

2. Select a button.

3. Press Delete to remove the button.

4. Click OK to exit the dialog box.

To save a command set:

1. Choose Palette > Save Command Set. The Save Actions dialog box appears.

2. Specify a name and destination for the saved set.

3. Click Save.

To load a command set:

1. Choose Palette > Load Command Set. A locate file dialog box appears.

2. Locate a saved command set.

3. Click Load.

Correcting Mistakes

Many people judge a program not only by how much it can do, but also by how much it can undo. Premiere allows up to 32 levels of undo. In other words, you can negate up to 32 of your most recent actions. If you change your mind yet again, you can redo the last undone action.

When undoing can't solve the problem, you may want to revert to the last saved version of the project or open an archived version.

To undo an action:

◆ Choose Edit > Undo (**Figure 2.81**).

If the last action can't be undone, the menu displays the grayed entry Can't Undo.

To redo an action:

◆ Choose Edit > Redo (**Figure 2.82**).

If the last action can't be undone, the menu displays the grayed entry Can't Redo.

To set the levels of undo:

1. Choose File > Preferences > Autosave/Undo.

   The Autosave / Undo panel of the Preferences dialog box appears.

2. Enter the number of actions that can be undone (**Figure 2.83**).

3. Quit and then restart Premiere to make the changes take effect.

Figure 2.81 Choose Edit > Undo to negate your last action.

Figure 2.82 Choose Edit > Redo to restore an undone action.

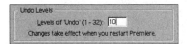

Figure 2.83 Enter the maximum number of undos.

WORKING
WITH CLIPS

When you import files into a project, those files appear as clips organized in bins. It is crucial to understand that clips—like everything else in a project—are simply graphical references to files on the hard drive. If you change or even delete a clip from the project, the source files remain untouched. To continue the musical-score metaphor from Chapter 2, it would be as though you removed the cello player's name from a list of musicians. The cellist will wait patiently, taking up space, just in case you change your mind.

Conversely, if you remove a source file from the drive (or even change a source file's name), the clip refer to a file that is no longer available. In the orchestra analogy, the cellist has left the concert hall. You may have included a part for a cello in the score, but if you want it to play, you'll have to get it back on the hard drive—or rather, get the cello player back in the orchestra pit.

In this chapter, you learn all the ways to open and view clips, whether they are video, audio, or still images. You learn how to precisely control the playback of clips by using the controllers in Premiere's new Monitor window. You also learn how to mark points of interest in the clip, including the most important marks of all: the in and out points.

Understanding the Monitor Window

Figure 3.1 The parts of the Monitor window.

The new Monitor window is not only one of the most noticeable improvements to Premiere, but also one of the most important. The Monitor window consolidates several of the older version's windows into a single, streamlined window (**Figure 3.1**).

The left side of the Monitor window displays the *Source view*, and the right side displays the *Program view*. Most editors agree that a source/program monitor is the best editing interface. The Monitor window resembles a traditional videotape editing suite or even a good flatbed film-editing table. But editors don't prefer this layout merely because it's familiar—this kind of interface also enables them to see the source and program clips side by side, which helps them make editing decisions. The interface also centralizes the essential editing controls.

Premiere's Source and Program views feature controllers, which you use to play back clips and to set editing marks. All these controls have single-stroke keyboard shortcuts— another time-saving feature that professional editors have come to expect from nonlinear editing tools.

In addition, the Monitor window incorporates the core editing controls. Four editing buttons located between the two views bring a new set of professional editing features to Premiere. The gang button at the top of the window allows you to gang-synch Source and Program views, so that they play simultaneously in a synchronized relationship. This feature is invaluable when you need to preview the timing of certain edits. When it's time to fine-tune the program, the Monitor window conveniently toggles to Trimming view (covered in Chapter 6).

Clearly, the new Monitor window isn't simply a cosmetic improvement. Except for special effects and audio mixing, you could do all your editing in the Monitor window alone, without even looking at the timeline.

Even if you are a fan of the old Premiere interface, the new look and functionality of the Monitor window are sure to win you over. Nevertheless, Premiere still permits you to customize your work space. You can still open clips in separate clip windows. You can even break the Monitor window in two, making it resemble the Preview and Controller windows of previous versions.

UNDERSTANDING THE MONITOR WINDOW

Modifying the Monitor Window

You can change the Monitor window to resemble previous versions of Premiere by separating program view from Source view and the controllers.

If your computer system supports a secondary computer monitor or television monitor, you might want to display the video separately from the controllers and other windows.

To change to a single view:

1. Click either Source or Program view to activate it.

2. From the Monitor window's pull-down menu, choose Single View (**Figure 3.2**).

   The Monitor window displays only the view that corresponds to the active controller (**Figure 3.3**).

To separate the view from the controllers:

◆ Click the Collapse button ⬇ to separate the view from the controllers (**Figures 3.4** and **3.5**).

✔ Tip

■ If you are modifying the Monitor window to resemble older versions of Premiere, also set the Preferences to open separate Clip windows by default, as explained in the section, Viewing Clips, later in this chapter.

Figure 3.2 Choose Single View from the Monitor window's pull-down menu.

Figure 3.3 If you use a single Monitor window, it displays the program when the program controller is active.

Figure 3.4 Click the Collapse button to separate the Monitor window into a Monitor view and Monitor controller.

Figure 3.5 The Monitor view and Monitor controller can be separated.

To view the program on another monitor:

1. Click the Collapse button ⏬ to separate the view from the controllers.

2. From the Monitor window's pull-down menu, choose Single View.

3. Drag the view to the second computer or television monitor.

4. Resize the window.

✔ Tip

■ You can also Command+click a source or program window to send the Monitor view to a television monitor. If you have no monitor attached to your system, double-click to return the window to your computer monitor.

Viewing Clips

Premiere's intuitive interface makes it simple to view a clip, no matter where it appears in your project.

To open a clip in Source view:

Do one of the following:

◆ Double-click a clip in a project, bin, or Library window.

◆ Drag it into Source view (**Figure 3.6**).

To view recently viewed clips with the Source View pull-down menu:

◆ Select the name of a previously viewed clip in the Source View pull-down menu (**Figure 3.7**).

✔ Tip

■ To save time, you can select multiple clips and drag them all to Source view. From then on, you can simply choose a clip from the Source View pull-down menu, rather than search through bins.

To open a clip in a separate clip window:

◆ Option+double-click a clip in a project, bin, or Library window; Source view; or a track of the Timeline window.

A separate clip window opens. This window works the same as a clip in Monitor window (**Figure 3.8**).

To make separate clip windows the default:

1. Choose Preferences > General / Still Image.

   The General / Still Image Preferences dialog box opens (**Figure 3.9**).

2. Choose Open movies in clip window (**Figure 3.10**).

VIEWING CLIPS

Figure 3.6 You can double-click a clip to open it in Source view, or you can drag it directly to Source view.

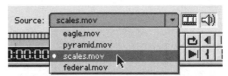

Figure 3.7 Choose a previously viewed clip from the Source View pull-down menu to reopen the clip.

Figure 3.8 A separate clip window.

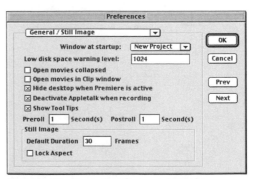

Figure 3.9 The General preferences dialog box.

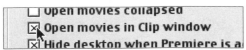

Figure 3.10 Choosing Open movies in Clip window makes separate clip windows the default.

Figure 3.11 Choose Open from the File menu.

Figure 3.12 Find the clip that you want to open, and click Open.

Figure 3.13 You can choose Project > Add This Clip to add an open clip to the project.

2. Choose Open movies in clip window (**Figure 3.10**).

3. Click OK.

This procedure reverses the default settings, so that double-clicking a clip opens it in a separate clip window, and Option+double-clicking a clip opens it in Source view.

To open a clip that is not in the project:

1. Choose File > Open (**Figure 3.11**).
The Open File dialog box appears.

2. Locate the clip that you want to view.

3. Click Open (**Figure 3.12**).

To add an open clip to the project:

Do one of the following:

◆ Drag an open clip to the project, bin, or Library window.

◆ Drag an open clip to an available track in the timeline.

◆ With the open clip selected, choose Project > Add This Clip (**Figure 3.13**).

VIEWING CLIPS

Working with Still-Image Clip Windows

Still-image files always open in a separate clip window. Because these files have only one frame, they do not have the same controller as audio or video clips. Instead of choosing an in and out point for still images, you simply set a *duration*—the length of time you want the still image to display in the program.

To set the duration of a still image:

1. Double-click a still-image clip to open it in a separate Clip window.

2. Click the Duration button (**Figure 3.14**). The Clip Duration dialog box appears.

3. Type a duration (**Figure 3.15**).

To set the default still-image duration:

1. Choose File > Preferences > General/Still Image (**Figure 3.16**).
   The General / Still Image dialog box appears.

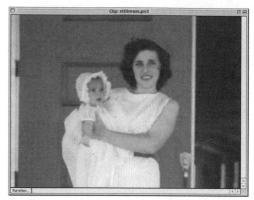

Figure 3.14 A still image's clip window has a Duration button.

Figure 3.15 Type a duration.

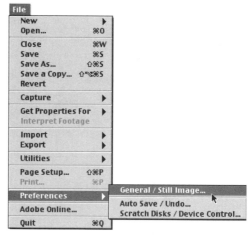

Figure 3.16 Choose File > Preferences > General / Still Image.

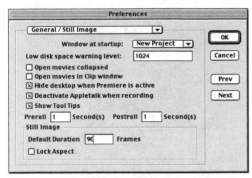

Figure 3.17 In the Still Image section, type a default duration.

2. In the Still Image section, type a duration to set the default duration for still images (**Figure 3.17**).

   All still images imported into the project have the default duration. Still images that are already in the project or timeline remain unaffected.

✔ Tips

- Any duration number that you enter in Premiere has a *threshold* of 100—that is, numbers 99 and below are interpreted as *frames*, and numbers 100 and above are interpreted as *seconds and frames*. The number 99, for example, is interpreted as 99 frames, or 3 seconds and 9 frames. The number 100 is interpreted as 1 second and 0 frames.

- You may also need to specify the way that Premiere treats the aspect ratio of a still image. See Chapter 2 for more information about how Premiere can interpret still images.

Using Audio Clips

Audio clips work the same as video clips in Source view. The separate clip window for audio, however, looks and operates slightly differently from the clip window for video.

To open an audio clip in Source view:

Do one of the following:

- Double-click an audio-only clip in the project, bin, or Library window, or drag it to Source view.

- To open an audio clip from the timeline, double-click the audio portion of the clip in the audio track.

The audio clip opens in Source view (**Figure 3.18**).

To open a separate Clip window for audio:

Option+double-click the audio clip in the project, bin, or Library window, or in an audio track of the timeline.

The audio clip opens in a separate audio clip window (**Figure 3.19**).

To change the audio waveform:

Click the Waveform button to display the audio-waveform in one of four ways (**Figure 3.20**).

An expanded setting shows more detail, but less of the audio (**Figure 3.21**).

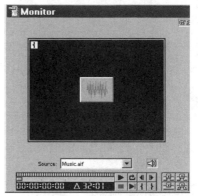

Figure 3.18 An audio clip in Source view. An audio icon appears in Source view instead of video.

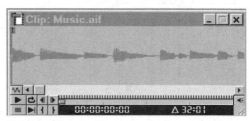

Figure 3.19 You can open an audio clip in a separate window to gain additional controls.

Figure 3.20 The Waveform button toggles among four settings.

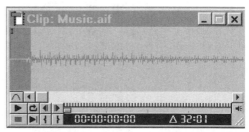

Figure 3.21 An audio clip viewed with the waveform set to an expanded view.

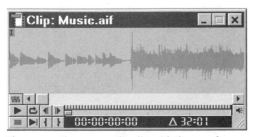

Figure 3.22 The same audio clip, with the waveform set to a more condensed view.

Figure 3.23 Click a point on the waveform to cue the playback line, which corresponds to the current time.

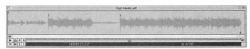

Figure 3.24 You can resize the audio clip window to display more of the waveform.

A more condensed setting shows more of the audio waveform, but less detail (**Figure 3.22**).

To cue the playback line in the audio clip window:

Click the point in the audio waveform where you want to cue the current time (**Figure 3.23**).

To view more of the audio waveform:

Drag the resize box in the corner of the audio clip window to increase the size of the window (**Figure 3.24**).

USING AUDIO CLIPS

Using Monitor Controllers

Not surprisingly, you use the controller below the Source view to play source clips and to mark the source's in and out points. You use the controller below the Program view to play the edited program and to mark the program's in and out points.

Whether you're controlling the source or the program, the buttons on the controllers work the same.

Because you have two controllers, always make sure that the controller you want to use is active. When a controller is active, the view above it has a highlighted border, and the current-time readout is green (**Figure 3.25**).

To change the count in the current-time display:

1. Command+click the current time.

2. Repeat step 1 until the current-time display shows the time unit that you want to use (**Figures 3.26** and **3.27**).

   Your options are:

   ◆ 24 fps timecode.

   ◆ 25 fps timecode.

   ◆ 30 fps drop-frame timecode.

   ◆ 30 fps non-drop-frame timecode.

   ◆ Frames/samples.

   ◆ Feet/frames 16mm.

   ◆ Feet/frames 35mm.

For more information on time measurements, see Chapter 17.

Figure 3.25 You can see that the Source view is active by the highlighted border around the image and the green time display.

Figure 3.26 Command+clicking the current-time readout toggles through the different time measurements. Here, the display is 30 fps non-drop-frame timecode...

Figure 3.27 ...and here, the display is 16mm feet and frames.

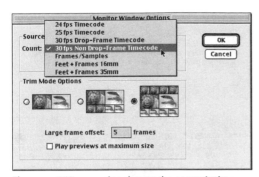

Figure 3.28 You can also change the source's time measurement from the Monitor Window Options dialog box.

To change the count in the Source controller:

1. From the Monitor pull-down menu, choose Monitor Window Options.

   The Monitor Window Options dialog box appears.

2. From the Source Count pull-down menu, choose the time measurement that you want to use (**Figure 3.28**).

✔ Tip

■ You can also change the program time display from the Timeline window's pull-down menu. See Chapter 5 for details.

Cueing Source and Program Views

You can cue the source and program to a particular frame number, also known as an *absolute time*. You can also cue them to a *relative time*. In other words, you can add frames to or subtract frames from the current time.

To cue the view to an absolute time:

1. Click the current-time readout for the view in the Monitor window to highlight it (**Figure 3.29**).

2. Type the number of the frame that you want to view.

3. Press Return (**Figure 3.30**).

   If the frame number that you entered exists, the view displays that frame.

✔ Tip

■ You can also highlight individual numbers in the current-time readout and change them to cue the view (**Figure 3.31**).

Figure 3.29 Click the current-time readout to highlight it.

Figure 3.30 Type a valid frame number that you want to be the new current time and then press Enter to cue to that frame.

Figure 3.31 You can also change individual numbers in the current-time readout.

Figure 3.32 To enter a relative time, type **+** or **–** and a number.

To cue the view to a relative time:

1. Click the current-time readout for the view in the Monitor window to highlight it.

2. Type a plus (+) or a minus (–) and a number (**Figure 3.32**).

   To cue the clip 30 frames after the current frame, for example, type **+30**. To cue the view 60 frames before the current frame, type **–60**.

   Numbers 99 and below are interpreted as frames. Numbers 100 and above are interpreted as seconds and frames. If you type **+99**, for example, the view is cued 99 frames (or 3 seconds, 9 frames) forward. If you type **+100**, the view is cued 1 second, 00 frames forward.

✔ Tip

- If the time that you enter in the current-time readout does not exist, the view is cued to the nearest available frame—either the first or the last frame of the clip or program.

Using Markers

During the editing process, you often need a way to mark important points in time. Markers allow you to visibly stamp these points in clips and in the program. *Markers* help you visually identify beats in a song, synchronize video with a sound effect, or note where a title should fade up. Although markers are visible in the source, program, and timeline, they are for your reference only and don't appear in the video during playback.

In each clip and in the timeline, you can add up to 10 numbered markers (0 through 9) and up to 999 unnumbered markers. You can quickly cue the clip or the program directly to a numbered marker or to consecutive markers.

When you add markers to a master clip, its markers are included with the clip when you add it to the timeline or when you create a subclip. The markers aren't added to existing subclips or instances of the clip that are already in the timeline. This means that each instance of the clip and each subclip can have a unique set of markers and aren't subject to unintentional changes.

Don't confuse source and program markers. Markers added to source clips appear in Source view and within the clip in the timeline. Markers added to the program appear in Program view and on the time ruler of the timeline (**Figure 3.33**).

To add a marker to a clip:

1. *Do one of the following:*

   ◆ Open a source clip in Source view or in a clip window.

   ◆ Click the clip in the timeline to select it.

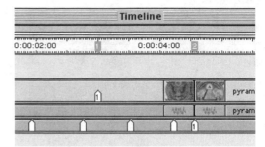

Figure 3.33 Source and program markers.

In	⌥⌘↑
Out	⌥⌘↓
Unnumbered	⌥⌘=
0	⌥⌘0
1	⌥⌘1
2	⌥⌘2
3	⌥⌘3
4	⌥⌘4
5	⌥⌘5
6	⌥⌘6
7	⌥⌘7
8	⌥⌘8
9	⌥⌘9

Figure 3.34 Choose a marker to mark a frame of the clip.

Figure 3.35 The marker is displayed for your reference whenever the clip is cued to the marked frame.

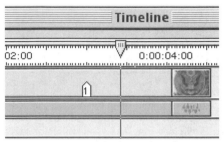

Figure 3.36 You also see the marker whenever the clip appears in the program.

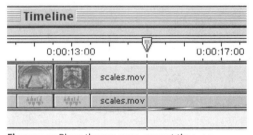

Figure 3.37 Place the program current time, as indicated by the edit line, at the point where you want to set the marker.

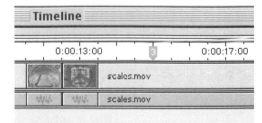

Figure 3.38 The program marker appears on the time ruler at the current time.

2. *Do one of the following:*

◆ In Source view or the clip window, go to a frame in the source clip to set a marker.

◆ If the clip is selected in the timeline, go to the point in time (also indicated by the edit line) where you want to add a marker to the selected clip.

3. Choose Clip > Set Marker.

4. From the menu, choose the marker that you want to add (**Figure 3.34**).

This marker appears in Source view whenever the clip is cued to the marked frame (**Figure 3.35**) or within the clip in the timeline (**Figure 3.36**).

To add a marker to the program:

1. Activate Program view or the Timeline window (see Chapter 5).

2. Make sure that no clips are selected in the timeline.

If a clip is selected, click it to deselect it.

3. In the time ruler, go to the point in time where you want to set the marker (**Figure 3.37**).

4. Choose Clip > Set Marker.

5. From the menu, choose the marker that you want to add.

The marker appears on the time ruler of the timeline (**Figure 3.38**).

To add markers on-the-fly:

1. *Do one of the following:*

◆ Play a source clip to add markers to a clip.

◆ Play the program to add markers to the time ruler.

(continued on next page)

2. *Do one of the following:*

◆ Press the asterisk key (*) in the number keypad, or press Option+Command+equal (=) on a regular keyboard to add unnumbered markers (**Figure 3.39**).

◆ Press Option+Command and a number to add numbered markers.

When you stop playback, the markers appear.

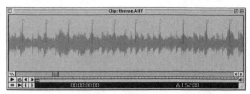

Figure 3.39 Press the asterisk key (*) to add unnumbered markers to a clip while it plays. You can tap in up to 999 beats of music, for example.

✔ Tips

■ Markers are helpful for marking where lines of dialogue or voiceover begin and end. Try using a numbered marker at the beginning of a line and an unnumbered marker at the end of a line. This technique not only conserves your limited numbered markers, but also makes it easy to identify pauses between lines (which often need to be cut) (**Figure 3.40**).

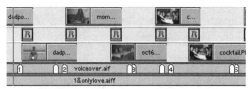

Figure 3.40 Use a combination of numbered and unnumbered markers to help you edit dialogue. You can see exactly where the lines of this voiceover start and end.

■ The zero marker has special uses with filters, titles, and the frame-hold feature. You may want to conserve the zero marker for these purposes.

To go to a marker in a clip:

1. *Do one of the following:*

◆ Activate Program view or the timeline. Make sure that no clips in the timeline are selected. If a clip is selected, click it to deselect it.

◆ Open a source clip, or click a clip in the timeline to select it.

2. *Do one of the following:*

◆ To go to a numbered marker, choose Clip > Go to Marker > *Marker #* (**Figure 3.41**).

In	⌘↑
Out	⌘↓
Next	⌘→
Previous	⌘←
0	⌘0
● 1	⌘1
2	⌘2
3	⌘3
4	⌘4
5	⌘5
6	⌘6
7	⌘7
8	⌘8
9	⌘9

Figure 3.41 The Go to Marker menu gives you several choices. If a clip has numbered markers, the markers are indicated by bullets.

Figure 3.42 Choose Clear Marker to delete the current marker or Clear All Markers to delete all the markers.

◆ To go to the next marker, choose Clip > Go to Marker > Next.

◆ To go to the preceding marker, choose Clip > Go to Marker > Previous.

◆ To go to the first marker, press Command+Option+up arrow.

◆ To go to the last marker, press Command+Option+down arrow.

To delete markers from a clip:

1. *Do one of the following:*

   ◆ Open the source clip.

   ◆ Click a clip in the timeline to select it.

2. Go to the marker that you want to delete. See the section, Cueing Source and Program Views, earlier in this chapter.

3. *Do one of the following:*

   ◆ Choose Clip > Marker > Clear Marker (**Figure 3.42**).

   ◆ Choose Clip > Marker > Clear All Markers.

To delete markers from the program:

1. Activate Program view or the timeline.

2. Make sure that no clips are selected in the timeline.

   If a clip is selected, click it to deselect it.

3. In the timeline, go to the marker that you want to delete.

4. *Do one of the following:*

   ◆ Choose Clip > Marker > Clear Marker.

   ◆ Choose Clip > Marker > Clear All Markers.

   ◆ This technique deletes only markers in the program and timeline, not markers within the clips in the timeline.

USING MARKERS

To make markers visible in the timeline:

1. From the Timeline pull-down menu, choose Timeline Window Options (**Figure 3.43**).

The Timeline Window Options dialog box appears.

2. *Do one of the following:*

◆ Check Show markers to make markers visible in the Timeline.

◆ Uncheck Show markers to conceal clip and program markers (**Figure 3.44**).

To shift program markers during editing:

1. From the Timeline pull-down menu, choose Timeline Window Options.

The Timeline Window Options dialog box appears.

2. *Do one of the following:*

◆ Check Block move markers, to shift program markers when a clip is inserted into the program in the timeline.

◆ Uncheck Block move markers, to leave program markers at fixed points on the time ruler (**Figure 3.44**).

Figure 3.43 Choose Timeline Window Options.

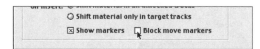

Figure 3.44 Check Show markers to make markers visible in the timeline, and check Block move markers to shift markers when you perform insert edits.

Figure 3.45 Click the Mark In or Mark Out button to set where the clip starts and ends. Icons appear in corresponding frames and in the shuttle bar of the controller.

Working with In Points and Out Points

Setting in points and out points is central to editing. An *in point* is where you want the clip to start playing, and the *out point* is where you want the clip to stop playing. The length of time between the in and out points is called the *duration*. When you edit, you set in and out points in both the source and the program.

You can accomplish this editing task in Premiere in several ways. This section explains how to use the controllers in the Monitor window. Later chapters teach you how to change the in and out points in the timeline.

Remember that because *clips* refers to media files, setting the source in and out point does not alter the files. You can always change in and out points, and the length of the source file is available for you to use.

To mark in and out points in the Monitor window:

1. *Do one of the following:*

    ◆ To mark edit points in the source, open a source clip in Source view or a clip window, or double-click a clip in the timeline.

    ◆ To mark edit points in the program, activate Program view or the Timeline window.

2. Go to the point in time where you want the clip to start.

3. Click the Mark In button (**Figure 3.45**).

4. Go to the point in time where you want the clip to end.

5. Click the Mark Out button (**Figure 3.45**).

(continued on next page)

WORKING WITH IN POINTS AND OUT POINTS

6. If you opened a source clip from the timeline, the Apply button appears above Source view Click the Apply button to make the changes that you made take effect in the timeline (**Figure 3.46**). If you do not open a clip in the program, the Apply button will not appear.

The program's in and out points are also displayed in the time ruler of the timeline (**Figure 3.47**).

Figure 3.46 If the clip is in the timeline, click the Apply button to make the changes take effect.

✔ Tip

■ When you mark the in and out points, notice how the duration ◬ changes. Knowing the duration can help you make editing decisions.

■ When you double-click a clip in the timeline, Premiere automatically sets an in and out point around the clip in the timeline.

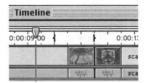

Figure 3.47 The program's in and out points are also displayed in the time ruler of the timeline.

To go to in and out points:

1. *Do one of the following:*

◆ To go to edit points in the source, open a source clip in Source view or a clip window, or double-click a clip in the timeline.

◆ To go to edit points in the program, activate Program view or the Timeline window.

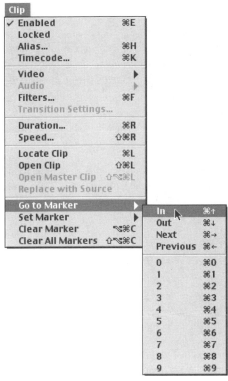

Figure 3.48 Choose Clip > Go to Marker > In or Clip > Go to Marker > Out.

Figure 3.49 When the clip is cued to an in point or out point, the appropriate icon appears in the view.

2. *Do one of the following:*

◆ To go to the in point, choose Clip > Go to Marker > In (**Figure 3.48**).

◆ To go to the out point, choose Clip > Go to Marker > Out.

When the clip is cued to an in or out point, the appropriate icon appears in the view (**Figure 3.49**).

To delete in and out points:

1. *Do one of the following:*

◆ To delete edit points from the source, open a source clip in Source view or a clip window, or double-click a clip in the timeline.

◆ To delete edit points from the program, activate Program view or the timeline window.

2. *Do one of the following:*

◆ To delete the in point, hold down the Option key while you click the Mark In button.

◆ To delete the out point, hold down the Option key while you click the Mark Out button.

◆ To delete both the in point and the out point, press G.

Using a Clip More Than Once in a Program

In previous versions of Premiere, whenever you used a clip (or parts of a clip) in the timeline more than once, every use of the clip was listed separately in the project. In the current version of Premiere, a clip is listed only once, no matter how many times you add it to the timeline.

The original clip is called a *master clip*, and each time you use it in the timeline, you create a new *instance* of the master clip. Because clip instances are part of the program, they are also referred to as *program clips*.

If you open program clips in Source view, the pull-down menu lists them, each with a unique name (**Figure 3.50**). Whenever you open a clip from the timeline, you are viewing a particular instance of the clip.

If you want to change a clip in the timeline by using the Source-view controls, make sure that you are viewing the correct instance of the clip.

Although clip instances can be manipulated independently, they still refer to a corresponding master clip, If you delete a master clip, you also delete its instances.

Figure 3.50 If you open program clips in Source view, they are listed in the Source View pull-down menu. Notice that each instance is identified differently.

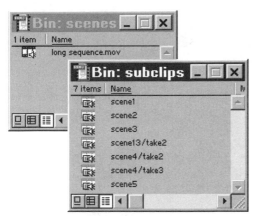

Figure 3.51 A master clip, and several subclips created from it.

Working with Subclips

If you want to name an *instance* of a clip, or if you want it to be listed separately in the program, you should create a *subclip*. A subclip is created from a portion of a master clip, Subclips provide you another way to organize your source materials.

You can create several subclips from a very long master clip, for example. Without subclips, you would have to search through the lengthy master clip to find the part that you want to use. In addition, without subclips, it would be more difficult to discern one instance of a master clip from another, because the instances would have nearly identical names. By creating subclips, you can define shorter, more manageable portions of the master clip. You can also name the subclips and organize them in bins (**Figure 3.51**).

Just as *master clips* refers to media, *subclips* refers to the master clip from which the clips were created. If the master clip is deleted, its subclips are also deleted. Otherwise, subclips function exactly like master clips.

In this book and elsewhere, the generic term *clip* refers to both master clips and subclips, unless making a distinction between those terms is important.

To create a subclip:

1. Open a master clip in Source view a or separate source clip window.

2. Mark the in and out points (the section, Working With In and Out Points, earlier in this chapter) to define the length of the subclip.

   Any markers that you set in the master clip are also included in the subclip.

(continued on next page)

3. Choose Project > Create > Subclip (**Figure 3.52**).

The Make Subclip dialog box opens.

4. In the Name field, type a name for the subclip (**Figure 3.53**).

5. From the Location pull-down menu, choose the project or bin where you want to save the subclip (**Figure 3.53**).

6. Click OK to create the subclip.

The subclip appears in the specified project or bin.

To create a subclip by copying:

1. Select a clip in a project, bin, or Library window.

2. Choose Edit > Copy.

3. Select a project, bin, or Library window.

4. Choose Edit > Paste.

To create a subclip by dragging:

1. Open a clip in Source view.

2. Set in and out points (the section, Working With In and Out Points, earlier in this chapter).

3. Drag the clip from Source view into a project, bin, or Library window (**Figure 3.54**).

✔ Tip

■ Copying, pasting, and dragging clips to the timeline creates another instance of the master clip, not a subclip.

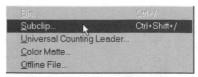

Figure 3.52 After you set the in and out points, choose Project > Create > Subclip.

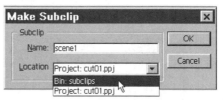

Figure 3.53 Name the subclip, and choose the project or bin where you want to save it.

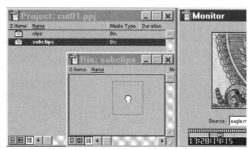

Figure 3.54 You can drag a clip to a project, bin, or Library window to create a subclip.

Figure 3.55 If the range of a subclip is too short, you can extend it by choosing Clip > Open Master Clip.

To extend the current start and end of a subclip:

1. Open a subclip in Source view or a Clip window.

2. Choose Clip > Open Master Clip (**Figure 3.55**).

   The subclip's associated master clip opens in Source view.

3. Follow the steps in any of the three preceding sections to create a subclip.

   The changes affect only how much of the master clip the subclip refers to. They do not directly affect the in and out points of the subclip or any instance of the subclip in the timeline.

✔ Tip

■ Subclips are also useful for creating a storyboard edit, as described in Chapter 4.

Using the Info Palette

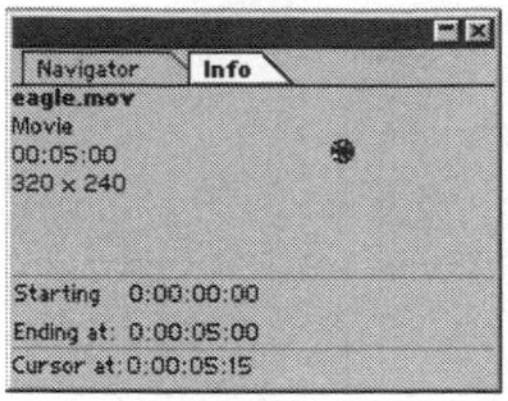

The Info palette can supply you a variety of information about a clip. The Info window can tell you basic information about a clip, like its type, duration, and whether it is being used in the program. You can use the Info window to help you set audio fade levels (Chapter 9), place objects in the Title window (Chapter 11), and set video fades (Chapter 12).

To use the Info palette:

1. *Do one of the following:*

♦ Choose Window > Info.

♦ Click the Info tab to activate the palette.

2. Click any clip.

The info window provides information about the clip (**Figure 3.56**).

Figure 3.56 The Info palette can provide you with essential information about the selected clip or other editing activities.

USING THE INFO PALETTE

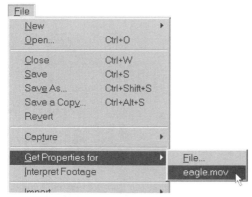

Figure 3.57 Choose Get Properties For.

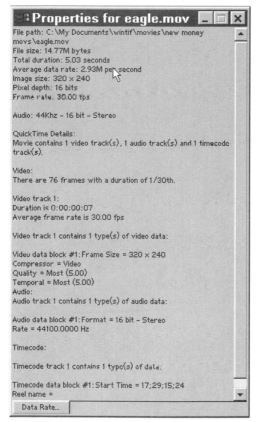

Figure 3.58 The Clip Properties window for a video clip.

Understanding Clip Properties

Getting clip properties allows you to view detailed information about any file in a supported format, even if that file is not part of the current project. Viewing a clip's properties can help you make decisions about the clip or troubleshoot a problem with it. You can discover whether a clip's data rate is appropriate for playback on the Internet, for example, or whether a clip has dropped frames.

To view the properties of a clip in the project:

1. If the clip is in the project, select it.

2. Choose File > Get Properties For > selected filename.

3. Choose the name of the clip that you selected (**Figure 3.57**).

   A Clip Properties window opens for the clip (**Figure 3.58**).

To view the properties of a clip that is not in the project:

1. Choose File > Get Properties For > filename.

2. Select the clip.

3. Click Open.

   A Clip Properties window opens for the clip (**Figure 3.58**).

To save the properties as a text file:

1. With the Clip Properties window open, choose File > Save As.

   The Save dialog box appears.

2. Type a file name.

3. Choose a destination for the file.

4. Click Save.

CREATING A PROGRAM

Now that you know how to set in and out points, you are ready to create an edited sequence of clips, called a *program*. You create a program by arranging clips in the timeline. You can review your work in the Program view on the right side of the Monitor window.

In other words, this is where the real editing begins.

Drag and Drop Vs. Monitor Controls

You can add clips to the timeline in either of two basic ways. Dragging and dropping is one way, and using the Monitor controls are the other. Each method has its advantages, so knowing both is wise.

Drag and Drop

The drag-and-drop method takes advantage of the computer's capability to display clips as objects that you can move and place by using the mouse. Most users find this technique to be the most intuitive and reassuringly similar to the way that Macintosh and Windows systems work (**Figure 4.1**).

Monitor Controls

Although this method is not as intuitive as dragging and dropping clips into the timeline, using the Monitor controls provides a great degree of flexibility and control. The Monitor window enables you to use a traditional editing technique called *three-point editing*. You can also perform four-point edits. (For more information on both techniques, see "Editing with the Monitor Controls" later in this chapter.) Because the Monitor's editing controls have single-stroke keyboard shortcuts, using them can be much faster than using the mouse (**Figure 4.2**).

Figure 4.1 Dragging video and audio from the Source View to the timeline.

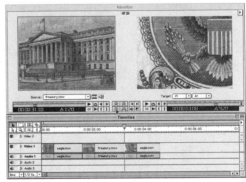

Figure 4.2 A typical three-point edit used to insert another clip into the middle of the clip added in **Figure 4.1**.

Choosing Source and Target Tracks

Video and audio material are often described as discrete *tracks* of information, due to the way that they are physically stored on traditional media, such as magnetic tape. Of course, digital files don't encode video and audio in the same way that tape does. Nevertheless, it's still helpful to think of video and audio as occupying tracks that you can manipulate separately. By selecting source and target tracks, you can add video only, audio only, or both video and audio to any combination of tracks in the timeline.

In drag and drop editing, you choose the source tracks by using the Take Video and Take Audio buttons, located under the Source view of the Monitor window (as explained in the following section, "To select source tracks"). You choose the destination, or *target* tracks, by simply dropping the clip in the timeline.

When you edit with the monitor controls, however, you must specify both the source and target tracks before you perform an edit. After all, you can choose any of several tracks in the timeline, and Premiere can't make this decision for you. You can select the video and audio tracks to which a clip will be added by using the Target menu under the Program view of the Monitor window (explained in the section "To select target tracks," later in this chapter).

By default, the source video and source audio are selected. Under the Program view, Video 1A and Audio 1 are selected as the target tracks. For more information about tracks in the timeline, see Chapter 5.

To select source tracks:

Under the Source view, *do any combination of the following:*

- To prevent the source video from being added to the timeline, click the Take Video icon so that it appears crossed out. To use the source video, click again to make the Take Video icon appear.

- To prevent the source audio from being added to the timeline, click the Take Audio icon 🔊 so that it appears crossed out. To use the source audio, click again to make the Take Audio icon appear (**Figure 4.3**).

If the source clip does not contain a track, the corresponding icon will not appear under the Source view.

To select target tracks:

Under the Program view, *do any of the following:*

- In the video Target track menu, choose the track in the timeline to which you want to add the source video (**Figure 4.4**).

- If you don't want to affect the target video track, choose None.

- In the audio Target track menu, choose the track in the timeline to which you want to add the source audio (**Figure 4.5**).

- If you don't want to affect the target audio track, choose None.

✔ Tip

- You can also choose a target track by clicking the name of a track in the timeline so that it becomes bold. Clicking the current target track's name deselects it, and it will no longer appear bold.

Figure 4.3 The Take Video and Take Audio icons indicate that source video and audio will be added to the program. If you don't want to add video or audio, click the icon to make it appear crossed out.

Figure 4.4 Choose a track in the video Target track menu.

Figure 4.5 Choose a track in the audio Target track menu.

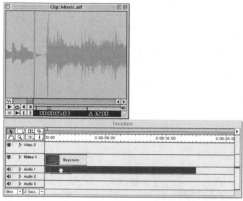

Figure 4.6 Both the Take Video and Take Audio buttons are selected.

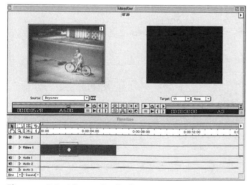

Figure 4.7 Only the Take Video is selected. Audio will not be added to the program.

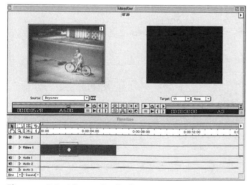

Figure 4.8 A video-only clip being dragged to an empty video track in the timeline.

Drag-and-Drop Editing

Wherever a source clip appears in Premiere, chances are that you can use the mouse to drag it into the timeline.

To add a source clip to the timeline from the Source View:

1. Open a source clip in the Source View of the Monitor window.

2. Set the In point and Out point in the source clip.

3. Make the Take Video icon visible to add source video to the program; make the Take Audio icons visible to add audio to the program (**Figures 4.6** and **4.7**).

   (See the section "Choosing Source and Target Tracks," earlier in this chapter.)

4. Drag the clip from the Source View to an unused portion of the timeline's video or audio track (**Figure 4.8**).

To add a clip to the timeline from a separate source clip window:

1. Open a separate clip window, as explained in the section "Viewing Clips" in Chapter 3.

2. Set the In point and Out point of the source clip.

(continued on next page)

3. Drag the clip to an unused portion of the timeline's video or audio track (**Figure 4.9**).

Both source video and audio (if present) are added to the timeline.

To add a clip to the program from a Project, Bin, or Library window:

1. Find a source clip in a Project, Bin, or Library window.

2. Drag the source clip to an unused portion of the timeline's video or audio track.

✔ Tip

■ If you want to add both video and audio to the program, make sure that you have enough space in both the video and audio tracks of the timeline. If one of the tracks is occupied, you won't be able to drop a linked clip there.

To add a clip between clips:

When you drag a clip, position the cursor between two clips in the timeline. An arrow appears above the next clip in the timeline (**Figure 4.10**).

When you release the mouse button, the new clip is added, and all the following clips shift forward in the timeline to make room for the new clip (**Figure 4.11**).

Figure 4.9 A separate audio clip window being dragged to an empty audio track of the timeline.

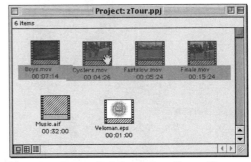

Figure 4.10 Drag a clip between two clips, until an arrow appear s above the following clip.

Figure 4.11 The following clips move forward in time to make room for the new clip.

Figure 4.12 You can drag a marquee around several clips to select them.

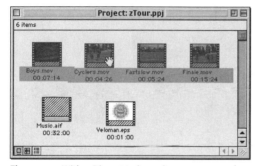

Figure 4.13 With a Bin set to icon view, you can make a storyboard and then drag it into the program or timeline.

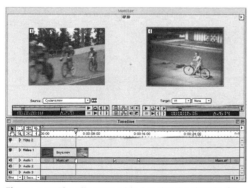

Figure 4.14 The clips are added to the timeline in the order in which they are arranged in the storyboard.

To add multiple clips to the program:

1. Select multiple clips in a Project, Bin, or Library window by dragging a marquee around the clips or by Shift+clicking several clips (**Figure 4.12**).

2. Drag the selected clips into the Program view or into an empty space in the timeline.

   When you release the mouse button, the clips are added to the program in the order in which they appear in the Bin.

✔ Tip

■ With a Bin set to Icon View, you can arrange clips or subclips in storyboard fashion. You may also want to mark In and Out points for the clips. You can then select and drag your entire "storyboard" into the timeline to create a program quickly (**Figures 4.13** and **4.14**).

DRAG-AND-DROP EDITING

Editing with the Monitor Controls

The Monitor window and its editing controls are among Premiere 5's most important new features. Before you can use them effectively, however, you must understand a few basic concepts.

Three-Point and Four-Point Editing

The *point* in the term *three-point editing* refers to In points and Out points. Technically, every edit has four points: source In, source Out, program In, and program Out. To add a clip to the program, you must define at least three of these four points in the Source and Program views. If you provide three points, Premiere figures out the fourth.

Most often, this means that you mark two In points and one Out point (**Figure 4.15**). Sometimes, however, it is more important to set where the clip ends than to set where it begins. In such a case, you mark one In point and two Out points. In the example shown in **Figure 4.16**, the editor has determined that the next clip must be start after the last clip in the timeline (program In) and end at a certain point in the music, at marker 2 (program Out). The editor also wants the source clip to end at a certain frame (source Out). The editor doesn't need to mark the source In, because it is determined by the program In.

You can also mark all four points. If the source duration differs from the program duration, Premiere asks whether you want to shorten the source clip or change the speed of the source clip to fit the program duration.

Figure 4.15 A common three-point edit. In this case, the most important edit points are the source In, source Out, and program In. The program Out doesn't have to be marked, because it is determined by the source Out.

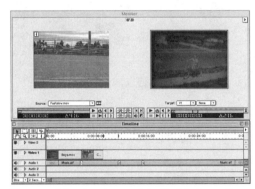

Figure 4.16 Another three-point edit, this time with a source Out, program In, and program Out.

Figure 4.17 A clip in the timeline before an insert or overlay edit. Note that the program In occurs in the middle of a clip in the timeline. The audio clip with markers will also help you see the results of the edit.

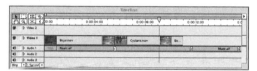

Figure 4.18 After a video insert. Everything after the In point is shifted forward in time to make room for the new clip, even if it means splitting a clip in two parts.

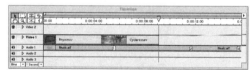

Figure 4.19 After a video overlay. The new clip replaces material in the timeline.

Figure 4.20 The Take Video button in the Source View.

Insert and Overlay

The Monitor controls allow you to use either of two methods to add clips to the timeline: insert and overlay.

When you *insert* a clip, the source clip is added at the designated point in the timeline, and all the subsequent clips are shifted forward in time to make room for the new clip (**Figures 4.17** and **4.18**).

When you *overlay* a clip, the source clip is added at the designated point in the timeline, replacing any clips that were already there (**Figure 4.19**).

Lift and Extract

The Monitor controls give you two methods of removing part of the program from the timeline: lift and extract.

The *Lift* button removes the defined range from the timeline, leaving a gap in the timeline.

The *Extract* button removes the defined range from the timeline and shifts all the later clips back in the timeline, closing the gap.

To perform a three-point edit:

1. View a source clip in the Source View of the Monitor window.

2. Click Take Video to use the source video in the program; click Take Audio to use the source audio in the program (**Figure 4.20**).

   (continued on next page)

3. In the Program view, select the target tracks where the source will be added (**Figure 4.21**).

4. Set any combination of three In and Out points in the Source and Program views (**Figure 4.22**).

5. Click either the Insert or Overlay button in the Monitor controls.

✔ Tip

■ If you do not specify an In or Out point in the Program view, the Edit Line serves as the In point. Using the Edit Line as the program In point can save time, especially when you are rough-cutting a sequence of clips.

To perform a four-point edit:

1. Mark all four edit points in the Source and Program views (**Figure 4.23**).

2. Select the source tracks by clicking the Take Video and Take Audio buttons.

3. Select the Target tracks in the Program view.

4. Click the Insert or Overlay button.

5. If the source duration and program duration are different, Premiere prompts you to choose one of the following:

◆ **Fit to Fill** changes the speed of the source clip to fit the specified duration in the program (**Figure 4.24**). Only the speed changes; the In and Out points stay the same. In **Figure 4.25**, the speed of the source clip has been slowed, making its duration long enough to fit in the range defined by the program In and program Out. If the source clip were too long, its speed would increase so that its duration would match the program duration.

Figure 4.21 Select Target tracks in the Program view. You can also select Target tracks in the timeline.

Figure 4.22 A typical three-point edit. Source video and program video1 are selected. A source In, source Out, and program In are marked.

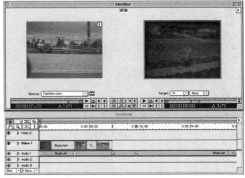

Figure 4.23 A four-point edit. Notice that the duration of the source and the program are different.

Figure 4.24 The Fit to Fill dialog box.

Figure 4.25 After performing the four-point edit using the fit to fill option.

Figure 4.26 In the timeline pull-down menu, choose Timeline Window Options.

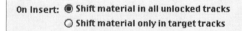

Figure 4.27 In the Timeline Window Options dialog box, choose the appropriate radio button.

◆ **Trim Source** changes the source Out point to fit the specified duration in the program. The In point and the speed of the clip are unaffected. (In other words, this option ignores the source Out and works like a three-point edit.)

◆ **Cancel Edit** stops the edit and makes no changes in the program.

Understanding Insert Edits

When you perform an insert edit, clips in the program shift later in time to accommodate the new clip. Several factors determine how the clips shift, and which tracks are affected. Your choice of source and target tracks can affect how an insert edit works (see "Choosing Source and Target Tracks," earlier in this chapter). In addition, you can choose to lock or unlock tracks (see "Locking Tracks" in Chapter 5). However, the primary factor that governs how insert edits work is found in the Timeline Window Options (to learn more about the Timeline Window Options, see Chapter 5).

To choose insert editing options:

1. In the Timeline window's pull-down menu, choose Timeline Window Options (**Figure 4.26**).

   The Timeline Window Options dialog box appears.

2. Next to On Insert, select the appropriate radio button (**Figure 4.27**):

   ◆ **Shift material in all unlocked tracks:** insert edits cause clips in all unlocked tracks of the timeline to shift later in time.

   ◆ **Shift material only in target tracks:** insert edits cause only clips in target tracks to shift later in time.

   (continued on next page)

✔ Tip

■ When you choose to shift material only in target tracks, be careful to select only the target tracks you want to affect. For example, if you want to insert edit source video only, make sure to select Take Video for the source clip, and None in the target audio menu. If you do select a target audio track, an insert edit will insert an empty space (equivalent to the duration of the inserted clip) into the selected audio track, shifting the audio clips in that track later in time. This oversight could cause unintentional loss of synchronization between video and audio (**Figure 4.28**).

To lift a range from the program:

1. Set an In and Out point in the Program view to define the range to be removed from the timeline (**Figure 4.29**).

2. Select the Target Tracks from which the range will be removed.

   You can select the Tracks in the Program view or in the timeline.

3. Click the Lift button  in the Monitor window (**Figure 4.30**).

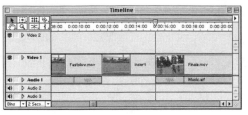

Figure 4.28 Careless track selection can cause you to accidentally insert empty space into a track and possibly result in a loss of synch.

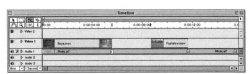

Figure 4.29 Before a lift or extract is performed. program In, program Out, and target tracks are set.

Figure 4.30 After the selected area is lifted. Notice that the area is removed, leaving a gap in the selected track.

Figure 4.31 After the selected area is extracted. Notice that subsequent clips in the selected track have been shifted back in the timeline.

To extract a segment of the program:

1. Set an In and Out point in the Program view to define the range to be removed from the timeline.

2. Select the Target Tracks from which the range will be removed.

   You can select the tracks in the Program view or in the timeline.

3. Click the Extract button 🔳 in the Monitor window (**Figure 4.31**).

EDITING
IN THE TIMELINE

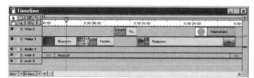

Figure 5.1 Parts of the timeline window.

Figure 5.2 Parts of the Navigator window.

As the name implies, the timeline window graphically represents the clips of the program arranged in time. The edit line of the timeline directly corresponds to the current time displayed in Program view. In the timeline, the program looks a lot like edited film. Like film, the timeline lays out the instances of clips before you. Unlike film, however, the timeline allows you to view any segment of the program instantly or to view the entire program at once. Yet the timeline isn't simply another way to look at or navigate through the program; it's also a way to edit. Editing in the timeline feels almost as tactile as editing film but is far more flexible and efficient than using razors and tape. You can select, move, rearrange, trim, cut, copy, and paste clips in the timeline (**Figure 5.1**). An associated tool, the new Navigator window, helps you find your way around the timeline (**Figure 5.2**).

Along with the rest of the Premiere interface, the timeline has undergone several significant changes from earlier versions. The new timeline looks much leaner and is more consistent with Adobe's other graphics software, such as Photoshop, Illustrator, and AfterEffects. In addition, the timeline has been reorganized and now incorporates a new editing model.

Customizing the Timeline's Appearance

You can customize the timeline window's appearance to fit your needs or simply your tastes.

To change the icon size and track format:

1. From the timeline window's pull-down menu, choose Timeline Window Options (**Figure 5.3**).

   The Timeline Window Options dialog box appears.

2. Click the radio button next to the icon size that you want to use (**Figure 5.4**).

   Choose among small, medium, and large icons for clips in video tracks.

3. Select the radio button next to the track format that you want to use (**Figure 5.4**):

   ◆ Icon view displays an icon for each time unit.

   ◆ Heads and Tails view displays an icon for the first and last time units of a clip, if the length of the clip allows.

   ◆ Name Only view displays no icons for clips in video tracks.

4. Check the Show Audio Waveforms check-box to display audio waveforms in the timeline (**Figure 5.4**); leave it unchecked to conceal this information.

   Checking Show Audio Waveforms makes waveforms visible when the audio track is expanded.

5. Click OK to close the Timeline Window Options dialog box and apply the changes.

Figure 5.3 Choose Timeline Window Options.

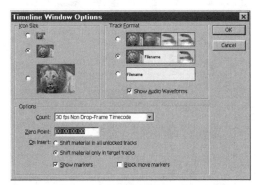

Figure 5.4 Choose an icon size for the video tracks, choose a track format for the video tracks, and specify whether audio waveforms are to be displayed.

Figure 5.5 Drag the split-window bar to reveal more video tracks or more audio tracks.

✔ Tip

■ To maximize both screen space and performance, display only the information that you need. Large icons, detailed track formats, and waveforms not only use up valuable screen space but also take longer to display. Excessive detail can result in an overcrowded screen and slow scrolling in the timeline.

To change the ratio of video and audio tracks displayed:

1. Drag the split-window bar, located on the right side of the timeline, between the video and audio tracks (**Figure 5.5**).

   The pointer changes to ↕ when you're at the correct place.

2. Drag down to reveal more video tracks or up to reveal more audio tracks.

   This procedure is helpful when a program has more tracks than the Timeline can display.

Customizing the Time Ruler

As you learned in Chapter 2, frames can be counted in several ways. The time ruler at the top of the timeline can display any of these time measurements. By default, the timeline starts at zero, but you can set it to start at any number.

To change the time count in the timeline:

1. From the timeline window's pull-down menu, choose Timeline Window Options (**Figure 5.6**).

   The Timeline Window Options dialog box appears.

2. From the Count pull-down menu, choose a time count (**Figure 5.7**).

To change the zero point:

1. From the timeline window's pull-down menu, choose Timeline Window Options.

   The Timeline Window Options dialog box appears.

2. In the Zero Point field, type the number you want the timeline to start at (**Figure 5.8**).

✔ Tip

■ An edited master tape typically contains information at the head of the tape, before the program starts. A common practice is to start the tape at 00:58:00:00. The program itself always begins at 01:00:00:00, which gives you 2 minutes from the beginning of the tape to the program start. The 2 minutes usually include 30 seconds of black, 1 minute of bars and tone, a 10-second slate, 10 more seconds of black, an 8-second countdown, and 2 seconds of black.

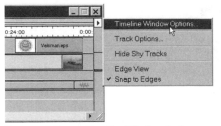

Figure 5.6 Choose Timeline Window Options.

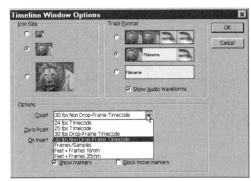

Figure 5.7 From the Count menu, choose a unit of measurement for the Time Ruler.

Figure 5.8 Type a number for the starting point of the Time Ruler.

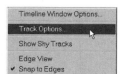

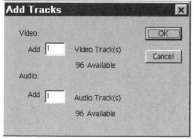

Figure 5.9 Choose Track Options.

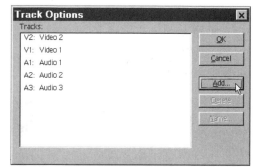

Figure 5.10 In the dialog box, click the Add button to add tracks.

Figure 5.11 Enter the number of video tracks and audio tracks that you want to add.

Adding, Deleting, and Naming Tracks

By default, the timeline opens with two video tracks and three audio tracks. Although this number is adequate for many projects, Premiere permits you to have as many as 99 video and 99 audio tracks in the timeline. What's more, you can now name all those tracks, so it's much easier to discern the sound-effects track from the music and dialogue tracks, for example.

To add tracks:

1. From the timeline window's pull-down menu, choose Track Options (**Figure 5.9**).

   The Track Options dialog box appears.

2. Click the Add button (**Figure 5.10**).

   The Add Tracks dialog box appears.

3. Enter the number of video tracks and audio tracks that you want to add (**Figure 5.11**).

4. Click OK.

5. Click OK to exit the Track Options dialog box.

To delete tracks:

1. From the timeline window's pull-down menu, choose Track Options.

   The Track Options dialog box appears.

2. Select the name of the track that you want to delete.

   You can delete only video track 2 and higher; you can delete only audio track 4 and later.

3. Click the Delete button to delete the track.

4. Click OK to exit the dialog box.

To name tracks:

1. From the timeline window's pull-down menu, choose Track Options.

   The Track Options dialog box appears.

2. *Do one of the following:*
   - ◆ Click the name of a track and then click the Name button.
   - ◆ Double-click the name of the track (**Figure 5.12**).

3. Type the name for the track (**Figure 5.13**).

4. Click OK.

   The track displays an abbreviated number and its new name.

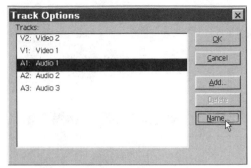

Figure 5.12 Double-click the name of a track, or select it and then click the Name button.

Figure 5.13 Type a name for the track.

Figure 5.14 Tracks with the eye icon 👁 will be seen in playback, and tracks with the speaker icon 🔊 will be heard.

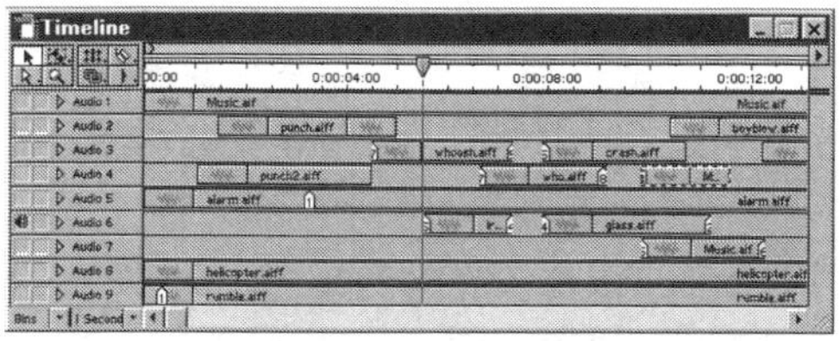

Figure 5.15 Monitoring only one track makes it easier to hear whether the sound effects are synched properly.

Monitoring Tracks

As you may already know, the term *monitor* can refer to a video screen or audio speaker. It is also used as a verb, meaning to see or hear, as in "to monitor the video and audio." In Premiere, you can monitor any combination of the tracks in the timeline. Only monitored tracks are included during playback and when you preview or export the program. Although you usually want to monitor all the tracks, at times, you want to monitor only certain tracks.

To monitor tracks:

Click next to the track name in the Timeline to reveal or hide the eye icon 👁 for video tracks and the speaker icon 🔊 for audio tracks.

The monitor icons indicate that the corresponding tracks are not shy (described later in this chapter) and will be seen or heard during playback (**Figure 5.14**). A track without a monitor icon will not be seen or heard during playback.

✔ Tips

- Option+click next to the track name in the timeline to reveal or hide all the speaker icons or all the eye icons, except for the Video 1A/1B tracks, which must be treated separately.

- Isolating a single audio monitor can be especially helpful when you are synching sound effects to video. (On an audio mixer, this procedure would be called *soloing* the track.) The other sound tracks often prevent you from hearing whether a sound effect is synched properly (**Figure 5.15**).

Locking and Unlocking Tracks

Locking a track protects the clips in the track from accidental changes. You can't move or modify the clips that are in the locked track. You also can't add clips to a locked track; the track's name appears dimmed in the Target Track menu. If you place the pointer or other tool on the locked track, it appears with a lock icon ◄ to indicate its locked status (**Figure 5.16**). Although you can't alter the clips in a locked track, you can still monitor those clips, and the track is included when you preview or export the program.

To lock and unlock tracks:

◆ Click next to the track name to display or hide the crossed-out pencil icon ✗ (**Figure 5.17**).

This icon indicates that the corresponding track is locked and can't be modified (or *written to*). No icon indicates that the track is unlocked.

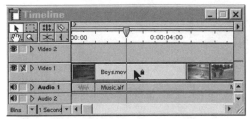

Figure 5.16 When you position the mouse pointer over a locked track, the lock icon appears.

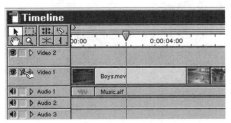

Figure 5.17 Click to make the crossed-out pencil icon appear, locking the track. Click again to make the icon disappear, unlocking the track.

Figure 5.18 Click the triangle to expand or collapse a track.

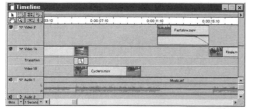

Figure 5.19 Expanding different types of tracks reveals different information.

Expanding and Collapsing Tracks

The capability to expand and collapse tracks is new to the Premiere Timeline, but it may be familiar to you from other programs or even the Macintosh desktop. Expanding the Video 1 track reveals a layout that resembles those of previous versions of Premiere. The Video 1A/1B tracks is discussed in more detail in Chapter 8.

To expand or collapse tracks:

◆ Click the triangle next to the track name to expand or collapse a track (**Figure 5.18**).

Depending on the type of track, expanding a track reveals different information (**Figure 5.19**). Expanding the Video 1 track reveals Video 1/A and 1/B tracks (see Chapter 7). Expanding video track 2 and higher reveals the fade linc (see Chapter 12). Expanding audio tracks reveals waveform, fade, and pan information (see Chapter 9).

EXPANDING AND COLLAPSING TRACKS

Displaying Shy Tracks

The capability to mark tracks as *shy* is another feature that makes the Timeline more consistent with other Adobe applications. Because conserving screen space is always an issue, shy tracks make it easy for you to quickly conceal tracks that you're not currently using. Whether they are hidden or visible, shy tracks are still included during playback and when you preview or output the program.

To reveal or conceal tracks:

1. Command+click the video-monitor icons 👁 and audio-monitor icons 🔊 to mark the tracks as shy (**Figure 5.20**).

   The monitor icons appear are outlined 👁 🔊 when the tracks are marked as shy.

2. To make your choice from the timeline window's pull-down menu, *do one of the following*:

   ◆ Choose Hide Shy Tracks.

   ◆ Choose Show Shy Tracks (**Figures 5.21** and **5.22**).

✔ Tip

■ If you're concentrating on video editing, mark most or all of the audio tracks as shy. Hide them until you need to view them again. If you're focusing on adjusting audio levels, mark the video layers as shy and hide those layers.

Figure 5.20 Command+click the eye icon 👁 to make a track shy.

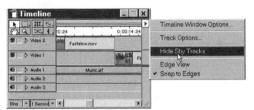

Figure 5.21 From the Timeline window's pull-down menu, choose Hide Shy Tracks to display fewer tracks in the timeline...

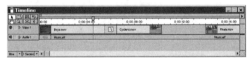

Figure 5.22 ...and the tracks marked as shy are hidden from view.

Figure 5.23 Open a Clip that's in the timeline.

Figure 5.24 After you make changes to the edit marks, you must click the Apply button for the changes to take effect.

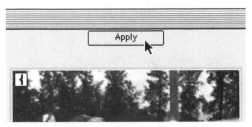

Figure 5.25 The clip in the timeline after the change is applied.

Opening a Clip in the Timeline

As you learned in Chapter 3, changing a master clip does not affect any instances of that clip that are already in the timeline. If you want to view a program clip, you can still open it in Source view or the Clip window, and you can change any of its editing marks by using the Controller.

To open and change a clip in the timeline:

1. Open a program clip (an instance of a clip in the timeline), using one of the methods described in Chapter 3 (**Figure 5.23**).

2. Using the Controller, make changes in the in point, the out point, or marked frames.

3. Click the Apply button to make the changes take effect in the clip in the timeline (**Figures 5.24** and **5.25**).

✔ Tip

- If you want to make the clip longer, you must have available space in the timeline. If another clip occupies the space after the clip that you want to extend, you have to use an alternative method. You can move the clips in the timeline to create enough room (explained later in this chapter), you can perform a ripple edit (see Chapter 6), or you can perform a three-point insert edit (see Chapter 4).

Getting Around the Timeline

You can navigate the program in the timeline in several ways. You can zoom in, zoom out, and scroll through the Timeline. You can also use the new Navigator palette to find your way.

To view part of the program in more detail:

Do one of the following:

◆ From the Time Unit pull-down menu, choose a smaller time increment (**Figure 5.26**).

◆ In the Navigator palette, drag the slider to the right (**Figure 5.27**) or click the Magnify icon ⬕.

◆ In the Tools palette, select the Zoom tool ⬕ and then click the part of the timeline that you want to see in more detail.

◆ In the Tools palette, select the zoom tool ⬕ and then drag a marquee around the area of the timeline that you want to see in detail (**Figure 5.28**).

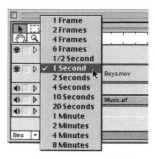

Figure 5.26 Choose a time unit from the pull-down menu. Smaller units give you a closer look at the timeline; larger units give you a wider view.

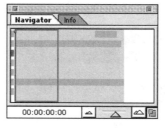

Figure 5.27 In the Navigator palette, drag the slider to the right to zoom in to the timeline, or click the Magnify icon.

Figure 5.28 Click a point in the timeline to zoom in one time unit at a time, or drag a marquee around the area you want to view more closely.

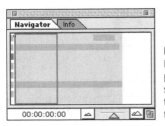

Figure 5.29
In the Navigator palette, drag the slider left, or click the Reduce icon to zoom out.

Figure 5.30 When you hold down the Option key, the Zoom tool displays a minus sign ⊖ and can be used to zoom out.

Figure 5.31 Use the scroll bar to scroll through the timeline.

Figure 5.32 Use the Hand tool to drag your view of the timeline to the right or left.

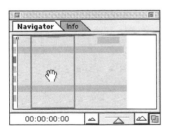

Figure 5.33 Drag the view box in the Navigator palette to change the view of the timeline.

To view more of the program in the timeline:

Do one of the following:

◆ From the Time Unit pull-down menu, choose a larger time increment.

◆ In the Navigator palette, drag the slider to the left or click the Reduce icon ⬇ (**Figure 5.29**).

◆ In the Tools palette, select the Zoom tool ⊕ and then Option+click the part of the timeline that you want to center in the wider view. When you press Option, the Zoom tool appears with a minus sign, to indicate that it will zoom out ⊖ (**Figure 5.30**).

✔ Tip

■ To zoom out quickly to view the entire program in the Timeline, press the back-slash key (\).

To scroll through the timeline:

Do one of the following:

◆ At the bottom of the timeline, click either the left or right scroll arrow to gradually move across a close view of the program (**Figure 5.31**).

◆ Drag the scroll box right or left to view a different part of the program (**Figure 5.31**).

◆ Click the scroll bar to the right or left of the scroll handle to shift the view one width of the timeline (**Figure 5.31**).

◆ In the Tools palette, select the Hand tool ✋ and then drag the program to the right or left (**Figure 5.32**).

◆ In the Navigator palette, drag the view box to the right or left to show another part of the timeline (**Figure 5.33**).

GETTING AROUND THE TIMELINE

To cue the Edit Line:

Do one of the following:

◆ Click the Time Ruler to move the Edit Line to that point in the timeline (**Figure 5.34**).

◆ In the Navigator palette, hold down the Shift key while you drag in the Navigator's miniature timeline (**Figure 5.35**).

◆ In the Navigator palette, highlight the time-code readout and then type a new time code (**Figure 5.36**).

◆ In Program view, use the Controller to move or cue the Edit Line, which corresponds to the current frame (see Chapter 3).

✔ Tip

■ Remember that you can use the program Controller to cue the Edit Line to an absolute or relative time position. You can also go to an in point, out point, or program marker (see Chapter 3).

Figure 5.34 Click the Time Ruler, and the Edit Line instantly cues to that point.

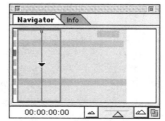

Figure 5.35 In the Navigator palette, Shift+drag in the miniature timeline to move the Edit Line in the actual timeline.

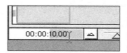

Figure 5.36 You can type a time code in the Navigator palette to cue the Edit Line to that point.

Figure 5.37 When a clip is selected, the border is highlighted with crawling ants.

Figure 5.38 Use the Range Select tool to drag a marquee around the clips that you want to select.

Selecting Clips in the Timeline

Not surprisingly, whenever you want to manipulate or affect a program clip in any way, you have to select it first.

To select a clip in the timeline:

1. Click a clip instance in the timeline to select it.

   When a clip is selected, its border has an animated highlight, sometimes described as crawling ants (**Figure 5.37**).

2. Click the clip again to deselect it.

To select multiple clips in the timeline:

Do one of the following:

◆ Hold down the Shift key while you click multiple clips in the timeline to select them.

◆ In the Tools palette, select the Range Select tool ⟦⟧ and then drag a marquee around the clips that you want to select (**Figure 5.38**).

✔ Tip

■ You can also Shift+click selected clips to deselect them. Shift+clicking is a common computer convention for adding to and subtracting from a selection.

Deleting Clips from the Timeline

If you can select a clip, it's a simple matter to delete it. The same is true of gaps between clips.

To delete a clip from the timeline:

1. Click the clip in the timeline to select it.

2. Press Delete.

✔ Tip

■ Only the selected clip is deleted. If you delete a video clip, for example, its linked audio remains in the timeline.

To delete more than one clip from the timeline:

1. In the Tools palette, select the Range Select tool ⌞⌟, or press M.

2. Drag a marquee around the clips in the timeline that you want to select (**Figure 5.39**).

3. To select additional clips, hold down the Shift key and click unselected clips; to deselect clips, hold down the Shift key and click selected clips.

4. Press Delete (**Figure 5.40**).

To delete a gap between clips:

1. Click an empty segment in a track of the timeline to select it (**Figure 5.41**).

2. Choose Edit > Ripple Delete (**Figures 5.42** and **5.43**).

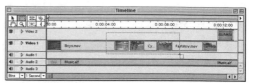

Figure 5.39 Use the Range Select tool to drag a marquee around the clips that you want to delete...

Figure 5.40 ...and press Delete to remove them from the timeline.

Figure 5.41 Click an empty segment to select it...

Figure 5.42 ...choose Edit > Ripple Delete...

Figure 5.43 ...and the gap is closed.

Figure 5.44 Uncheck Enabled to disable the clips.

Figure 5.45 Disabled clips appear with a hatched pattern of backslashes.

Enabling and Disabling Clips

Disabling a clip in the timeline prevents it from appearing during playback and when you preview or export the program. Disabling a clip is useful if you want to keep the clip in the program but want to exclude it temporarily. You might want to disable a single audio clip to hear what the program sounds like without it, for example. You can still move and make other changes in a disabled clip.

To disable or enable a clip:

1. Select one or more clips in the timeline (explained earlier in this chapter).

2. Choose Clip > Enabled (**Figure 5.44**).

   A check indicates that the clip is enabled. No check indicates that the clip is disabled. Disabled clips appear in the timeline with a hatch pattern of backslashes over them (**Figure 5.45**). Notice that backslashes on a disabled clip slope down to the right.

Locking and Unlocking Clips

Locking a clip protects it from any unintentional changes. You can't move or modify locked clips. Locked clips appear in the timeline with a hatch pattern of slashes over them. Notice that slashes on a locked clip slope down to the left. Although you can't alter locked clips, you can monitor them, and they're still included when you preview or export the program.

To lock a clip:

1. Select one or more clips in the timeline (explained earlier in this chapter).

2. Choose Clip > Locked (**Figure 5.46**).

   A check indicates that the clip is locked. No check indicates that the clip is unlocked. Locked clips appear in the Timeline with a hatch pattern of slashes (**Figure 5.47**).

✔ Tip

■ You can also lock an entire track to protect it from unintentional changes (explained earlier in this chapter).

Figure 5.46 Check Locked to lock the clip.

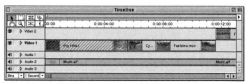

Figure 5.47 Locked clips appear with a hatched pattern of slashes. Compare this pattern with that of a disabled clip.

Figure 5.48 The video and audio portions of a linked clip move together in the timeline.

Using Linked Clips

When a clip has both video and audio, it is known as a *linked clip*. When you move a linked clip in the timeline, the video and audio portions of the clip move together (**Figure 5.48**). Similarly, when you change the edit marks of a linked clip, the video and audio tracks both change—unless you deliberately treat them separately.

The link helps you keep the video and audio synchronized. Even if your video and audio were recorded separately (as in a film shoot), you can create an artificial link, or *soft link,* between video and audio. If you've ever edited film and magnetic tape, you know how convenient linked clips are.

Nevertheless, it's still possible to lose synch between the tracks of a linked clip. Fortunately, Premiere alerts you to the loss of synch by tagging the affected clips in the timeline. Premiere even tells you exactly how much the clips are out of synch and provides easy ways to restore it.

Although the link is usually an advantage, Premiere permits you to override the link, if necessary. You can even break the link, if you want.

To perform the tasks described in this chapter, you need to understand how linked clips behave in the timeline. In later chapters, you learn to tackle more advanced tasks related to synch and links.

Moving Clips in the Timeline

You can manipulate clips directly in the timeline to shift and rearrange them. You can move individual or multiple clips or entire tracks of clips.

To move a clip in the timeline:

1. Drag selected clips to an unused part of the timeline.

2. Linked video and audio move together (**Figure 5.49**).

To nudge a clip frame by frame:

1. Select a clip in the timeline.

2. Press the right- or left-arrow key to move the clip one frame at a time in the timeline.

   If you nudge the video or audio portion of a linked clip, you lose synch between the two.

✔ Tips

- As you discovered in Chapter 4, a linked clip can be dragged to the timeline only where both video and audio tracks are unoccupied, because linked video and audio tend to move in corresponding tracks in the timeline (video 1 and audio 1, for example). To override the link, hold down the Option key while you drag the linked clip in the timeline. If one track is occupied, Premiere shifts part of the linked clip to the next empty track, allowing you to drag the linked clip to that point in time (**Figure 5.50**).

- You can still drag a clip between two clips, as you learned in Chapter 4.

Figure 5.49 Linked clips usually move in corresponding video and audio tracks...

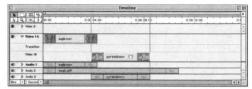

Figure 5.50 ... but if you Option+drag, one track can shift to an empty track.

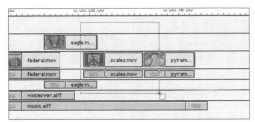

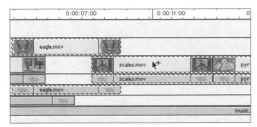

Figure 5.51 Use the Range Select to select multiple clips.

Figure 5.52 When you drag the selected clips, the Range Select tool becomes the Move icon.

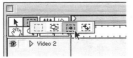

Figure 5.53 Select the Track tool from the Tools palette.

Figure 5.54 Click a clip to select that clip and all the following clips in that track.

To move a range of clips in the timeline:

1. In the Tools palette, select the Range Select tool ⌐⌐.

2. Drag a marquee around the clips that you want to select (**Figure 5.51**).

3. Drag the selection to an unused part of the timeline.

   When you drag the selection, the tool changes to the Move icon ↖⁺ (**Figure 5.52**).

To move all the clips in a track:

1. In the Tools palette, choose the Track tool ⊕ (**Figure 5.53**).

2. Click a clip in the timeline.

   All the clips in the track from that clip forward are selected.

3. Drag the selected clips to shift their position in the timeline (**Figure 5.54**).

✔ Tip

- Be careful: The Track tool ignores any links between audio and video. Whenever you use the Track tool, it's easy to lose synch between video and audio. (Synch and linked clips are explained earlier in this chapter.)

To move all the clips in multiple tracks:

1. In the Tools palette, choose the Multitrack tool 🔢 (**Figure 5.55**).

2. Click a clip in the timeline (**Figure 5.56**). All the clips in all tracks from that clip forward are selected.

3. Drag the selected clips to shift their position in the timeline.

✔ Tip

■ As usual, you can add to or subtract from your selection by Shift+clicking the Timeline. When you use the Track tool 🔢, add another track to your selection by Shift-clicking a clip in another track. Deselect a track by Shift+clicking it. Your selection can also start at different points in different tracks (**Figure 5.57**).

Figure 5.55 Select the Multitrack tool in the Tools palette.

Figure 5.56 Clicking a clip selects that clip and all the clips from that point on in the timeline.

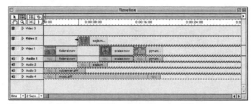

Figure 5.57 You can Shift+click clips in different tracks, starting at different points in the timeline.

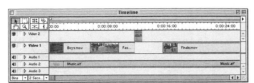

Figure 5.58 These two clips may look aligned when the timeline is zoomed out...

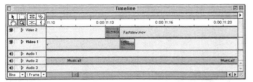

Figure 5.59 ...but a closer look reveals otherwise.

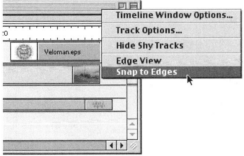

Figure 5.60 Choose Snap to Edges to activate the feature.

Using Snap to Edges

When you move clips in the timeline, you usually want to align them precisely. You may want a title in video track 2 to start right after the clip in track 1 ends, for example. When you place a sound effect, you may want to align a marker in a video clip with a marker in an audio clip. Or you may want to move a clip exactly where you placed the Edit Line. When you create transitions, the proper alignment of clips is critical. Unless you zoom in for a very close view of the program or continually consult the Info window, precise placement of clips in the timeline can be difficult (**Figures 5.58** and **5.59**).

The timeline provides an easy way to align clips, through a feature called *Snap to Edges*. When Snap to Edges is activated, clips behave as though they're magnetized; they tend to snap to the edge of another clip, to a marker, and to the Edit Line. Snap to Edges also works when you're trimming clips in the timeline (covered in Chapter 6). When Snap to Edges is off, the clips move smoothly past one another as you drag them in the timeline. Because Snap to Edges is so convenient, most editors leave it on most of the time.

To toggle Snap to Edges on and off:

From the timeline window's pull-down menu, choose Snap to Edges (**Figure 5.60**).

When Snap to Edges is checked ✔, it is on; when it is unchecked, it is off.

To use Snap to Edges:

1. From the timeline window's pull-down menu, choose Snap to Edges.

2. *Do one of the following*:

   ◆ Drag a clip in the timeline close to the edge of another clip, a marker, or the Edit Line.

   ◆ Position the Selection tool (the standard pointer) over a marker within a clip in the timeline until the pointer turns blue (**Figure 5.61**).

   As you drag the clip or the marker, it snaps to the edges of other clips, other markers, and the Edit Line.

✔ Tips

■ When Snap to Edges is on, it's easy to use clip markers to cut video to the beat of music or to synch sound effects to video (**Figure 5.62**)

■ Occasionally, several edges are so close together that Snap to Edges makes it difficult to place the Clip properly. In these infrequent cases, you should zoom into the timeline, so that competing edges appear farther apart. Alternatively, of course, you can turn off Snap to Edges and disable its magnetic effect.

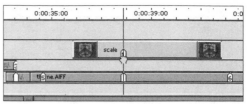

Figure 5.61 Drag a marker to make it snap to other markers, the Edit Line, or to the edges of other clips.

Figure 5.62 Markers and Snap to Edges make it easy to cut video to the beat of the music or to synch sound effects to video.

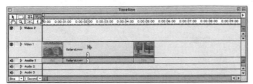

Figure 5.63 Use the Razor tool to split a clip.

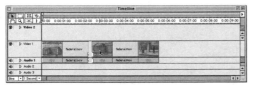

Figure 5.64 Splitting a clip results in two individual clips.

Figure 5.65 Click a clip in the timeline to split all the clips at that point in time.

Figure 5.66 All the clips are split, doubling the number of clip instances.

Splitting a Clip

Sometimes, you need to cut a clip in the timeline into two or more pieces. You may want to apply a filter effect to one part of a shot but not to another, for example. When you split a clip, of course, each piece becomes an independent program clip. When you split a linked clip, both the video and audio tracks are split.

To split a clip with the Razor:

1. In the Tools palette, select the Razor tool.

2. Click a clip in the timeline at the point where you want to split it (**Figure 5.63**).

   The clip is split into two individual clips at that point (**Figure 5.64**).

To split clips in multiple tracks:

1. In the Tools palette, select the Multirazor tool.

2. Click the point in the timeline where you want to split the clips in all tracks (**Figure 5.65**).

   All unlocked clips in all unlocked tracks are split at the same point in the timeline (**Figure 5.66**).

To split clips at the Edit Line:

1. Position the Edit Line at the point where you want to split the clip (**Figure 5.67**).

2. Choose Edit > Razor at Edit Line (**Figure 5.68**).

   All unlocked clips in all unlocked tracks are split at the same point in the timeline (**Figure 5.69**).

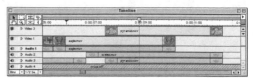

Figure 5.67 Position the Edit Line where you want to split the clips...

Figure 5.68 ...choose Edit > Razor at Edit Line ...

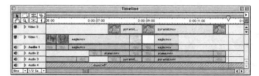

Figure 5.69 ...and the clips are split at that point in the timeline. Notice that the locked clip remains unaffected.

SPLITTING A CLIP

Match Frame Edits

Splitting a clip creates a cut that is visible in the timeline but invisible in playback. This kind of cut is called a *match-frame edit*. Because the viewer can't detect a match-frame edit, effects such as speed changes and filters appear to be seamless.

Figure 5.70 Select an empty track or a clip that you want to replace.

Figure 5.71 The pasted clip replaces the clip that had been in the timeline.

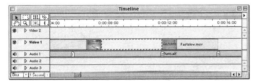

Figure 5.72 Select the gap where you want to paste the clip.

Figure 5.73 Premiere changes the out point of the clip so that it fits into the selected space.

Cutting, Copying, and Pasting Clips

As you would expect of any computer program, Adobe Premiere uses copy and paste functions. However, you might be pleasantly surprised by Premiere's powerful paste commands. In this section, you learn how to copy a clip's contents.

To paste a clip:

1. Click a clip in the timeline to select it.

2. *Do one of the following:*
   - ◆ Choose Edit > Copy to leave the selected clip in the timeline.
   - ◆ Choose Edit > Cut to remove the selected clip from the timeline.

2. *Do one of the following:*
   - ◆ Select an empty segment in an appropriate track in the timeline.
   - ◆ Select a clip in the timeline that you want to replace with the pasted clip (**Figure 5.70**).

3. Choose Edit > Paste.

   The clip either appears in the empty track of the timeline or replaces a clip in the timeline (**Figure 5.71**).

To use the Paste to Fit command:

1. Click a clip in the timeline to select it.

2. *Do one of the following:*
   - ◆ Choose Edit > Copy to leave the selected clip in the timeline.
   - ◆ Choose Edit > Cut to remove the selected clip from the timeline.

3. Select an empty segment in a track of the timeline (**Figure 5.72**).

4. Choose Edit > Paste to Fit (**Figure 5.73**).

To use the Paste Custom command:

1. Click a clip in the timeline to select it.

2. *Do one of the following:*
   - ◆ Choose Edit > Copy to leave the clip in the timeline.
   - ◆ Choose Edit > Cut to remove the clip from its current position.

3. Choose Edit > Paste Custom.

   The Paste Custom Settings dialog box appears (**Figure 5.74**).

4. Click the Content radio button.

5. Choose an option from the pull-down menu in the Content section of the Paste Custom dialog box (**Figures 5.75** and **5.76**).

   Animations dynamically illustrate the effect of each option, as follows:
   - ◆ **Normal** works the same as an ordinary paste.
   - ◆ **Move Source Out** works the same as Paste to Fit, by changing the source out point to fit into the space in the timeline.
   - ◆ **Move Destination In Point** changes the next clip's in point to accommodate the pasted clip.
   - ◆ **Move Source In Point** changes the source clip's in point to fit the clip into the space in the timeline. The source out point remains unchanged.
   - ◆ **Move Destination Out Point** changes the out point of the preceding clip to accommodate the pasted clip.
   - ◆ **Change Speed** changes the speed of the clip to fit it into the space in the timeline. The source in and out points remain unchanged.
   - ◆ **Shift Linked Tracks** shifts the following clips and their linked tracks forward in time to accommodate the pasted clip.

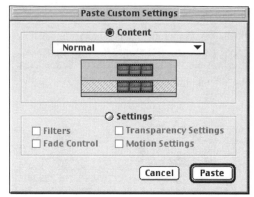

Figure 5.74 Choose Edit > Paste Custom for the Paste Custom Settings dialog box.

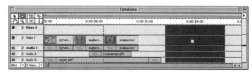

Figure 5.75 Click the Content radio button to paste the content of the clip, as opposed to its settings. Animations dynamically illustrate how each option works.

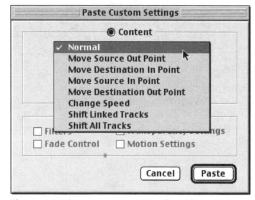

Figure 5.76 Choose a paste option from the pull-down menu.

Figure 5.77 Drag to select the range of the program that you want to block-copy.

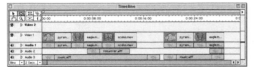

Figure 5.78 Option+drag the selection to an empty part of the timeline, and drop a copy of all the clips in the selected area.

◆ **Shift All Tracks** shifts the following clips in all tracks forward in time to accommodate the pasted clip.

6. Click Paste.

To block-copy a range of the program:

1. In the Tools palette, select the Block Select tool ⟐.

2. Drag to select the part of the program that you want to block-copy (**Figure 5.77**).

3. Option+drag the selection to an empty part of the Timeline (**Figure 5.78**).

   The block-copy function copies the selected area in all tracks; you can't limit the effect to certain tracks.

✔ Tip

■ If you don't hold down the Option key, you create a virtual clip instead of block-copying the selection. For more information about virtual clips, see Chapter 7.

CUTTING, COPYING, AND PASTING CLIPS

REFINING THE PROGRAM

After you assemble a rough cut, you can refine it by making adjustments to the in and out points of the clips in the program—a process known as *trimming*. Although you already know several ways to trim program clips, the techniques in this chapter expand your repertoire. You learn to trim clips by using tools in the timeline as well as Trim view in the Monitor window.

If you're familiar with previous versions of Premiere (or if you have experience with other editing software), you'll be pleased with how Trim view has been integrated into the Monitor window. You'll also appreciate two useful new tools that allow you to perform slip and slide edits.

This chapter also covers techniques that deal with the link between video and audio. You learn how to trim linked video and audio separately to create split edits. You also learn how to create—and break—a link between video and audio. In addition, you learn how to detect when audio and video are out of synch and how to correct the problem.

Using Timeline Trimming Vs. Trim View

Making an adjustment to a clip's in point or out point is called *trimming*. You can trim a clip by manipulating it in the timeline or by activating Trim view. Although you can use either method to perform some editing tasks, each method has unique features.

Figure 6.1 Trimming a clip directly in the timeline.

Timeline Trimming

Trimming in the timeline relies on using the mouse to move the edges of a program's clips, thereby changing their in or out points (**Figure 6.1**). By selecting different tools, you can perform ripple edits, rolling edits, or simple trims. You can also slip or slide clips—something that you can't do in Trim view. Like all timeline editing, trimming in the timeline is quick and intuitive. The precision of the edit, however, depends partly on the detail of your view of the timeline. Also, this kind of trimming doesn't permit you to preview the changes before you make them final.

Figure 6.2 Trimming in Trim view.

Trim View

When you activate Trim view, the Monitor window switches to an editing mode designed for trimming clips in the program (**Figure 6.2**). Like trimming in the timeline, trimming in Trim view lets you perform ripple edits and rolling edits. Although this method is not as intuitive as the timeline, Trim view gives you more precise control. Trim view also provides a large view of the edit as you make adjustments and allows you to preview the changes.

✔ Tip

■ You can't extend an in point or an out point beyond the limits of the master clip, of course. If Premiere doesn't let you trim any farther, you're probably out of source material.

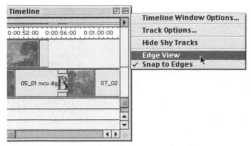

Figure 6.3 Choose Edge View to see the changes as you make them.

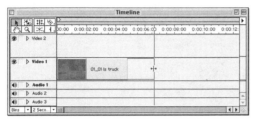

Figure 6.4 When you position the mouse pointer at the edge of a clip, the pointer becomes the Trim tool.

Trimming in the Timeline

The left edge of a clip in the timeline is the in point, or *head*; the right edge is the out point, or *tail*. You can trim the edges of clips in the timeline with the Trim, Ripple, Rolling, Slip, and Slide editing tools. If you want to view the edge frames (the in and out points) as you trim them, activate Edge Viewing.

To view edges:

From the Timeline pull-down menu, check Edge View to view the edge frame (the in point or out point) as you trim (**Figure 6.3**).

Uncheck the option to turn this feature off.

Program view displays the edge frame as you trim.

To trim with the Trim tool:

1. Make sure that the Selection tool is selected.

2. *Do one of the following:*

   ◆ Position the mouse pointer on the left edge of a clip in the timeline to trim the in point.

   ◆ Position the mouse pointer on the right edge of the clip to trim the out point.

   The pointer becomes the Trim tool ✛.

3. Drag the Trim tool to the left or right to change the clip's in or out point (**Figure 6.4**).

(continued on next page)

TRIMMING IN THE TIMELINE

If Edge View is active, you can view the edge frame in Program view (see the previous section "To view edges").

When you release the mouse, the clip's in or out point changes (**Figure 6.5**).

✔ Tip

- If Snap to Edges is active, edges snap to other edges, markers, or the edit line as you trim. This situation is often advantageous, but if it prevents you from trimming to the frame you want, turn off Snap to Edges (see the section "Using Snap to Edges" in Chapter 5).

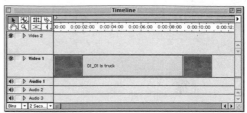

Figure 6.5 When you release the mouse, the new in point or out point corresponds with the edge of the clip.

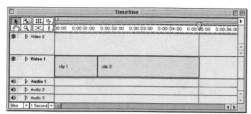

Figure 6.6 The clips before the edit...

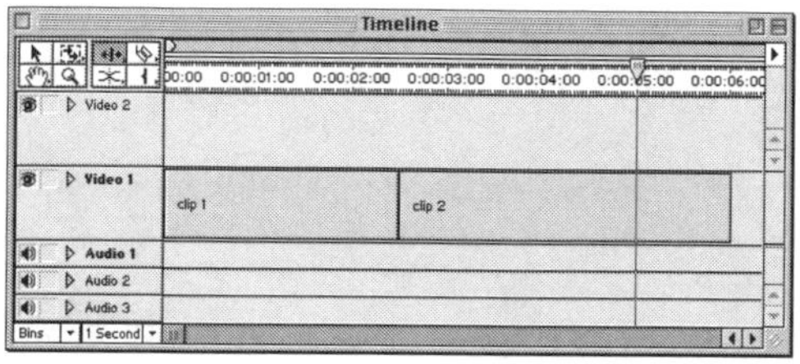

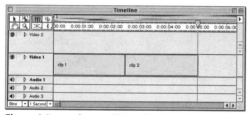

Figure 6.7 ...and the clips after a ripple edit...

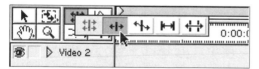

Figure 6.8 ...or after a rolling edit.

Figure 6.9 Select the Ripple Edit tool.

Making Ripple and Rolling Edits

When two clips are side by side in a track in the timeline, you can perform a ripple or rolling edit. You can make ripple or rolling edits by using tools in the timeline or by using Trim view.

Ripple Edits

In a *ripple edit*, you change the duration of one clip but do not affect the duration of the adjacent clips. After you ripple-edit the edge of the clip, all the adjacent clips shift in the timeline to compensate for the change, in a ripple effect. Therefore, the total length of the program changes (**Figures 6.6** and **6.7**). You can ripple-edit an out point in the timeline, or you can ripple-edit both the in and out points in Trim view.

Rolling Edits

In a *rolling edit*, you change the out point of one clip while you change the in point of the adjacent clip. In other words, you make one clip shorter while you make the adjacent clip longer. One clip rolls out, while the other rolls in. Therefore, the total length of the program remains the same (**Figure 6.8**).

To perform a ripple edit in the timeline:

1. In the Tools palette, select the Ripple Edit tool ╫ (**Figure 6.9**).

2. Position the mouse pointer on the out point (right edge) of the clip that you want to change.

(continued on next page)

The mouse pointer becomes the Ripple Edit tool (**Figure 6.10**).

3. Drag to the left to shorten the clip or to the right to lengthen it.

   The subsequent unlocked clips shift in the timeline to compensate for the edit (**Figure 6.11**).

✔ Tip

- All unlocked clips shift after a ripple edit. If you don't want a clip to move in the timeline, lock the clip.

To perform a rolling edit in the timeline:

1. In the Tools palette, select the Rolling Edit tool ⊞ (**Figure 6.12**).

2. Position the mouse pointer between the two adjacent clips that you want to change.

   The mouse pointer becomes the Rolling Edit tool (**Figure 6.13**).

3. Drag to the left or right to trim the out point of the first clip and the in point of the second clip by the same number of frames (**Figure 6.14**).

   If View Edges is active, you can see the edge frames in the Monitor window as you trim.

✔ Tip

- You can use a rolling edit to adjust the point at which you split a clip with the Razor. If you weren't precise when you split the clip, simply use the Rolling Edit tool to move the cut point to the left or right.

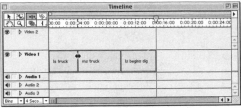

Figure 6.10 Position the Ripple Edit tool on the out point of the first clip, and drag left or right.

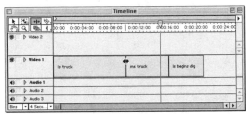

Figure 6.11 After the ripple edit, subsequent clips shift to compensate for the trimmed clip.

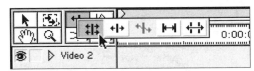

Figure 6.12 Select the Rolling Edit tool.

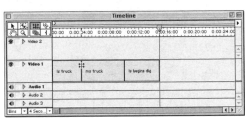

Figure 6.13 Position the Rolling Edit tool between two clips, and drag left or right.

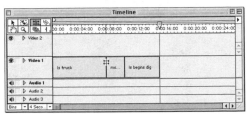

Figure 6.14 Both clips are trimmed by the same number of frames.

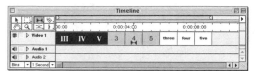

Figure 6.15 Notice how the frames of the clip in the center look before the slip edit...

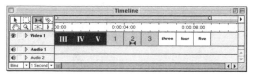

Figure 6.16 ... and after the slip edit.

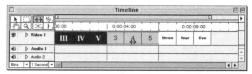

Figure 6.17 When slide edit the clip in the center...

Figure 6.18 ...one of the adjacent clips gets shorter, while the other gets longer.

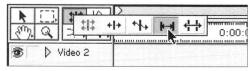

Figure 6.19 Select the slip tool.

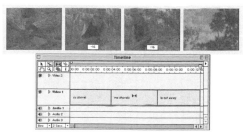

Figure 6.20 Slip the center clip without affecting the adjacent clips.

Making Slip and Slide Edits

When you have three clips side by side in the Timeline, you can perform slip edits and slide edits. These useful timeline editing tools are new additions to Premiere.

Slip Edits

In a *slip edit*, you change both the in point and the out point of a clip at the same time, without altering the adjacent clips. It's like you're viewing part of the clip through a space between the two other clips; when you slip the center clip back and forth, you get to see a different part (**Figures 6.15** and **6.16**).

Slide Edits

In a *slide edit*, the duration of the clip remains the same as you shift it in the timeline. When you drag, or slide, the clip to the left, the preceding clip gets shorter as the following clip gets longer. When you slide the clip to the right, the preceding clip gets longer as the following clip gets shorter (**Figures 6.17** and **6.18**).

To slip a clip:

1. In the Tools palette, select the Slip tool ⊬ (**Figure 6.19**).

2. Position the mouse pointer on a clip that is between two other clips in the timeline.

   The mouse pointer changes to the Slip tool ⊬ .

3. Drag left or right to change the clip's in and out points without changing the clip's duration or position in the timeline (**Figure 6.20**).

To slide a clip:

1. In the Tools palette, select the Slide tool ⊢ (**Figure 6.21**).

2. Position the mouse pointer on a clip that is between two other clips in the timeline.

   The mouse pointer changes to the Slide tool ⊢ .

3. Drag right or left to shift the clip in the timeline.

   The out point of the preceding clip and the in point of the following clip change in relation to the sliding clip (**Figure 6.22**).

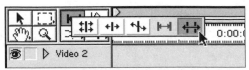

Figure 6.21 Select the Slide tool.

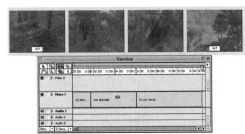

Figure 6.22 As you slide the center clip in the timeline, the adjacent clips adjust accordingly.

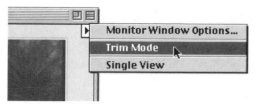

Figure 6.23 Choose Trim Mode...

Figure 6.24 ...and the Monitor window switches to Trim mode.

Using Trim View

Trim view lets you make ripple and rolling trims with numerical precision and permits you to preview your edit before you apply it. Unlike trimming in the timeline, editing in Trim view lets you ripple-edit an in point.

To activate Trim view:

From the Monitor pull-down menu, choose Trim View (**Figure 6.23**).

The Monitor window switches to Trim view (**Figure 6.24**). The way that this view appears on your screen depends on how you set the Trim Mode options, which are explained in the section "To customize Trim view," later in this chapter .

To deactivate Trim view:

Do one of the following:

◆ In the Monitor pull-down menu, deselect Trim View.

◆ In the timeline window, click the time ruler.

To find the cut you want to trim:

Do one of the following:

◆ Position the edit line (the program's current time) on or before the cut you want to trim, and activate Trim view.

◆ In Trim view, click the Previous Edit button ▣ or Next Edit button ▣ .

To ripple-edit in Trim view:

1. *Do one of the following:*

 ◆ In Trim view, click the image on the left to trim the out point of the first clip.

 ◆ Click the image on the right to trim the in point of the second clip.

(continued on next page)

USING TRIM VIEW

The controls under the active side of the Trim view are highlighted.

2. To trim frames of the active clip (**Figure 6.25**), *do any of the following:*

Figure 6.25 The active controls in Trim view.

- ◆ Click the Left Single-Frame Trim button ◀ to trim one frame to the left.

- ◆ Click the Left Five-Frames Trim button ◀ to trim five frames to the left (or the number of frames that you set in the Trim Mode options).

- ◆ Click the Right Single-Frame Trim button ▶ to trim one frame to the right.

- ◆ Click the Right Five-Frame Trim button ▶ to trim five frames to the right (or the number of frames that you set in the Trim Mode options).

- ◆ Using the numeric keypad, type a positive number to add frames to the selected view, or type a negative number to subtract frames from the selected view.

- ◆ Drag the jog control below the selected view to trim.

As you trim frames, the number of trimmed frames appears next to the delta symbol **Δ**. Trimming to the left subtracts from an out point or adds to an in point. Trimming to the right adds to an out point or subtracts from an in point.

✔ Tip

- ■ In Trim view, you can ripple-trim either clip or both of them. Switch between trimming the left and right clip simply by clicking the view that you want to trim.

Figure 6.26 When you drag between the two views in Trim view, you can perform a rolling edit.

To perform a rolling edit in Trim view:

1. Click between the two views to activate them both.

2. *Do any combination of the following:*

   ◆ Click the Left Single-Frame Trim button ⬛ to trim one frame to the left.

   ◆ Click the Left Five-Frame Trim button ⬛ to trim five frames to the left (or the number of frames that you set in the Trim Mode options).

   ◆ Click the Right Single-Frame Trim button ⬛ to trim one frame to the right.

   ◆ Click the Right Five-Frame Trim button ⬛ to trim five frames to the right (or the number of frames that you set in the Trim Mode options).

   ◆ Using the numeric keypad, type a positive number to trim to the right, or type a negative number trim to the left.

   ◆ Place the mouse pointer between the two views, so that the pointer becomes the Rolling Edit tool, and drag left or right to trim (**Figure 6.26**).

   As you trim frames, the number of trimmed frames appears next to the delta symbol Δ. Trimming to the left moves the cut earlier in time. Trimming to the right moves the cut later in time.

✔ Tip

■ In Trim view, you can switch between ripple and rolling edits before you apply the edit.

USING TRIM VIEW

To preview the trimmed edit:

◆ Click the Play Edit button ⏩ to preview the trimmed edit.

To apply the trimmed edit:

Do one of the following:

◆ Click the Next Edit or Previous Edit button to apply the edit and continue trimming other cuts.

◆ Exit Trim view by deselecting Trim View in the Monitor pull-down menu or clicking the time ruler.

To cancel the trim edit:

◆ Click the Cancel Edit button ⊠.
Any changes (Δ) are reset to zero.

To customize Trim view:

1. From the Monitor window pull-down menu, choose Monitor Window Options (**Figure 6.27**).
   The Monitor Window Options dialog box opens.

2. In the Trim Mode section of the dialog box (**Figure 6.28**), *choose one of the following display options:*

   ◆ The first option displays the out frame of the left clip and the in frame of the right clip.

   ◆ The second option displays large edge frames as well as the frames before and after the edge frames.

   ◆ The third option displays large edge frames as well as the first and fifth frames before and after the edge frames.

Figure 6.27 Choose Monitor Window Options to customize Trim view.

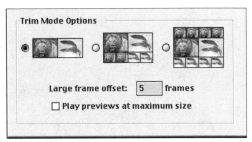

Figure 6.28 In the Trim Mode section of the Monitor Window Options dialog box, customize Trim view.

3. Type a number of frames for the Large Frame offset (the number of frames that are trimmed when you use the multiple-frame trim buttons).

By default, these buttons trim five frames.

4. Choose Play Previews at Maximum Size to make trimming previews appear at the largest size that fits in the Monitor window.

Deselect this option to make trimming previews play at the program frame size that you set in the Program settings.

Working with Links

As you learned in earlier chapters, changing a linked clip usually affects both its video and audio. A link helps you keep the video and audio synchronized.

At times, however, you want to manipulate the two parts of a linked clip separately. You might want to employ a traditional editing technique called the split edit or L-cut. Sometimes, you want to break the link altogether, so that the video and audio can be manipulated independently. Or you may want to create a link between two clips that aren't linked. In film production, for example, the image and sound are recorded separately. After they are digitized, you can create a link to synchronize the two elements in the timeline.

Trimming with Link Override

In a *split edit* or *L-cut*, the video and audio have different in points or out points. A dialogue scene is a good example. First, you see and hear a person talking, in synch. Then, you hear a person's voice but see the person to whom that person is talking. In this case, the video out point occurs earlier than the audio out point. In the timeline, the video and audio would form an L shape—hence the name *L-cut*.

Split edits are a great way to make your edits feel much smoother. You can make a split edit by using the Monitor editing controls or by using the Link Override tool in the timeline. Link Override temporarily overrides, or ignores, the link between video and audio while you use the tool. When you finish using Link Override, the video and audio link is intact.

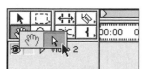

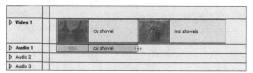

Figure 6.29 Select the Link Override tool.

Figure 6.30 With Link Override, you can trim only the video or the audio of a linked clip.

Figure 6.31 When you finish using the Link Override tool, the video and audio retain their link but have different in or out points.

To trim with Link Override:

1. *Do one of the following:*
   - In the Tools palette, select the Link Override tool (**Figure 6.29**).
   - With the Selection tool selected, hold down the Option key while you perform the following steps.

2. Position the mouse pointer on the edge of the video or audio portion of a linked clip.

   The mouse pointer becomes an outlined version of the Trim tool.

3. Drag to trim the edge without trimming the linked edge (**Figure 6.30**).

4. In the Tools palette, select the Selection tool again.

   The video and audio are still linked but have different in or out points (**Figure 6.31**).

✔ Tip

- As you learned in Chapter 3, you can also use Link Override to move the audio or video of a linked clip to a different task. Be careful not to lose synch, however.

WORKING WITH LINKS

Breaking and Creating Links

You can break or create links in the timeline. When you do so, however, you affect only the instances of the clips in the timeline: The links of the master clips and their associated files on the drive are unaffected.

To break a link:

1. In the timeline, select the video portion of a linked clip.

2. Choose Edit > Break Link (**Figure 6.32**).

   The clips in the timeline unlink and move independently. The master clip retains its link (**Figure 6.33**).

To create a soft link:

1. In the Tools palette, select the Soft Link tool  (**Figure 6.34**).

2. Click a video clip and then click an audio clip (or vice versa).

   When you position the mouse pointer on the second clip, the Soft Link tool appears (**Figure 6.35**). After you click the second clip, the clips are linked in the timeline, but the master clips and their associated files on the drive remain separate.

✔ Tips

- You can also create a soft link by clicking the first clip and then Shift+clicking the second clip.

- Soft links are great for synching film footage with audio. Just mark the frame in the film where the slate (clapper board) closes, mark the sound of the slate mark, align the marks, and link the clips.

Figure 6.32 Choose Edit > Break Link to eliminate the link between audio and video in the timeline.

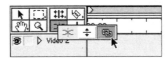

Figure 6.33 When the link is broken, video and audio move independently in the timeline. Premiere does not alert you to a loss of synch.

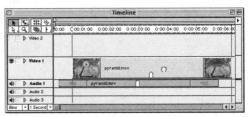

Figure 6.34 Select the Soft Link tool.

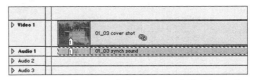

Figure 6.35 Before you click the second clip, the Soft Link tool appears.

WORKING WITH LINKS

Figure 6.36 When linked clips are out of synch, a red triangle appears on each portion of the clip.

Figure 6.37 Highlight the out-of-synch number.

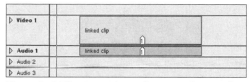

Figure 6.38 When you release the mouse button, the clips shift into synch.

Keeping Synch

During the course of editing, you may inadvertently lose synch between linked video and audio. Fortunately, Premiere alerts you when linked clips are out of synch, and it provides a simple way to correct the problem.

To detect a loss of synch:

◆ A red triangle appears at the left edge of linked video and audio that are out of synch (**Figure 6.36**).

To restore synch:

1. Click the red out-of-synch triangle, and hold down the mouse button.

2. Drag to highlight the number next to the red triangle (**Figure 6.37**), and release the mouse button.

   If there is available space in the track, the clip shifts in the timeline to resynchronize with the linked portion (**Figure 6.38**).

To restore synch by using other methods:

If clicking the out-of-synch indicator is not a practical way to re-synch the clips, you can use many other techniques to solve the problem.

You can *do any of the following:*

◆ Move a clip manually with the Link Override tool.

◆ Nudge the clip with the arrow keys.

◆ Use the Track tool to shift all the clips in a track back into synch.

◆ Open the source clip and edit it into the program again.

(continued on next page)

✔ Tip

- Prevention is the best medicine. Avoid loss of synch by locking clips or tracks that shouldn't be moved; use the Track tool cautiously; create a soft link between clips that require a synched relationship; and use markers as synch marks that you can use to visually check alignment.

TRANSITIONS

Figure 7.1 A transition from one shot to another.

A *transition* is the way one clip visually replaces the next. Although the cut is the most basic transition, the term *transition* often refers to a more gradual change from one clip to another (**Figure 7.1**). Adobe Premiere ships with 75 customizable transitions, including an array of dissolves, wipes, and special effects. You can even create your own transitions.

Because it's a palette, the Transition palette can be grouped or docked with other palettes, and it can be customized to display just the information you need. You can save and load custom sets of transitions and specify a default transition, available at the click of a button.

As you saw in Chapter 5, the timeline lets you view transitions in the expanded A/B roll style or in the collapsed, single-track style.

Ordinarily, you use a transition in the traditional manner, to change completely from one shot to the next. You can also customize transitions to achieve effects that aren't, strictly speaking, transitions. By using a feature called virtual clips, you can layer transitions to create complex effects.

This chapter covers how to create transitions; Chapter 8 addresses how to play them back. Because transitions are digitally created effects, you have to render them before you can watch them in real time.

Transitions Palette

The Transitions palette lists 75 customizable transitions. You can customize the palette to display more or less information about the transitions and to temporarily hide transitions that you don't need. You can also save and load custom sets of transitions.

To open the Transitions palette:

◆ Choose Window > Show Transitions or click the Transitions palette's tab to make it the active palette.

To customize the Transitions palette:

From the Transitions palette pull-down menu (**Figure 7.2**), choose among the following options:

◆ Check Animate to animate the transition icons. Animations illustrate how each transition works. In the animated icon, A represents the first clip, and B represents the second.

◆ Uncheck Hide Descriptions to display large icons with brief descriptions of each transition (**Figures 7.3** and **7.4**).

◆ Check Sort by Name to display the transitions in alphabetical order.

✔ Tip

■ Although Premiere 5.1 has many more options than previous versions did, one option is missing: You can no longer type a letter to jump to that letter in the list of transitions.

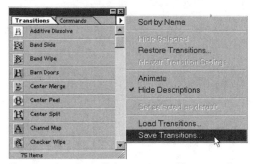

Figure 7.2 Use the pull-down menu to choose options.

Figure 7.3 You can view the Transitions window with no descriptions and small icons.

Figure 7.4 You can also view the Transitions window with large icons and brief descriptions.

TRANSITIONS PALETTE

Figure 7.5 Select a transition or range of transitions to hide.

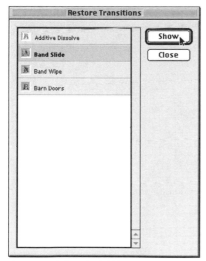

Figure 7.6 Choose Hide Selected to hide selected transitions or Restore Transitions to put hidden transitions back on the list.

Figure 7.7 Select the hidden transitions, and click Show to restore them to the list.

To reorder transitions:

1. Drag a transition to a new position in the list.

2. To put the transitions back in alphabetical order, from the Transitions pull-down menu choose Sort by Name.

To hide transitions:

1. To select a transition, *do one of the following:*

- ◆ Click a transition to select it.
- ◆ Shift+click another transition to select a range of transitions (**Figure 7.5**).

2. From the Transitions palette's pull-down menu, choose Hide Selected (**Figure 7.6**).

3. Repeat steps 1 and 2 as needed.

The items are temporarily removed from the list but not from the Plug-Ins folder, and can be restored to the list at any time.

To display hidden transitions:

1. From the Transitions palette's pull-down menu, choose Restore Transitions.

A list of the hidden transitions appears.

2. To select a transition, *do one of the following:*

- ◆ Click a transition to select it.
- ◆ Shift+click another transition to select a range of transitions.

3. Click Show to restore the selected transitions to the Transitions palette (**Figure 7.7**).

4. Repeat steps 2 and 3 as needed.

5. When you finish, click Close.

TRANSITIONS PALETTE

To save a set of transitions:

1. Hide the transitions that you do not want to include in the saved set.

2. From the Transitions palette's pull-down menu, choose Save Transitions (**Figure 7.8**).

3. Choose a name and destination for the saved set (**Figure 7.9**).

   If you're using Windows, use the .PFX extension.

4. Click Save.

To load a set of transitions:

1. From the Transitions palette's pull-down menu, choose Load Transitions.

2. Double-click the saved set to load it.

Figure 7.8 Choose Save Transitions to save the current list of transitions as a separate file, or choose Load Transitions to use an already-saved set.

Figure 7.9 Choose a name and location for the transition set.

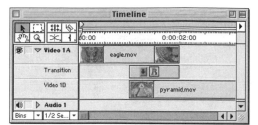

Figure 7.10 A transition viewed in the expanded Video1 track.

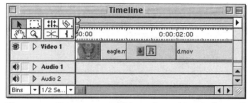

Figure 7.11 The same transition, viewed in a collapsed Video1 track.

A/B Roll Vs. Single-Track Transitions

You can add transitions only to Video 1 track, in either an expanded or collapsed view. The expanded Video 1 track resembles that of previous versions of Premiere and represents transitions in an A/B roll layout. Starting with Premiere 5, however, you can choose to view transitions in single-track mode. You can achieve the same results using either layout, but each requires a different approach (**Figures 7.10** and **7.11**).

Expanded-Track Transitions

When you expand the Video 1 track, it reveals Video 1A, 1B, and a transitions track. This layout emulates a traditional A/B-roll editing suite. In A/B roll editing, transitions are accomplished by playing two source tapes (A and B) at the same time, and transitioning between the two with a switcher. The tracks of the expanded view correspond to this editing model. The expanded-track method tends to be easier to understand visually. The tracks do take up more screen space, however, and require you to assemble clips in alternating A and B tracks, in checkerboard fashion.

Single-Track Transitions

In the collapsed Video1 layout, transitions are applied to a single track. What appears to be overlapping frames in the expanded view is not visible in the collapsed view. Because the frames that are being used to create the transition are not visible in the timeline, it can be harder to understand how to define a transition, how to plan for it, and how to adjust it. However, it consumes less window space and allows you to avoid alternating tracks but takes some getting used to. Also, it simply hides the expanded track. For this reason, you should know how to alternate between methods, not just choose between them.

Expanded-Track Transitions

In an expanded-track transition, clips in the A and B tracks overlap, and a transition is positioned between the overlapping areas. When you add a transition, Premiere automatically sizes it to the overlapping area, and transitions properly between one clip and the next. If you adjust the duration of the transition, Premiere automatically trims the corresponding clip to compensate for the change and ensure that the transition will work properly.

Even though Premiere usually makes these adjustments automatically, at times, you will have to adjust a transition manually. You should understand a few basic concepts about the proper arrangement of a typical transition: track direction and clip alignment (**Figures 7.12, 7.13,** and **7.14**). When you understand these rules, you can creatively break them.

Track Direction

To work properly, a transition must be set to switch from the first clip to the second clip. If the first clip is in track A, the transition must be set to switch from A to B, and vice versa. Transitions set in the opposite direction won't look correct during playback. A track-selector button indicates how the transition is set. This button is visible on the transition in the timeline (if the view is large enough) and in the transition settings.

Alignment

Ideally, the transitions should be aligned with the edges of the clips used in the transitions. Premiere attempts to align transitions automatically, but they can still be out of alignment. Transitions that aren't aligned properly may not look correct during playback, particularly if the clip in track A is out

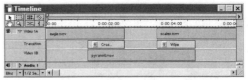

Figure 7.12 Track direction and alignment usually are set by Premiere, but not always.

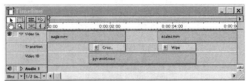

Figure 7.13 Incorrect track direction makes the transition look incorrect when it plays.

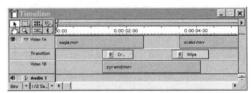

Figure 7.14 Incorrect alignment also prevents the transition from looking right.

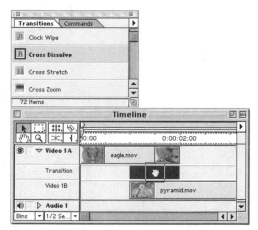

Figure 7.15 Drag a transition from the Transitions palette to the Transitions track.

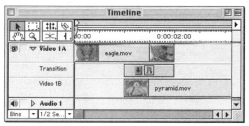

Figure 7.16 Premiere automatically adjusts the track direction and alignment.

of alignment. A clip in track A supercedes a clip in track B if no transition is provided between them. Therefore, if a clip in A extends beyond the edge of a transition, you see an unwanted cut to A during playback. Conversely, if a transition extends beyond the overlap, the empty track appears as an unwanted black image during the transition. Go ahead and deliberately misalign a transition to see the result.

✔ Tip

- Turn on Snap to Edges to help you align transitions and clips, as explained in Chapter 5.

To add a transition to the expanded track:

1. Arrange clips in track A and B so that part (or all) of the clips overlap in the timeline.

   The amount by which the clips overlap determines the duration of the transition.

2. Drag a transition from the Transitions palette to the Transitions track, between the overlapping clips (**Figure 7.15**).

   Premiere automatically sets the alignment and direction of the transition (**Figure 7.16**).

3. If you need to, trim the transition or the clips.

   If you trim the transition, Premiere trims the edge of the corresponding clip to compensate.

4. If you need to, adjust the transition settings, as described later in this chapter in the Transitions Settings section.

✔ Tip

- To trim a transition without affecting a clip, hold down the Command (Mac) or Ctrl (Windows) key as you trim.

EXPANDED-TRACK TRANSITIONS

Collapsed-Track Transitions

In essence, a transition in a collapsed Video1 track works the same as it does in an expanded track, but the frames that are used in the transition are hidden from view.

Premiere approaches collapsed-track transitions in two ways.

◆ **Premiere sizes the transition to the overlap.** That means you have to arrange the clips in expanded view: place them in alternating tracks, and extend their edges to overlap. When you add the transition in collapsed view, Premiere sizes the transition to the overlapping frames. This is practically the same as working with A/B tracks, except that the clips are collapsed for the final step.

◆ **Premiere sizes the overlap to the transition.** Without overlapping the clips in advance, you can add a transition to adjacent clips in a collapsed Video1 track. You must know, however, that each clip has enough extra footage to create the overlap. In other words, the first clip must have frames available after the current out point; and the second clip must have more frames before the current in point. When you add a transition, Premiere uses these "hidden" frames to create the transition. (If you expand the track, you can see how Premiere automatically places the clips in alternating tracks and extends the edges to overlap.) When you adjust the length of the transition, Premiere automatically s the corresponding clip, provided 'that enough frames are available. The initial duration of the transition is the same as the default transition's duration. (For information on setting the duration of the default transition, see the following sections .)

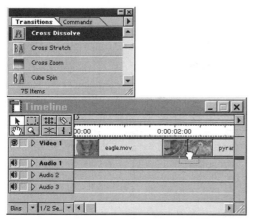

Figure 7.17 Drag a transition from the Transitions palette to the cut between two clips in the collapsed Video1 track.

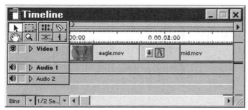

Figure 7.18 The transition appears in the collapsed track.

To add a transition to a collapsed track:

1. To check the clips, *do one of the following:*
   - ◆ Make sure that the clips have enough trimmed frames to accommodate the default transition duration.
   - ◆ In expanded view, extend the out point of the first clip and the in point of the second clip so that the clips overlap.

2. Drag a transition to the cut between two clips in the collapsed Video1 track (**Figure 7.17**).

   If the clips overlap, the transition covers the duration of the overlapping frames.

   If the clips do not overlap, the transition is the default transition (**Figure 7.18**).

3. If you need to, adjust the duration of the transition.

4. If you need to, adjust the transition settings.

✔ Tip

- ■ Adjusting the placement of the transition can be tricky in collapsed view. If you get confused, don't be afraid to examine the transition in expanded view.

Default Transitions

You can set a transition that you use frequently as the default transition and apply it quickly, without going to the Transitions palette. The default transition also defines the initial duration of transitions added to the collapsed Video1 track.

Figure 7.19 Select a transition that you frequently use to specify as the default.

To set the default transition and duration:

1. From the Transitions palette, choose the transition that you want to set as the default (**Figure 7.19**).

2. From the Transitions palette's pull-down menu, choose Set Selected As Default (**Figure 7.20**).

3. Type a default duration for the transition (**Figure 7.21**).

   When the transition is in the timeline, you can change the duration.

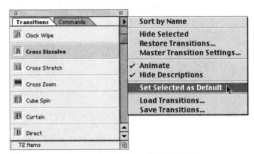

Figure 7.20 Choose Set Selected As Default.

To add the default transition:

1. Position the Edit Line where two clips meet or overlap (**Figure 7.22**).

2. *Do one of the following:*

   ◆ Click the Default Transition button 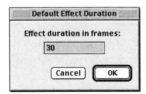 in the Monitor window (**Figure 7.23**).

   ◆ Viewing the expanded Video1 track, Command+Option+Shift+click (Cntrl+Option+Shift+click for Windows) the Transition track between two overlapping clips.

   If not enough trimmed frames are available for Premiere to create the transition, a warning appears, and you must adjust the clips before you can proceed (**Figure 7.24**).

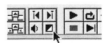

Figure 7.21 Type a duration for the default transition.

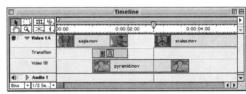

Figure 7.22 Position the edit line where you want to add the default transition.

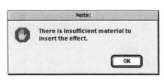

Figure 7.23 Click the Default Transition button.

Figure 7.24 Premiere will warn you if it does not have enough frames to create the transition.

Figure 7.25 Choose Master Transition Settings from the Transitions palette's pull-down menu to change the initial settings for a transition.

Figure 7.26 Choose Transition Settings from the Clip menu to adjust a particular transition.

Transitions Settings

Each transition has several customizable settings that affect the way that it looks during playback. The specific settings depend on the particular transition. The Transitions Settings dialog box can show a sample of the transition, in which A represents the first clip and B represents the second; or it can show representative frames from the program.

To change the default settings for a transition:

1. To select the transition *do one of the following:*
   - ◆ Double-click the transition in the Transitions palette.
   - ◆ Select the transition in the Transitions palette, and then choose Master Transition Settings from the palette's pull-down menu (**Figure 7.25**).
2. Adjust the settings.
3. Click OK.

To change settings for a single instance of a transition:

1. To select the transition *do one of the following:*
   - ◆ Double-click the transition in the Timeline.
   - ◆ Select the transition in the timeline and then choose Clip > Transition Settings (**Figure 7.26**).
2. Adjust the settings.
3. Click OK.

TRANSITIONS SETTINGS

To adjust transition settings:

In the Transition Settings dialog box, change any of the available settings for a particular transition (**Figure 7.27**):

◆ Check the Show Actual Sources checkbox to show the starting and ending frames of the clips in the transition.

◆ Drag the start and end sliders to define the initial and final appearances of the transition. Ordinarily, a transition starts at 0 and ends at 100. Hold down the Shift key to set both sliders to the same value and move them together.

◆ Click the track selector to determine which clip starts the transition. The arrow points down to switch from track 1A to track 1B; it points up to switch from 1B to 1A. This button is also available on the transition in the timeline.

◆ Click the Forward/Reverse button ![F][R] to make the transition play forward or backward. The Clock Wipe transition, for example, can play clockwise or counterclockwise (**Figure 7.28**).

◆ Click the Anti-Aliasing button to smooth the edge or border of a transition. Clicking this button cycles through the options Low (smoother) ![icon], High (smoothest) ![icon], and Off (rough) ![icon].

◆ Click the small arrows, or edge selector, around the transition thumbnail to select the orientation of the transition. You can choose the direction of a wipe, for example.

◆ Drag the Border slider to adjust the width of an optional border (**Figure 7.29**).

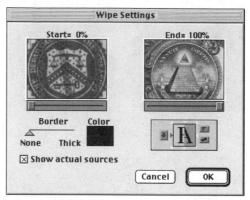

Figure 7.27 Wipe settings.

Figure 7.28 A closer view of your options.

Figure 7.29 You can add a border. Here, the starting slider has been moved to 50 percent so you that can see what the border will look like.

Figure 7.30 Some transitions have a point of origin that you can drag.

Figure 7.31 Some transitions have custom settings.

Figure 7.32 The custom settings for Slash Slide allow you to choose the number of slashes.

◆ If you add a border, click the color swatch to select a color for the border by using the color picker.

◆ Drag the handle in the Start or End image to set the center point of the transition. The handle represents the center of an Iris transition, for example (**Figure 7.30**).

◆ Click the Custom button (if available) to define settings specific to that transition. You can define the number of slashes in the Slash Slide transition, for example (**Figures 7.31** and **7.32**).

Special Transitions

Most transitions included with Premiere operate along the same lines and use similar settings. A few transitions, however, work a little differently than the rest. Because these transitions can't all be covered in the limited scope of this book, the following list describes the ones that you give special attention:

◆ **Channel Map** uses specialized custom settings to manipulate the red, green, blue, and alpha channels of the image.

◆ **Displace** can be used as an ordinary transition or in combination with your own displacement map.

◆ **Gradient Wipe** and **Image Mask** both require separate bitmapped images to work. These transitions are worth looking up in your user guide.

◆ **Motion** can use motion settings in the transition. (You learn to save motion settings in Chapter 13.)

◆ **QuickTime Transition** uses QuickTime's built-in effects to achieve a variety of transitions with minimal computer processing.

◆ **Transition Factory** allows you to create your own transitions. Refer to Factory.PDF in the Premiere folder for more information.

Figure 7.33 This effect was created by a series of circle wipes and nested virtual clips.

Virtual Clips

A *virtual clip* is a clip that refers to a range of clips in the timeline. Although the virtual clip is created from multiple clips, transitions, and effects in multiple tracks, it is represented as a single clip. You can edit, reuse, and apply effects to virtual clips as you would to any other clip.

By allowing you to represent complex sequences as a single clip, virtual clips can benefit you in several ways. You can repeat complex sequences easily, for example, and apply different settings to each instance. Or you can update all the instances of the virtual clip at the same time, by adjusting the sequence to which it refers.

In addition, you use virtual clips to layer transitions. Ordinarily, you can create a transition between only two clips at a time. If you create a virtual clip from those two clips, however, you can use the virtual clip in another transition, thereby layering the effect. For that matter, you can create virtual clips from other virtual clips. Premiere allows you to *nest* as many as 64 levels of virtual clips (**Figure 7.33**).

Because the clips that you use to create a virtual clip are almost like another program in the timeline, you should keep them separate from your main program. Set aside space at the beginning or end of the timeline for the clips that you'll use to create virtual clips. Make sure that you do not include this material when you output your final program.

To create a virtual clip:

1. In the Tools palette select the Block Select tool  (**Figure 7.34**).

2. Select the part of the timeline that you want to include in the virtual clip (**Figure 7.35**).

3. Position the Block Select tool inside the selected area.

   The Virtual Clip tool ♨ appears.

4. Drag the block to an available space in the timeline (**Figure 7.36**).

✔ Tips

- After you create a virtual clip, lock the clips from which it was created. This procedure protects them (and the related virtual clip) from accidental changes (see Chapter 3).

- Double-clicking a virtual clip scrolls the timeline to the virtual clip's source clips.

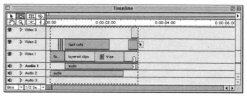

Figure 7.34 Select the Block Select tool.

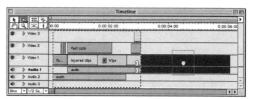

Figure 7.35 Drag the Block Select tool to select part of the program.

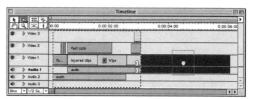

Figure 7.36 Drag the selection with the Virtual Clip tool to create a virtual clip in an available part of the timeline.

Previewing Transitions and Effects

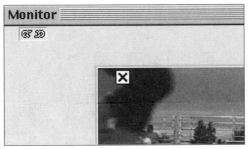

Figure 8.1 Program view displays an X in the corner of the image if the effect has not been previewed.

As you know, you can watch your program play back at any time in the Program view of the Monitor window. This works great for a sequence of cuts, because the source clips are on the hard drive and ready to play. But you may have noticed that your program won't instantly play transitions or other effects, such as filters, motion effects, or superimposed clips. Instead, Program view displays an X in the corner of the image, indicating that you still need to preview the effects (**Figure 8.1**).

To *preview* effects, your computer must create them digitally, and that can take time. The complexity of the effect, the size of the source files, and the speed of your computer all influence the processing time. The attributes of the preview—frame size, audio quality, frame rate, and so on—are determined by the project settings, which you learned to set back in Chapter 2.

In this chapter, you learn how to preview your work, including transitions and other effects. You also learn how to manage preview files.

Preview Effects

You can preview effects in several ways. By *scrubbing* the time ruler (option+dragging the edit line), you can preview an effect immediately, but not at final playback speed. If you want to see the effect at final playback speed, you can render a preview file. You can also preview an effect by using RAM, which processes the effect on the fly.

To render a preview of part of the program, you must define the area with the *work-area bar,* a shaded bar located in a thin band near the top of the Timeline window.

To preview by scrubbing the Time Ruler:

◆ Hold down the Option (Mac) or Alt (Windows) key as you drag the edit line in the time ruler (**Figure 8.2**).

The top of the edit line changes from a triangle to a down arrow. The program, including effects, is visible in Program view. Audio does not play while you scrub.

To preview the work area:

1. To set the work-area bar over the part of the program that you want to preview, *do any of the following:*

   ◆ Drag the work-area bar over part of the program (**Figure 8.3**).

   ◆ Drag the edges of the work-area bar to resize the bar (**Figure 8.4**).

   ◆ Option+click the *work-area band* (the "track" for the work-area bar) to size the bar over a contiguous series of clips.

   ◆ Double-click the work-area band to set the bar to the width of the Timeline window.

Figure 8.2 Hold down the Option or Alt key as you drag the Edit Line to view effects right away. The top of the Edit Line becomes an arrow.

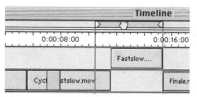

Figure 8.3 Drag the work-area bar over the area that you want to preview.

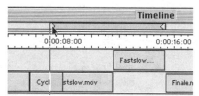

Figure 8.4 Drag the edges of the work-area bar to resize it.

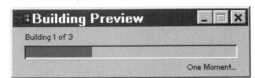

Figure 8.5 Premiere estimates the time required to process the effects.

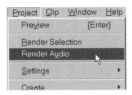

Figure 8.6 Choose Project > Render Audio to preview audio effects only.

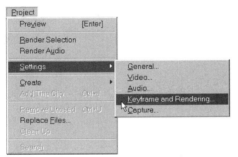

Figure 8.7 Open the Keyframe and Rendering settings.

Figure 8.8 Check Preview to RAM.

2. *Do one of the following:*

◆ Choose Project > Preview.

◆ Press Return.

A window appears, predicting the approximate processing time, based on the current operation (**Figure 8.5**).

To preview audio only:

1. Set the work-area bar over the audio that you want to preview (see the preceding section).

2. Choose Project > Render Audio (**Figure 8.6**).

Previewing to RAM

With Premiere 5.1 or later, you can use the RAM in your computer to preview effects. If you have enough RAM, this method gets quick results. Previewing to RAM doesn't create a preview file, however, so you have to preview the effect each time to load it into RAM and view it. Also, if the processing demands are too high, frames may be dropped during playback. Because previewing to RAM doesn't use the standard playback mechanism, the frame rate may differ from that of the project. For these reasons, use relatively small frame sizes (320x240 or 240x180) when you preview to RAM. Preview to RAM for quick processing but a rough approximation of an effect. Use a standard preview for slower processing but a more accurate preview.

To preview to RAM:

1. Choose Project > Settings > Keyframe and Rendering (**Figure 8.7**).

2. The Keyframe and Rendering panel of the Project Settings dialog box appears.

3. Check the Preview to RAM checkbox (**Figure 8.8**).

4. Click OK to exit the dialog box.

PREVIEWING EFFECTS

Previewing Files

When you create a preview, Premiere automatically creates a temporary file, called a *preview file*. You can designate where preview files are stored by choosing a *scratch disk*, the disk Premiere uses to store temporary files. You can also use your computer's RAM to preview files faster.

When you preview effects below the work area, a dark band appears below the work-area band and above the previewed effects. This band indicates that a preview file exists for the effects in this area and can be played back. If you make any changes in the program in this area, the indicator disappears, and you have to preview the area again to view the changes.

For this reason, the scratch disk may accumulate preview files that have become obsolete during the editing process. You can delete all the preview files, if you no longer want them. Any previews that are in use, however, will have to be rendered again.

When you save your project, any preview files that you created are associated with the project. When you open the project again, Premiere attempts to locate the preview files. If the preview files are present, you can still view the previewed portions of your program. If the preview files have been deleted from your drive since you saved the project, Premiere will be unable to locate them. In such a case, you can still open the project, but you will have to preview any effects that you want to view.

Preview files are considered to be temporary files. Deleting them affects only whether you have to preview effects. If the preview files match the final output settings, however, they can save you time in exporting a final movie.

Figure 8.9 Choose Files > Preferences > Scratch Disks.

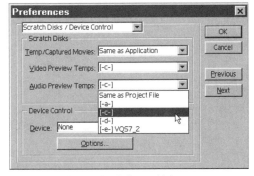

Figure 8.10 Choose the disk on which you want to store preview files.

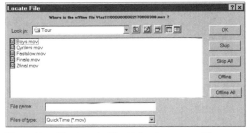

Figure 8.11 The Locate File dialog box opens if preview files are missing.

To choose a scratch disk for previews:

1. Choose File > Preferences > Scratch Disks / Device Control (**Figure 8.9**).

2. The Scratch Disks / Device Control panel of the Preferences dialog box appears.

3. From the Video Preview Temps and Audio Preview Temps pull-down menus, choose a disk on which store the preview files (**Figure 8.10**).

4. Click OK.

✔ Tip

■ Because this disk will play back audio / video files, it should be a relatively large, fast disk. If you have several volumes, put the Premiere application, media files, and preview files on separate volumes.

To open a project with missing preview files:

1. Open an existing project (see Chapter 2). If preview files are missing, a Locate File dialog box opens (**Figure 8.11**).

2. To find the file, *do one of the following:*
   ◆ Allow Premiere to locate the missing preview file.
   ◆ Navigate to the missing preview file.

3. To replace the file, *do one of the following:*
   ◆ Click Select (Mac) or OK (Windows) to replace the missing file with the selected file.
   ◆ Click Offline to replace the missing file with an offline file.
   ◆ Click All Offline to replaces all missing files with offline files without being prompted for confirmation.

(continued on next page)

PREVIEWING FILES

- ◆ Click Skip Preview File to disassociate the missing preview file from the project.
- ◆ Click Skip All Preview Files to disassociate all missing preview files from the project without being prompted for confirmation.

✔ Tip

- ■ If you deleted the preview files, you can choose Skip All Preview Files. Do not choose Skip All. Skip All skips all missing files, not just your preview files, and could cause your project to remove references to files that you need. If this happens, don't panic. Just close the project without saving it, open it again, and take care to make the correct choices.

MIXING AUDIO

In Chapter 3, you learned that you can have as many as 99 tracks of audio. But even if you use only two tracks, you will probably need to make subtle adjustments in their relative volumes, or *gain levels*. You accomplish this task, known as *mixing*, by directly manipulating audio in the timeline. In addition, Premiere provides a wide range of audio-processing controls to correct or enhance audio—a process called *audio sweetening*.

The current version of Premiere features greatly expanded audio-processing capabilities. Adobe added pan controls for clips in the timeline and refined the existing fade controls. Not only does Premiere offer several new audio filters, but also allows you to keyframe many of them so that their effects change over time. Premiere also preserves audio quality better by using an enhanced rate conversion process.

Although they don't take nearly as long to process as video effects, most audio effects must be previewed to be heard (see Chapter 8).

Adjusting Gain

You can adjust the overall *gain level*, or volume, of a clip in the timeline by using a menu command. You can also adjust the gain at any point in the clip by using the fade line.

To adjust the overall gain:

1. Select an audio clip in the timeline.

2. Choose Clip > Audio > Gain (**Figure 9.1**).

3. The Level Control Gain dialog box opens (**Figure 9.2**).

4. To choose a gain value *do one of the following:*

   ◆ Type a value for the gain.

   ◆ Click Normalize to have Premiere calculate a gain value automatically.

   A value more than 100 amplifies the audio; a value less than 100 *attenuates* the audio clip, making it quieter.

5. Click OK.

✔ Tip

■ The Compressor/Expander audio filter gives you more control of audio gain.

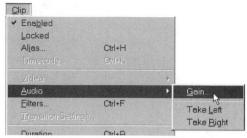

Figure 9.1 After you select a clip in the Timeline, choose the Gain command.

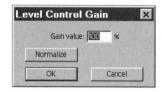

Figure 9.2 Type a gain level, or click Normalize to have Premiere to calculate a value.

Controlling Audio Quality

As you must with video or still-images, you must maintain audio quality at every step of the production process: recording, digitizing, processing, and export. At each step, your goals are to capture and maintain a strong signal without distorting it and to minimize noise. Audio engineers like to call achieving these goals maintaining a good *signal-to-noise ratio*; you might think of it as keeping the sound loud and clear.

If you use good recording and digitizing techniques, preserving audio quality in the editing and export process will be that much easier.

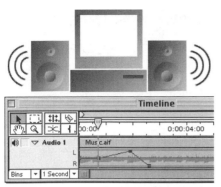

Figure 9.3 Panning audio distributes monophonic audio to both speakers...

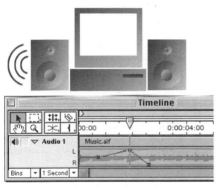

Figure 9.4 ...to the left speaker only...

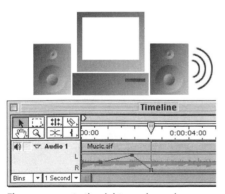

Figure 9.5 ...or to the right speaker only.

Using Audio Pan and Fade Controls

When you expand the audio tracks, you obtain access to the fade and pan controls. The red line represents the fade control; the blue line, the pan control. You can fade and pan the audio by altering the position and slope of these lines. You do this by adding a control point, or *handle,* to the line and dragging it to a new position. The line slopes up or down in a connect-the-dots fashion to represent the fade and pan. Every clip has a handle at its beginning and end, but you can add an unlimited number of handles for precise control of the audio.

Fading

The red fader (often called the rubber band) controls the level of the audio clip. By default, the fader appears in the middle of the clip, at the normal gain level of 100. You can drag a handle anywhere from 0, at the bottom of the clip, to 200, at the top of the clip.

Panning

The blue line, or pan control, controls how the monophonic (mono) audio of a clip is distributed between the left and right stereo speakers. By default, the pan control appears in the middle of the clip, indicating that the pan is centered, or equally distributed between the two speakers. Dragging a control handle to the top pans the audio to the left speaker; dragging it to the bottom pans the audio to the right speaker. An expanded track displays a blue L and R to remind you how the line corresponds to the speakers (**Figures 9.3** to **9.5**).

✔ Tip

■ You can use the Paste Custom command to copy and paste pan and fade adjustments from one clip to another.

Fading

The fade control gives you precise control of the audio levels. You can fade up, fade out, change levels over time, or cross-fade audio. Starting with Premiere 5.0, you can adjust the levels in increments of 1 percent—a big improvement from the 10 percent increments of previous versions.

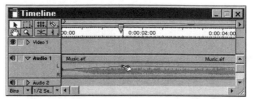

Figure 9.6 Use the finger pointer to create and drag a control handle.

To create and use a fade handle:

1. With the Selection tool selected, position the pointer on the red fade line where you want to create a fade handle.

    The pointer changes to a white finger icon with red +/- 🔴 to indicate that you are about to add a fade handle.

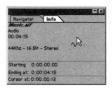

Figure 9.7 The Info palette displays updated information about a fade handle as you drag.

2. Click to create a fade handle.

    A handle (red dot) appears on the fade line.

3. Drag the fade handle up or down to change the level of the audio at that point or side to side to change the handle's position in time (**Figure 9.6**).

To delete a fade handle:

Drag a fade handle all the way outside the audio track, and release the mouse button. The fade handle disappears.

✔ Tip

■ Activate the Info palette before you use the fade handle. As you drag a handle, you can see the current level value update in the Info palette (**Figure 9.7**).

Performing Subtractive Mixing

When you adjust audio levels, follow the principle of *subtractive mixing*. In subtractive mixing, you favor reducing (subtracting) gain levels over increasing (adding) them. First, establish a strong, representative audio level for the program. Then, whenever possible, try to decrease the gain of a clip in relation to the others. Avoid increasing levels in relation to other clips. Adding gain increases not only the signal (the sounds that you want) but also the noise (the sounds that you don't want, such as buzz and hiss), and can even introduce distortion.

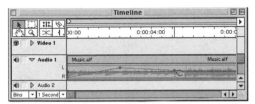

Figure 9.8 The finger pointer turns gray when you are about to grab a handle.

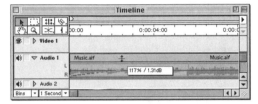

Figure 9.9 Hold down the Shift key to drag a fade handle in increments of 1 percent.

To move an existing fade handle:

1. With the Selection tool selected, position the pointer on the red fade line where you want to create a fade handle.

   The pointer changes to a gray finger icon with red +/- ✌ to indicate that you are about to move a fade handle (**Figure 9.8**). If the finger is white, you are about to create a new handle.

2. Drag the fade handle up or down to change the level of the audio at that point or side to side to change the handle's position in time.

To fade in increments of 1 percent:

1. With the Selection tool selected, position the pointer over the fade handle you want to adjust.

   The pointer changes to a gray finger icon with red +/- ✌ to indicate that you are about to move a fade handle (**Figure 9.8**).

2. Hold down the Shift key, so that the finger icon changes to the Fade Adjustment tool ✌.

3. Still holding down the Shift key, drag the handle up or down.

   A numeric display appears, indicating the current fade level. As long as you hold down the Shift key, you can drag beyond the top or bottom of the audio track, allowing you to adjust the level in increments of 1 percent (**Figure 9.9**).

FADING

163

To fade two handles simultaneously:

1. In the Tools palette, select the Fade Adjustment tool (**Figure 9.10**).

2. Position the Fade Adjustment tool between the two handles you want to adjust.

3. Drag up or down to move both handles, shifting the level between the two (**Figure 9.11**).

To create two adjacent fade handles:

1. In the Tools palette, select the Scissors tool >< (**Figure 9.12**).

2. Click the fader where no handles are present.

   Two adjacent handles appear, although they may be too close together for you to see both (**Figure 9.13**).

3. In the Tools palette, select another tool (such as the Selection tool).

4. Adjust the handles as needed.

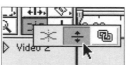

Figure 9.10 Select the Fade Adjustment tool.

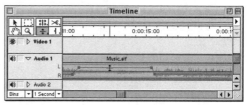

Figure 9.11 Drag with the Fade Adjustment tool to shift the level between two handles.

Figure 9.12 Select the Scissors tool.

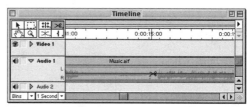

Figure 9.13 Click the line to create two adjacent handles.

FADING

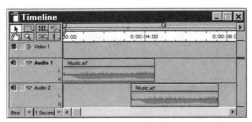

Figure 9.14 Overlap the audio clips in Expanded view.

Figure 9.15 Select the Cross-Fade tool.

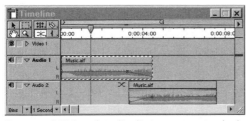

Figure 9.16 Click each audio clip to create a standard audio cross-fade.

Creating Cross-Fades

A *cross-fade* occurs when one audio clip fades out (grows silent) while another audio clip fades in (becomes audible). You can manipulate fade handles manually to create a cross-fade, or you can use Premiere's Cross-Fade tool to create simple cross-fades quickly.

To use the Cross-Fade tool:

1. Overlap two audio clips in time, displayed in Expanded view (**Figure 9.14**).

2. In the Tools palette, select the Cross-Fade tool ✕ (**Figure 9.15**).

3. Click one audio clip.

4. Click the other audio clip.

   When you position the pointer over the second clip, the Cross-Fade tool appears. After you click, Premiere creates a standard cross-fade (**Figure 9.16**).

Cross-Fading Audio Linked to Video

Because a cross-fade requires two audio clips to overlap, audio linked to video initially seems to present a problem: The linked video prevents you from dragging the audio clip to another track to overlap the audio (**Figure 9.17**).

If you apply what you learned in Chapter 6, however, you can easily overcome this problem by temporarily overriding the link between video and audio. This override permits you to move and trim the audio independently. At the same time, you retain the link between the video and audio, which helps you keep them in synch. Although split edits and link override are discussed in Chapter 6, the topics are worth reviewing in the context of audio mixing.

Figure 9.17 Initially, audio clips with linked video can't be made to overlap.

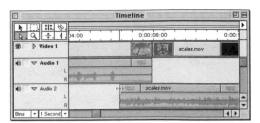

Figure 9.18 Activating a link override allows you to move and trim the audio clips independently.

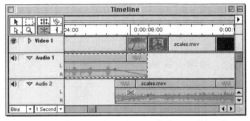

Figure 9.19 After you deactivate a link override, the links are restored, and you can create cross-fades as needed.

To cross-fade audio linked to video:

1. To override the link, *do one of the following:*
   - In the Tools palette, select the Link Override tool.
   - With the Selection tool selected, hold down the Option key (Mac) or the Ctrl key (Windows) while you perform the following steps.

2. Drag one audio clip to another track.

   Do not shift the clip in time (horizontally); if you do, the clip loses synch with the linked video.

3. Trim the edges of one or both of the audio clips, so that they overlap (**Figure 9.18**).

4. *Do one of the following:*
   - Release the Option or Ctrl key to revert to the Selection tool.
   - Select the Selection tool or the Cross-Fade tool.

5. Create a cross-fade manually or with the Cross-Fade tool, as explained earlier in this chapter (**Figure 9.19**).

Panning and Stereo

The current version of Premiere gives you the same control of panning that you have of fading. You can pan mono audio over time and adjust it in increments of 1 percent. Stereo audio clips, however, do not display a blue pan line. Even though stereo audio clips appear in a single track, you can still use each stereo channel with the Take Left and Take Right commands.

To pan an audio clip:

1. With the Selection tool selected, hold down the Option key (Mac) or Ctrl key (Windows) as you position the pointer on the blue pan control where you want to create a pan handle.

The pointer becomes a pointing finger with blue arrows 🖝.

2. Still holding down the Option or Ctrl key, drag the pan handle up to pan the audio left or down to pan the audio right (**Figure 9.20**).

To pan in increments of 1 percent:

1. With the Selection tool selected, hold down the Option key (Mac) or Ctrl key (Windows) as you position the pointer on the fade handle you want to adjust.

The pointer changes to a gray finger icon with blue arrows 🖝 to indicate that you are about to move a pan handle. If white, you are about to create a new handle.

2. Still holding down the Option or Ctrl key, hold down the Shift key: the finger icon changes to the Pan Adjustment tool 🖝.

3. Still holding down the Option or Ctrl and Shift keys, drag the handle up or down (**Figure 9.21**).

A numeric display indicates the current pan level. Pan center is at 0 percent. If you press Option+Shift or Ctrl+ Shift, you can

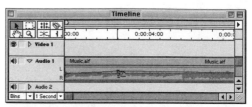

Figure 9.20 Holding down the Option key allows you to create and move a handle on the blue pan line.

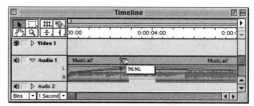

Figure 9.21 Pressing Option+Shift allows you to adjust the pan in increments of 1 percent.

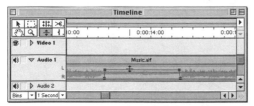

Figure 9.22 Select the Fade Adjustment tool.

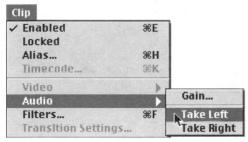

Figure 9.23 Holding down the Option key when the Fade Adjustment tool is selected allows you to adjust two pan handles simultaneously.

Figure 9.24 Choose Take Left or Take Right to use one channel of a stereo clip.

drag beyond the top or bottom of the audio track. This lets you to adjust the pan in increments of 1 percent.

To move two pan handles simultaneously:

1. In the Tools palette, select the Fade Adjustment tool (**Figure 9.22**).

2. Press the Option key as you position the Fade Adjustment tool between the two pan handles you want to adjust.

   Holding down the Option key allows you to use the Fade Adjustment tool as a Pan Adjustment tool.

3. Drag up or down to pan both handles at the same time (**Figure 9.23**).

✔ Tip

■ You can use the Pan, Fill Right, or Fill Left audio filters to pan audio, but you don't see their effects in the expanded audio track.

To use one stereo channel of a clip:

1. In the Timeline select a stereo audio clip.

2. To choose a channel *do one of the following:*
   ◆ To use only the left channel, choose Clip > Audio > Take Left (**Figure 9.24**).
   ◆ To use only the right channel, choose Clip > Audio > Take Right.

   A blue pan line appears in the audio clip.

3. Pan the single channel as needed.

✔ Tip

■ You can use Take Left and Take Right commands to manipulate stereo audio tracks separately, by applying Take Left to one copy of the clip and Take Right to another copy. If audio was recorded only in the left or right stereo channel, the appropriate Take command mixes the audio to mono and plays it from both speakers (unless you then pan it).

PANNING AND STEREO

169

Audio Filters

Audio filters not only filter out unwanted sounds but also can enhance or alter audio, and create special effects. You can apply multiple filters to the same clip, and you can alter their effects over time. You can even apply the same filter to a single clip more than once, using different settings each time.

Like other filters, the audio filters are located in Premiere's Plug-Ins folder. You can also add filters offered by other manufacturers. Because you apply audio filters in almost the same way that you do video filters, this section covers the topic briefly, leaving some details for Chapter 10.

To apply or remove audio filters:

1. Select an audio clip in the Timeline.

2. Choose Clip > Filters (**Figure 9.25**). The Audio Filters dialog box appears (**Figure 9.26**).

3. In the right column of the Audio Filters dialog box, select the filter that you want to apply.

4. Click Add to add the filter to the Current column.

5. If the filter has customizable settings, select your options.

6. If available, add and edit keyframes to alter the filter over time.

   Keyframes for audio filters work the same as they do for video filters (see Chapter 10 for details).

Figure 9.25 Select an audio clip in the Timeline, and choose Clip > Filters.

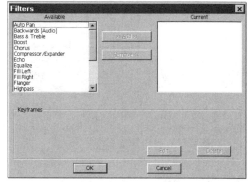

Figure 9.26 Choose filters from the Audio Filters dialog box.

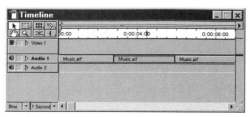

Figure 9.27 A thin line indicates that a filter has been applied to a clip.

7. If you need to remove a filter, select a filter in the Current column, and click Remove.

8. Repeat steps 3 to 6 to add additional filters to the clip.

   The order of the filters influences the final effect.

9. If you want to change the order of the filters, drag a name of a filter in the right column of the dialog box to a new position in the list.

10. Click OK to exit the Filter dialog box.

    A thin stripe appears at the top of the clip in the timeline, indicating that you applied a filter to it (**Figure 9.27**).

Using Audio Filters

Premiere currently offers 21 audio filters, including 11 new filters—too many to cover in detail in this section. Instead, the section lists the audio filters arranged by general category. For more specific information, consult the online help system (discussed in Chapter 2).

Filters to pan audio: AutoPan, Pan, Fill Left, Fill Right, Swap Left & Right.

Filters to correct or enhance audio: Bass & Treble, Boost, Compressor/Expander, Echo, Equalize, High Pass, Low Pass, Noise Gate, Notch/Hum, Parametric Equalization.

Filters to add depth, tone, color, or special effects: Backwards, Chorus, Flanger, Multi-Effect, Multitap Delay, Reverb.

Audio Processing

Now that you are familiar with the ways in which you can adjust audio, you should know how Premiere processes it. Knowing the order in which Premiere processes audio can influence the way that you plan your adjustments. Premiere processes audio in the following order:

1. The Audio settings you selected (Chapter 2), regardless of the clips' original audio settings.

2. Audio filters.

3. Pan and fade adjustments.

4. Adjustments resulting from the Clip > Audio > Gain command.

Figure 9.28 The audio settings control processing options.

Logarithmic Fades and Enhanced Rate Conversion

Remember the Enhanced Rate Conversion and Logarithmic Audio Fade options in the audio settings, discussed in Chapter 2 (**Figure 9.28**)?

When Premiere processes audio, it first converts, or *resamples*, the audio to the sample rate that you specified in the audio settings. Enhanced Rate Conversion determines the level of quality used in converting to a higher sample rate (*upsampling*) or to a lower sample rate (*downsampling*). Set Enhanced Rate Conversion to Off for faster processing but lower quality; Better for medium speed and quality; or Best for maximum quality but slower processing.

When you choose Logarithmic Audio Fades, Premiere processes gain levels according to a logarithmic scale; when the option is unselected, Premiere processes gain changes by using a linear curve. Conventional volume controls also use a logarithmic scale, which emulates the way that the human ear perceives audio gain increases and decreases. Logarithmic fades sound more natural but require more processing time.

Working with Filters

Just as a cinematographer adds filters to the lens of a camera to enhance or alter the image, you can add digital filters to clips in the timeline. Premiere ships with dozens of customizable video filters, which you can apply to clips in any number or combination. You can use filters to subtly correct a clip or dramatically stylize it (**Figure 10.1**).

Like the clip itself, Premiere filters are dynamic—that is, they can change settings and intensity over time. In the current version of Premiere, you can change the effect of most filters over time by using keyframes.

As with all effects, you must preview a filtered clip to see its effects in real time (see Chapter 8). Depending on their number and complexity, filters can add considerable processing time to previewing or exporting a final movie.

Filters are stored in Premiere's Plug-Ins folder. Adobe and other manufacturers offer other filters that are designed for, or compatible with, Premiere. You can add compatible plug-in filters by dragging them to the Plug-Ins folder when Premiere is not running. When Premiere starts, the names of the filters are displayed in the splash screen as they load.

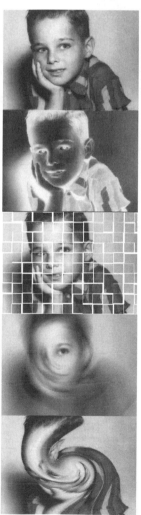

Figure 10.1 Here is just a few examples of what filters can do to images.

✔ Tip

■ Add filters to titles that you create in Premiere to add dramatic effects or movement.

To add filters to clips:

1. *Do one of the following:*

   ◆ Select a clip in the timeline.

   ◆ Use the Range Select tool to select multiple clips in the timeline.

2. Choose Clip > Filters (**Figure 10.2**). The Filters dialog box appears (**Figure 10.3**).

3. *Do one of the following:*

   ◆ Select a filter from the Available list on the left and then click Add.

   ◆ Double-click the filter in the Available list.

   If the filter has customizable controls, the Settings dialog box appears (**Figure 10.4**). The Settings dialog box of each filter differs.

4. *Do one of the following:*

   ◆ If the Settings dialog box appears, specify the settings for the entire clip (if you don't want to make different settings for other keyframes).

   ◆ Specify the settings for the first keyframe (if you do want to make different settings for other keyframes).

5. Add and set other keyframes for the clip (as described in "To set Keyframes" later in this chapter).

6. If you want, you can repeat steps 1 through 5 to add more filters to the same clip.

   Each filter that you apply appears in the Current list on the right.

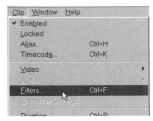

Figure 10.2 Select a clip and choose Clip > Filters.

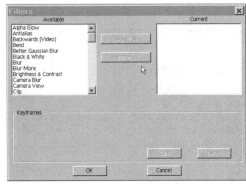

Figure 10.3 The Filters dialog box lists the available filters on the left, and the currently applied filters on the right.

Figure 10.4 Each filter, such as Brightness and Contrast, has a unique Settings dialog box.

FILTERS

7. Click OK to apply the filters.

A thin blue line appears at the top of the filtered clip in the timeline, indicating that you applied a filter to it.

✔ Tip

■ You can preview the effects of some filters in the filter's Settings dialog box. The Zoom tool, Hand tool, and Collapse button work the same as they do for the Transparency settings, as explained in Chapter 12.

To remove filters:

1. Select a clip in the timeline.

2. Choose Clip > Filters.

The Filters dialog box appears.

3. Select a filter from the Current list.

4. Click Remove.

5. Repeat steps 3 and 4 for any other filters that you want to remove.

6. Click OK to apply the changes.

To edit filters:

1. Select a clip to which filters have been applied.

2. Choose Clip > Filters.

The Filters dialog box appears.

3. Select a filter in the Current list.

4. Click the Edit button.

5. Add, change, or delete any of the settings at any keyframe.

6. Click OK to apply the changes.

✔ Tip

■ You can copy and paste filters by using the Paste Custom command.

FILTERS

Keyframes

If the selected filter's settings can be changed over time, a keyframe timeline appears, and the Edit button is active. If the Edit button is grayed-out, you can affect only the first keyframe.

The keyframe timeline represents the entire duration of the clip, from in point to out point. A triangle on the timeline represents a keyframe—a point in time where you define the settings for a filter. Every clip has a keyframe at its beginning and ending; this keyframe cannot be deleted. When you select a keyframe by clicking it, it is highlighted, and the window displays the selected keyframe's name and position in time. When you move a keyframe's position in the time-line, you can see the frame's current position in Program view. By adding and manipulating keyframes, you can change the effects of a filter as the clip plays.

To set keyframes:

1. Add one or more filters to a clip, as described earlier in this chapter.

2. In the Filter dialog box, select a filter's name in the Current list.

   A keyframe timeline appears near the bottom of the Filter dialog box. If the Edit button is active, you can define keyframes for the filters.

3. *Do one of the following:*
   - ◆ Click an empty part of the keyframe timeline to create a new keyframe and specify its settings (**Figure 10.6**).
   - ◆ Select an existing keyframe and click Edit to change the settings for the filter at that point in time (**Figure 10.7**).

   The filter's Settings dialog box appears.

Figure 10.5 Most of the filters applied to a clip can change as the clip plays.

Keyframes

Keyframe is a term borrowed from traditional animation. In a traditional animation studio, a senior animator might draw only the *keyframes*—what the character looks like at key moments in the animation. The junior animators then draw the rest of the frames, or *in-betweens*. The same principle applies to computer animations: if you supply the keyframes, the computer program determines the in-between frames. When you think about it, every handle on an audio fade line is like a keyframe. You define the gain-level values at particular points in time, and Premiere interpolates all the values in between, in a linear progression. When you apply a motion setting to a clip, you use keyframes to animate its position on the screen (Chapter 13). By adding keyframes to a filter, you can define the effects of a filter at different points in the clip, thereby animating the effects of the filter over time (**Figure 10.5**).

KEYFRAMES

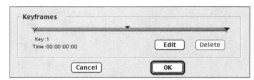

Figure 10.6 Click an empty part of the timeline to create a new keyframe.

Figure 10.7 Click an existing keyframe to change its settings.

Figure 10.8 Different settings at keyframes 1, 2, and 3 cause the image to change over time.

4. In the filter's Settings dialog box, specify the settings for the current keyframe, and click OK to exit the Settings dialog box.

5. *Do either of the following:*

- ◆ Select a keyframe and click Delete to remove the keyframe.

- ◆ Drag a keyframe left or right to change its position in the keyframe timeline.

    You can see the position of the keyframe in Program view in the Monitor window as you drag.

6 Repeat steps 2 through 4 to set all the keyframes you want.

7. Click OK to exit the Filters dialog box.

    The filter settings change as the clip plays (**Figure 10.8**).

KEYFRAMES

Filter Order

When a clip has more than one filter, Premiere applies the filters in the order in which they appear in the Current list, from top to bottom. Because each filter adds to the effect of the preceding one, the order of the filters determines the cumulative effect. Changing the order of filters can change the final appearance of the clip (**Figures 10.9** and **10.10**).

To change filter order:

◆ In the Filters dialog box, drag a filter up or down in the Current list to change its position in the list (**Figure 10.11**).

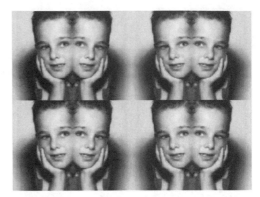

Figure 10.9 The Mirror filter followed by the Replicate filter results in this image...

Figure 10.10 ...and in this image when the filter order is reversed.

Figure 10.11 Drag a filter's name to change its position in the list.

Figure 10.12 A clip with the Crystallize filter set to 10 looks like this when previewed at 320x240...

Figure 10.13 ...and it looks like this when it's previewed at 640x480. The filter settings are the same but the crystals now appear half the size relative to the clip.

Filters and Image Size

Some filters—such as Pointillize, Crystallize, and Image Pan filters—use settings expressed in pixels. The pixel settings of these filters remain constant, even if you change the size of the video image. Therefore, the apparent effects of these filters change according to the image size (**Figures 10.12** and **10.13**). Size-relative filters become a concern if you preview these filters at a different image size than the final output, or if you use smaller source clips as proxies for larger clips.

✔ Tip

- You can use the Image Pan filter to simulate a motion-control camera panning over parts of a clip's image. You often see this effect in documentaries that use still images. Because the Image Pan filter settings are expressed in pixels, however, the effects are relative to the size of the clip. If you apply the Image Pan filter to a smaller proxy clip, you have to reset the filter when you replace the proxy with a larger source clip.

CREATING TITLES

Although Premiere accepts files created with other applications, it also has its own powerful tool for creating text and graphics. In the Title window, you can create graphics that include straight lines, shapes, or text in any font that's available on your computer. You can easily manipulate the color, transparency, and arrangement of these objects, apply a drop shadow, or include an alpha channel so that you can superimpose the title over other clips.

Although the Title window doesn't look very different from previous versions of Premiere, it does incorporate a couple of welcome new features: rolling and crawling text. Now you don't need to use motion settings or the Image Pan filter to create these common effects.

Admittedly, Premiere's Title window may not be as flexible as a dedicated graphics program such as Adobe Illustrator, but it does share one important characteristic with that program. Like Illustrator, Premiere creates object-oriented (vector-based) graphics. Unlike some of the other images you create in Premiere (color mattes and counting leaders, for example), titles are independent files you save separately from your project. Like other source files, you can open more than one Title window at a time, and you can use titles in any project or Library window.

The Title Window and Menus

Whenever you create or change a title clip, it opens in a Title window. The Title window includes a drawing area and a set of tools for creating and editing text and graphics. When the window is active, a Title menu appears in the menu bar. Like the other windows, the Title window also has options that you can access through the Windows menu.

Figure 11.1 Choose File > New > Title.

To create and save a new title:

1. Choose File > New > Title (**Figure 11.1**). The Title window appears (**Figure 11.2**).

2. Create text and graphic objects for the title, as described in the following sections.

3. Choose File > Save As to display the Save dialog box.

4. Specify a location and name for the title.

5. Click Save.

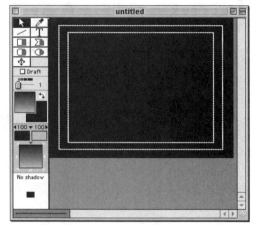

Figure 11.2 The Title window includes a drawing area and tools for creating text and graphics.

To add the title to the current project:

Do one of the following:

- Select an open Title window and choose Project > Add This Clip (**Figure 11.3**).

- Drag the Title window to a Project or Bin window or to the timeline.

- Select File > Import > File, and select the title in the import dialog box to import it.

The duration of the title is determined by the default still-image duration (see Chapter 3).

Figure 11.3 With the Title window active, choose Add This Clip or drag the title into your project.

✔ Tip

■ When you drag a title to a Bin or Project window or to the timeline, Command+drag so that you don't accidentally select any of the objects in the title and move them instead.

To open and save an existing title:

1. Double-click a title in the timeline or in a Project, Bin, or Library window.

   The title opens in a Title window.

2. Make changes in the objects in the Title window.

3. *Do one of the following:*
   ◆ Choose File > Save to save the title with the changes.
   ◆ Choose File > Save As to save another version of the title as a separate file.

✔ Tip

■ When you edit and save a title, you are saving changes in a source file, not just an single instance of the title. Whatever changes you save appear in every instance of the title in the project and timeline. If another project uses the same title, it also reflects the changes.

THE TITLE WINDOW AND MENUS

Title-Window Options

Because they are tucked away in the Windows menu, the Title-window options can be easy to overlook. Nevertheless, these options control several important attributes of titles.

Drawing Space

The *drawing space* determines the size of the title clip. The size of the Title window doesn't need to match the final output size, however. Objects that you create this window are vector-based, so Premiere can scale the title to the output size without making the edges look jagged.

Aspect Ratio

The *aspect ratio* of the title usually matches that of the program. As you learned in Chapter 1, conventional video has a 4:3 aspect ratio. If the aspect ratio differs from the project, the title will appear distorted—unless you also apply the Image Pan filter (for more information about the Image Pan filter, see your Adobe Premiere User Guide or the online help system).

Action Safe and Title Safe

A computer screen allows you to see more of the video image than a television screen does. Televisions *overscan* the image, cropping off the outer edges. Because the amount of overscan differs from one television set to the next, important elements of the image should not appear close to the edges of the screen. Important subjects should remain within the inner 90 percent of the image—an area called the *action-safe* area. Titles should remain within the inner 80 percent of the image—an area called the *title-safe* area. The Title window can display guides to help you keep titles within the title-safe area.

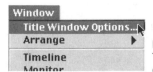

Figure 11.4 Open the Title Window Options dialog box.

Figure 11.5 The Title Window Options dialog box allows you to control several aspects of the title.

NTSC-Safe Colors

A color that looks great on a computer screen may not be *NTSC-safe* and may appear to be "noisy" or to "bleed" on a television screen. Premiere can automatically adjust colors that are destined for television.

Background Color and Opacity

The Title-window options allow you to use an opaque background or to use the background as an alpha channel. As you learn in Chapter 12, you can use the alpha channel to make the background transparent and superimpose the title over another clip.

To set Title-window options:

1. With a Title window active, choose Window > Title Window Options (**Figure 11.4**).

   The Title Window Options dialog box appears (**Figure 11.5**).

2. *Do any combination of the following:*
   - ◆ Check 4:3 Aspect to ensure the title clip has the same aspect ratio as a conventional TV set: 4 across to 3 down.
   - ◆ Type the horizontal (h) and vertical (v) dimensions of the Title window, expressed in pixels.

   If the 4:3 Aspect box is checked, Premiere provides the second number to preserve a 4:3 ratio.
   - ◆ Check Show Safe Titles to display title-safe and action-safe guides.
   - ◆ Check NTSC Safe Colors to automatically shift the colors of the title that are outside the NTSC color space into the NTSC color space when the title is rendered.

(continued on next page)

TITLE-WINDOW OPTIONS

- ◆ Click the color-swatch rectangle to open the color picker, and then choose a background color for the title.
- ◆ Check the Opaque box to make the background color opaque. Leave this box unchecked to use the background as an alpha channel (see Chapter 12).

When you finish choosing options, click OK to close the dialog box.

The currently selected Title window and subsequent titles use your selections (**Figure 11.6**).

✔ Tip

- ■ When the Title window is active, you can type **W** to quickly change to a white background or **B** to change to a black background.

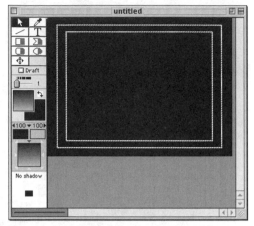

Figure 11.6 This Title window has been set to have a 320x240 drawing space (a 4:3 aspect ratio) and to display action-safe and title-safe area guides.

Figure 11.7 Drag the clip image into the Title window to use the frame marked 0 (or the in point) as a background frame.

Background Clips

You can place a reference frame of video in the background of the Title window. The background frame allows you to preview how the title will look when you superimpose it over a video clip.

The background frame itself is not saved as part of the title; it's merely a helpful reference, which you can use or remove at any time.

You can set the marker 0 on the frame of the clip that you want to use as a background frame. Otherwise, the first frame of a video clip serves as the background frame.

To use a background clip:

1. Create or open a Title window, as explained in the preceding sections.

2. Open a video clip, using any of the methods that you learned in Chapter 3.

3. Cue the current frame to the frame that you want to use as a background frame in a Title window.

4. Choose Clip > Set Marker > 0 to set the frame as the background frame.

5. Drag the frame of the clip into an open Title window.

6. When the border of the drawing area is highlighted, release the mouse button.

   The frame marked 0 appears in the background of the title as a reference (**Figure 11.7**). If you do not set a zero marker, the in point acts as the background clip.

To remove a background clip:

◆ When a Title window with a background clip is active, choose Title > Remove Background Clip (**Figure 11.8**).

✔ Tips

■ To change the background frame, simply set the marker 0 to a different frame in the clip.

■ Use the Eyedropper tool to load colors from the background clip into the foreground or shadow color.

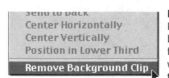

Figure 11.8
Remove the background frame when you want to view the title without it.

BACKGROUND CLIPS

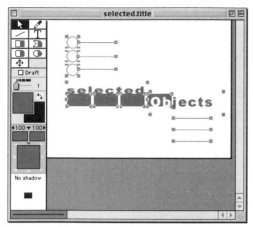

Figure 11.9 The objects on the left are selected and display control handles. The objects on the right are not selected.

Objects and Attributes

The following sections explain how to create text and graphic objects. The attributes that are unique to each kind of object are addressed first. Later sections deal with attributes that are relevant to both text and graphics. You can set most attributes before or after you create an object.

To set attributes for objects before you create them:

1. In the Title window, make sure that no objects are selected (see " Objects" later in this chapter).

   Selected objects appear with control handles around them (**Figure 11.9**).

2. Choose object attributes such as color, opacity, and gradient.

   New objects have these attributes unless you change them later.

Draft Mode

If the Title window displays and updates objects slowly, you can work in draft mode. Draft mode displays text and graphic objects faster but at lower quality. Draft mode affects only the display in the Title window, not the final output.

To use draft mode to increase display speed:

◆ In the tools area of the Title window check Draft to display objects in draft mode. Uncheck Draft to display the objects at full quality (**Figures 11.10** and **11.11**).

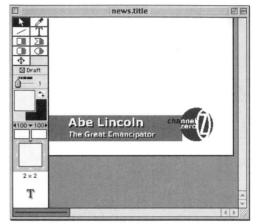

Figure 11.10 In normal mode, objects display with smooth edges and transparency.

Figure 11.11 In draft mode, transparency is not displayed, and edges look jagged.

Figure 11.12 Select the Type tool to create text.

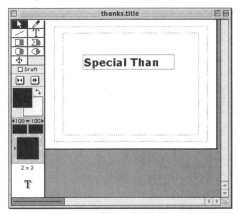

Figure 11.13 Click in the drawing area, and begin typing.

Figure 11.14 When you click away, the new text object uses the current attributes, such as color and opacity.

Text Objects

You can create text objects that contain any font that's available on your computer, including PostScript and TrueType fonts. The font must be loaded and available on the computer whenever you open the Title window.

Attributes that are unique to titles include font, size, style, justification, and orientation. You can also precisely control kerning and leading.

To create a text object:

1. Select the Type tool T (**Figure 11.12**).

2. Click anywhere in the drawing space to position the top-left corner of the text object.

    A blinking insertion point appears, prompting you to type.

3. Type the text (**Figure 11.13**).

4. When you are finished typing, click outside the area of the text object.

    The text object uses the current attributes. You can change these attributes at any time (**Figure 11.14**).

✔ Tip

■ Not all fonts look like letters. By loading special fonts—known as symbols, ornaments, and dingbats—you can easily create useful graphic elements. You can use these fonts just as you do other fonts, and you won't have to draw a thing (**Figure 11.15**).

To resize the text bounding box:

1. Select the Selection tool.

2. Click the text object to select it.

   Four corner handles appear, representing the bounding box for the text.

3. Drag any of the handles to change the size of the text object's bounding box (**Figure 11.16**).

   The text in the box reflows to accommodate the new size of the box (**Figure 11.17**).

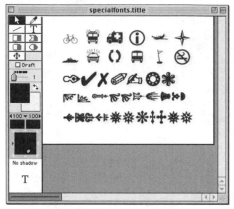

Figure 11.15 Use symbols, ornaments, and dingbat fonts to create special characters.

Figure 11.16 Drag a handle to resize the bounding box.

Figure 11.17 The text reflows to fit into the resized bounding box.

Figure 11.18 Option+drag the bounding box to stretch the proportions of the text object.

Figure 11.19 When you release the mouse button, the text appears with different proportions.

To stretch type:

1. Select the Selection tool.

2. Click the text object to select it.

3. Option+drag any of the object handles to stretch the vertical and horizontal scale of the text object.

   The mouse pointer becomes the Stretch tool as you Option+drag (**Figure 11.18**). When you release the mouse button, the text appears with different horizontal and vertical proportions (**Figure 11.19**).

TEXT OBJECTS

Text Attributes

You can set most text attributes before you create a text object. If you want to edit the text (or adjust the kerning or leading), you must select all or part of the text. After you learn how to select text, you can adjust its attributes.

To select text for editing:

To select text, *do any of the following:*

◆ Select the Selection tool, and click the text object to change the entire text object (**Figure 11.20**).

◆ Select the Selection tool, and double-click the text object to quickly switch to the Type tool and set an insertion point (**Figure 11.21**).

◆ Select the Type tool T , and click the text object to position the insertion point in the text.

◆ Select the Type tool, and drag to select a range of text (**Figure 11.22**).

✔ Tip

■ You can also press the left- and right-arrow keys to move the insertion point.

To set font, style, and size:

1. Select all or part of the text, using the methods described in the preceding section.

2. *Do any of the following:*

   ◆ Choose Title > Font, and then select a font for any selected text and any new text (**Figure 11.23**).

   ◆ Choose Title > Style; then choose any styles that you want to apply to selected text and any new text (**Figure 11.24**).

   ◆ Choose Title > Size; then select a point size for any selected text and any new text (**Figure 11.25**).

Figure 11.20 You can select the entire text to edit the text...

Figure 11.21 ...you can set the insertion point...

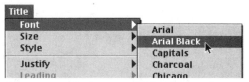

Figure 11.22 ...or you can select a range of characters.

Figure 11.23 With all or part of the text selected, choose a font...

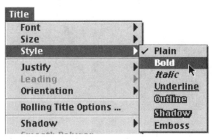

Figure 11.24 ... choose a style...

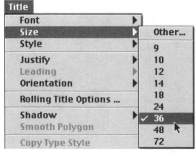

Figure 11.25 ... or choose a size for the selected text.

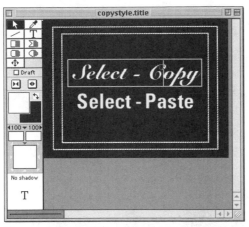

Figure 11.26 Place the insertion point in text that has the attributes you want to apply to other text.

Figure 11.27 Choose Title > Copy Type Style.

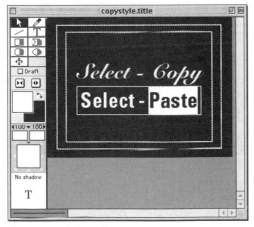

Figure 11.28 Select other text...

To copy and paste a type style:

1. Place the insertion point in the text that has the attributes you want to copy (**Figure 11.26**).

2. Choose Title > Copy Type Style (**Figure 11.27**).

3. Select the characters of the text to which you want to copy the attributes (**Figure 11.28**).

(continued on next page)

TEXT ATTRIBUTES

4. Choose Title > Paste Type Style (**Figure 11.29**).

Attributes (font, size, color, and so on) are copied to the selected text (**Figure 11.30**).

To justify text in the text object:

1. Position the insertion point (the blinking cursor) in the line of text that you want to justify.

2. *Do one of the following* (**Figure 11.31**):

◆ Choose Title > Justify > Left to position the line of text flush left in the bounding box.

◆ Choose Title > Justify > Right to position the line of text flush right in the bounding box.

◆ Choose Title > Justify > Center to horizontally center the text in the bounding box.

The selected text object is justified within its bounding box (**Figure 11.32**).

Figure 11.29 ...choose Title > Paste Type Style...

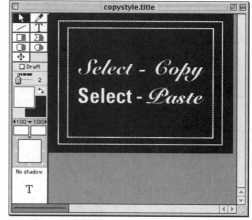

Figure 11.30 ...and the text takes on the same attributes.

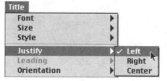

Figure 11.31 Choose a justification option for the selected text.

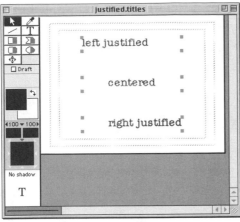

Figure 11.32 You can justify text left, right, or centered in its bounding box.

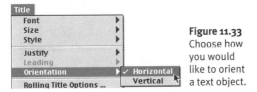

Figure 11.33 Choose how you would like to orient a text object.

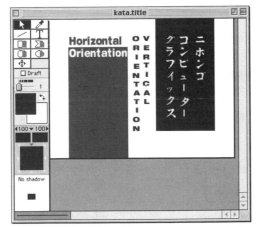

Figure 11.34 You can orient text vertically instead of horizontally.

To change text orientation:

1. Select a text object.

2. *Do one of the following* (**Figure 11.33**):

   ◆ Choose Title > Orientation > Horizontal to orient the text horizontally from left to right.

   ◆ Choose Title > Orientation > Vertical to orient the text vertically from top to bottom and from right to left (**Figure 11.34**).

TEXT ATTRIBUTES

Kerning

Kerning is a typesetting term that describes the space between characters. The Title window allows you to adjust the spaces between two letters or a range of letters.

To adjust kerning:

1. *Do one of the following:*

   ◆ Drag to highlight a range of characters in the text.

   ◆ Click between characters to place the insertion point in the text.

   Kerning buttons appear below the Draft checkbox in the tools area of the Title window (**Figure 11.35**).

2. *Do any combination of the following:*

   ◆ Click the Decrease Kerning button to move letters closer together (**Figure 11.36**).

   ◆ Click the Increase Kerning button to move letters farther apart (**Figure 11.37**).

3. Click outside the text object to deselect it and apply the changes.

✔ Tip

■ You can use easy keyboard shortcuts to kern text. Press Option+left arrow to decrease kerning; press Option+right arrow to increase kerning.

Figure 11.35 When you edit text, the kerning buttons appear.

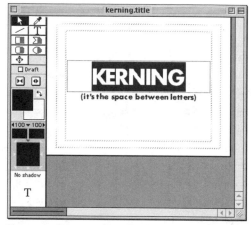

Figure 11.36 You can decrease the space between the selected characters...

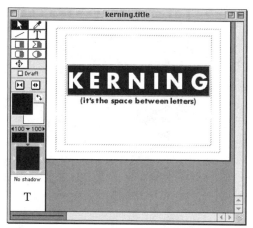

Figure 11.37 ...or increase the space between the selected characters.

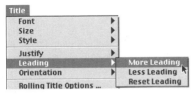

Figure 11.38 You can increase or decrease the leading.

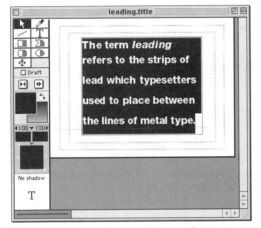

Figure 11.39 You can increase the space between lines of text...

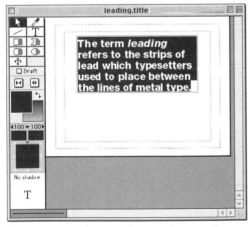

Figure 11.40 ...or decrease the space between lines.

Leading

Leading (which rhymes with *wedding*) is a typesetting term that describes the space between lines of text. If a single title object contains more than one line of text, you can adjust the space between the lines.

To adjust leading:

1. Select a text object.

2. Choose one of the following commands (**Figure 11.38**):
   - ◆ Title > Leading > More Leading to increase the space between lines (**Figure 11.39**)
   - ◆ Title > Leading > Less Leading to decrease the space between lines (**Figure 11.40**)
   - ◆ Title > Leading > Reset Leading to restore the default leading for the font

✔ Tip

- ■ You can also use a keyboard shortcut to adjust leading. Press Option+down arrow to increase leading; press Option+up arrow to decrease leading.

LEADING

Rolls and Crawls

In a title *roll*, text moves up the screen. Title rolls are frequently used in a final credit sequence or to present lengthy text on-screen.

A title *crawl* moves across the screen horizontally—typically, from right to left. A news bulletin is a classic example of a title crawl, and very large crawling type is often used for a dramatic opening title.

Previous versions of Premiere required you to use motion settings or the image pan filter to create rolls or crawls; now, these effects are built-in features of the Title window. Bear in mind, however, that you can roll or crawl only text, not graphic objects.

To create a text roll or crawl:

1. Select the Rolling Title tool ⊕ (**Figure 11.41**).

2. Drag in the drawing space to specify the area of the rolling text object (**Figure 11.42**).

3. Drag the bottom-right corner to resize the object at any time.

4. Type the text for the roll or crawl (**Figure 11.43**).

5. Press Return to create a new line or extra space for a roll; press the spacebar to create extra space for a crawl.

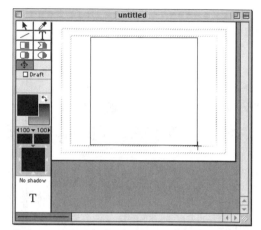

Figure 11.41 Select the Rolling Title tool to create rolling or crawling text.

Figure 11.42 Drag in the drawing space to define an area for the rolling or crawling text.

Figure 11.43 Type the text, making sure to include line breaks or spaces when necessary.

Figure 11.44 Choose Title > Rolling Title Options.

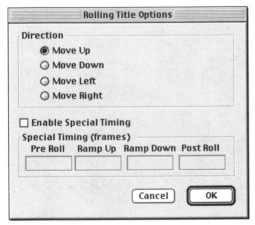

Figure 11.45 In the Rolling Title Options dialog box, choose a direction for the type to move, and select any special timings that you want to use.

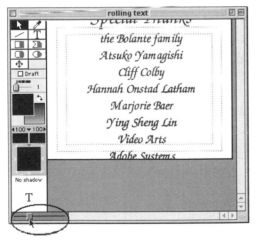

Figure 11.46 Drag the slider at the bottom of the Title window to see how the roll or crawl will look during playback.

6. With the rolling title still selected, choose Title > Rolling Title Options (**Figure 11.44**).

   The Rolling Title Options dialog box appears (**Figure 11.45**).

7. In the Direction section, choose a direction for the type to move.

8. Choose Enable Special Timings to gain more control of the motion.

9. If you choose Enable Special Timings, type any of the following values:

   ◆ In the PreRoll text box, type the number of frames for which you want the text to appear motionless after the title's in point.

   ◆ In the RampUp text box, type the number of frames that the title will use to accelerate to full speed.

   ◆ In the RampDown text box, type the number of frames that the title will use to decelerate to a full stop.

   ◆ In the PostRoll text box, type the number of frames for which you want the text to appear motionless until the title's out point.

To preview rolls and crawls:

◆ Drag the slider in the bottom-left corner of the Title window (**Figure 11.46**).

All rolling and crawling text objects play back. You cannot preview special timings by dragging the slider, however.

If the title uses a background clip, the clip that contains the frame is used as the duration of the roll or crawl, and it plays back as you drag the slider.

Graphic Objects

The Title window includes tools for creating graphic objects: straight lines, rectangles, ellipses, and polygons. You can create shapes that are *framed* (outlines only) or *filled* (filled with the current color). You can control the thickness of lines and framed objects and specify whether polygons have sharp or rounded corners. As usual, you can change an object's position, shape, color, and other attributes at any time.

To create a line:

1. Select the Line tool (**Figure 11.47**).

2. *Do one of the following:*
   - Drag in the drawing space to draw a line at any angle or length (**Figure 11.48**).
   - Shift+drag to constrain the angle to 45-degree increments.

✔ Tip

- After you use a tool once, it reverts back to the selection tool. However, if you double-click a tool, it will highlight in black and remain selected until you choose another tool (**Figure 11.49**).

To create a rectangle, round-cornered rectangle, or ellipse:

1. *Do one of the following:*
   - Click the left side of a shape tool to create a framed shape.
   - Click the right side of a shape tool to create a filled shape (**Figure 11.50**).

2. *Do one of the following:*
   - Drag in the drawing area to draw the shape (**Figure 11.51**).
   - Shift+drag to constrain the dimensions to perfect circles, squares, or squares with rounded corners.

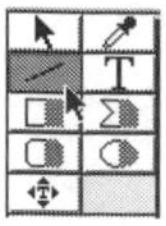

Figure 11.47 Select the Line tool.

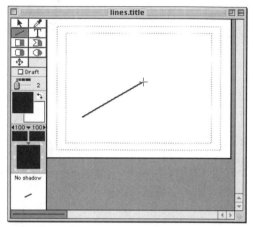

Figure 11.48 Drag in the drawing space to create a line of any angle or length.

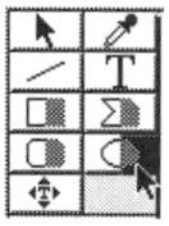

Figure 11.49 Double-clicking a tool will highlight it in black, and cause it to remain selected until you choose another tool.

Figure 11.50 Click the left side of a shape tool to create framed objects; click the right side to create filled objects.

GRAPHIC OBJECTS

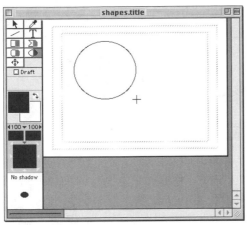

Figure 11.51 With a shape tool selected, drag in the drawing area to create framed and filled shapes.

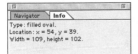

Figure 11.52 You can see the exact size and position of a selected object In the Info window.

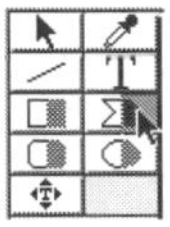

Figure 11.53 Select the Framed or Filled Polygon tool.

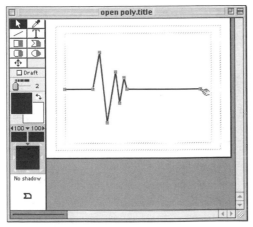

Figure 11.54 Click to create corner points, and click the first point to close the shape.

✔ Tip

■ Look in the Info window for information on the exact size and position of the objects that you create in the Title window (**Figure 11.52**).

To create a polygon:

1. *Do one of the following:*
   - ◆ Click the left side of the Polygon tool to create a framed polygon.
   - ◆ Click the right side of the Polygon tool to create a filled polygon (**Figure 11.53**).

2. Position the Polygon tool in the drawing area and click to create the first corner point of the shape.

   A line segment connects the corner point to the Polygon tool.

3. Position the Polygon tool and click to set the next corner point.

4. Repeat steps 2 and 3 until you are ready to set the last corner point.

5. *Do one of the following:*
   - ◆ Click the first corner point to close the shape (**Figure 11.54**).

     A dot appears next to the Polygon tool to indicate that it is positioned over the first point.

   - ◆ Double-click to place the last point and create an open framed polygon.

     You cannot leave a filled polygon open.

GRAPHIC OBJECTS

203

To smooth a polygon:

1. Select a polygon object (**Figure 11.55**).

2. Choose Title > Smooth Polygon (**Figure 11.56**).

   The selected polygon toggles from sharp corners to smoothed corners (**Figure 11.57**).

To edit a graphic object:

1. With the Selection tool, click a shape to select it.

2. Position the mouse pointer on the shape's handle so that the finger pointer appears.

3. Drag the handle to resize the object, or reposition a corner of a polygon or move one end of a line.

   Option+drag to constrain the dimensions of a shape or the angle of a line.

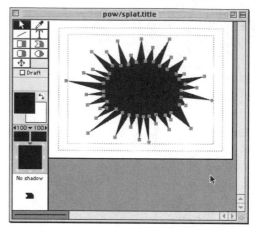

Figure 11.55 Select a polygon that has sharp corners, like this "pow" shape.

Figure 11.56 Choose Smooth Polygon...

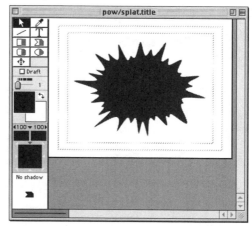

Figure 11.57 ... to turn it into a "splat" shape.

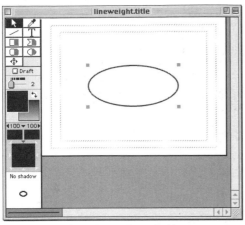

Figure 11.58 Select a line or framed object.

Figure 11.59 Drag the line-weight slider...

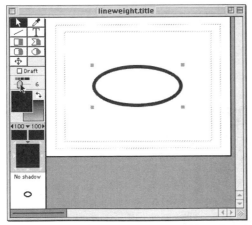

Figure 11.60 ... to change the thickness of the selected lines and framed shapes.

To change the line weight of a line or framed object:

1. With the Selection tool, click the line or framed object that you want to select (**Figure 11.58**).

2. In the tools area of the Title window, drag the line-weight slider to change the selected line weight (**Figure 11.59**).

   The thickness of the line or framed object changes according to your adjustments (**Figure 11.60**).

✔ Tip

■ You can still select and move the corner points of a polygon, even if you selected smooth corners.

To change a framed object to a filled object, or vice versa:

1. With the Selection tool, click the graphic object to select it (**Figure 11.61**).

2. To change a graphic object choose one of the following commands (**Figure 11.62**):
   - ◆ Title > Convert to Filled.
   - ◆ Title > Convert to Framed.

   The select object changes, according to your choice (**Figure 11.63**).

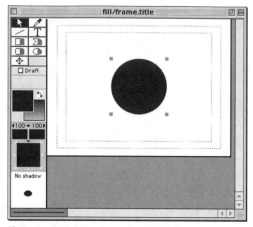

Figure 11.61 Select a framed or filled shape...

Figure 11.62 ... and choose the appropriate Convert command...

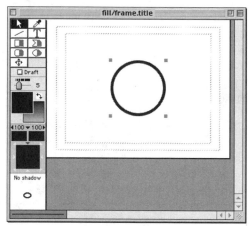

Figure 11.63 ...to change a framed shape to a filled shape, or vice versa.

Figure 11.64 Choose the appropriate Create command to create a filled copy of a framed object, or vice versa.

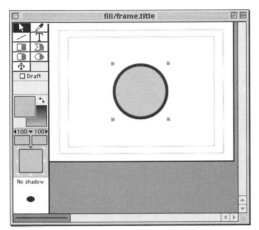

Figure 11.65 Move or change the attributes of the copy to distinguish it from the original object.

To duplicate a framed object as a filled object, or vice versa:

1. With the Selection tool, click the graphic object to select it.

2. To create a framed or filled version of a graphic object, choose one of the following commands (**Figure 11.64**):

   ◆ Title > Create Framed Object to create a framed copy of a filled object.

   ◆ Title > Create Filled Object to create a filled copy of a framed object.

   The new copy appears in the same position as the original.

3. Move or change the attributes of the copy to distinguish it from the original (**Figure 11.65**).

GRAPHIC OBJECTS

Objects

Although selecting and moving objects in Premiere is both intuitive and consistent with the techniques of most graphic programs, a few techniques may not be so obvious. Premiere can also center objects automatically or align objects to the bottom of the title-safe area.

In addition to positioning objects, you can control how they are layered. Initially, the most recently created object appears in front of the others, but you can change the stacking order.

Figure 11.66 You may want to select multiple objects so that you can move them together.

To select objects:

Do one of the following:

◆ With the Selection tool, click an object to select it.

◆ Shift+click with the Selection tool to select additional objects and to deselect them.

◆ Choose Edit > Select All to select all the objects in the Title window (**Figure 11.66**).

◆ Press period (.) to select the next object higher in the stacking order.

◆ Press comma (,) to select the next object lower in the stacking order.

To move objects:

1. Select the objects that you want to move.

2. *Do one of the following:*

◆ Drag them to a new position in the drawing area.

◆ Press the arrow keys to nudge them 1 pixel at a time.

OBJECTS

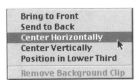

Figure 11.67 Select objects and then choose an alignment command.

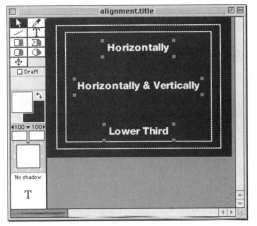

Figure 11.68 You can align objects horizontally, vertically, or to the bottom of the title-safe area.

To align objects:

1. Select the objects that you want to align.

2. Choose one of the following commands (**Figure 11.67**):

   ◆ Title > Center Horizontally.

   ◆ Title > Center Vertically.

   ◆ Title > Position in Lower Third to place the object at the bottom of the title-safe area.

   The selected title repositions according to your choice (**Figure 11.68**).

✔ Tip

■ Identification titles (like the ones that you see in newscasts, sports broadcasts, and documentaries) are usually positioned in the bottom third of the screen, aligned with the bottom of the title-safe area.

To change the stacking order:

1. Select the object that you want to reorder (**Figure 11.69**).

2. To change the stacking order, choose one of the following commands (**Figure 11.70**):

   ◆ Title > Bring to Front to bring an object to the foreground, higher in the stacking order (**Figure 11.71**).

   ◆ Title > Send to Back to send an object to the background, lower in the stacking order.

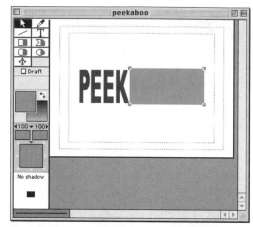

Figure 11.69 Select an object you want to reorder.

Figure 11.70 Choose a command in the Title menu...

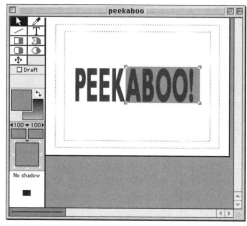

Figure 11.71 ...to change it's stacking order.

Figure 11.72 Drag the Shadow Offset control to create a drop shadow for the selected object.

Figure 11.73 The object's shadow reflects your adjustments.

Figure 11.74 To remove the shadow from the selected object, drag the shadow completely outside the Shadow Offset control area.

Figure 11.75 Choose one of three types of shadows.

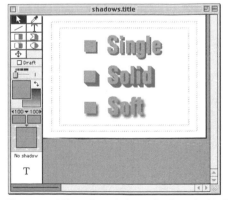

Figure 11.76 The selected object displays the kind of shadow that you select.

Drop Shadows

You can add a drop shadow to both graphic and text objects. This effect can set an object apart from the background or impart a sense of dimension. Like the object with which it's associated, a shadow can have any color, opacity, or gradient.

To add a shadow:

1. Select the objects to which you want to apply a shadow.

2. In the lower left corner of the Title window, drag the Shadow Offset control to set the shadow's angle and distance from the object (**Figure 11.72**).

   The Shadow Offset control indicates how the shadow looks for the selected object (**Figure 11.73**).

To remove a shadow:

1. Select an object that has a shadow.

2. Drag the Shadow Offset control outside or to the center of the control area, until it displays the message *No Shadow* (**Figure 11.74**).

To choose a shadow type:

1. Select an object that has a shadow.

2. Choose Title > Shadow.

3. From the Shadow submenu, choose a type of shadow (**Figure 11.75**):

   ◆ Single to create a simple drop shadow.

   ◆ Solid to create a shadow that is connected to the object, simulating extruded, three-dimensional text.

   ◆ Soft to create a soft-edged drop shadow.

   The shadow of the selected object reflects your choice (**Figure 11.76**).

Color, Opacity, and Gradients

You can independently control the color and opacity of any object or its shadow. Both color and opacity can gradually change from one end of an object or shadow to the other—an effect called a *gradient*.

To set object and shadow color:

1. *Do one of the following:*
   - Select an entire object.
   - Select a range of text.

2. *Do one of the following:*
   - Click the object color (the top-left color swatch) to open the color picker for the object.
   - Click the shadow color (the bottom-right color swatch) to open the color picker for the shadow (**Figure 11.77**).

3. Choose a color from the color picker.

4. Click OK to exit the color picker and apply the change.

To swap the object and shadow colors:

Click the swap icon (the curved double arrow between the object and shadow color swatches) (**Figure 11.78**).

✔ Tips

- Press Z to reset the object and shadow colors to the default colors.

- Dragging one color swatch to another color swatch copies the color from one to the other.

Figure 11.77 Double-click the top-left color swatch to choose the object color, or click the bottom-right color swatch to choose the shadow color.

Figure 11.78 Click the swap icon to switch the object and shadow colors.

Figure 11.79 Choose a starting color and an ending color, and click a triangle to choose the direction of the gradient.

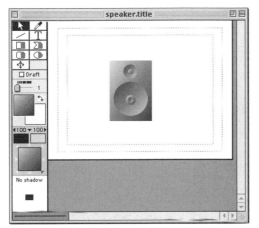

Figure 11.80 This audio-speaker icon consists of several objects that have color gradients.

To set a color gradient:

1. *Do one of the following:*
   ◆ Select an object.
   ◆ Select a range of text.

2. *Do one of the following:*
   ◆ Click the object color swatch to affect the object color.
   ◆ Click the shadow color swatch to affect the shadow color.

   The selected color swatch overlaps the other.

3. Click the Beginning Color (the leftmost color swatch below the object and shadow color) and then choose a color from the color picker.

4. Click the Ending Color (the rightmost color swatch below the object and shadow color) and then choose a color from the color picker.

5. Click one of the triangles around the gradient sample to set the direction of the gradient (**Figure 11.79**).

   The object displays the color gradient from beginning color to ending color, in the direction that you specify (**Figure 11.80**).

✔ Tips

■ If an object has both a color gradient and an opacity gradient, both gradients must go in the same direction.

■ To quickly eliminate the color gradient, drag the beginning color to the ending color, or vice versa. You can also eliminate a color gradient by dragging a color to the gradient sample.

COLOR, OPACITY, AND GRADIENTS

To set opacity:

1. Select an object, or select a range of text.

2. Click the object color swatch, or click the shadow color swatch.

3. Click the triangle between the beginning and ending opacity values to select an overall opacity (**Figure 11.81**).

Figure 11.81 Click the center triangle to set the overall opacity for the selected object.

✔ Tips

- You can set an object's opacity to Clear to make it transparent when you superimpose the title over video (see Chapter 12). A clear object cuts through an opaque object in the title (**Figure 11.82**).

Figure 11.82 You can set an object's opacity to Clear to cut through another object and reveal the underlying clip.

- If a transparent object doesn't look transparent, the object may have a drop shadow. In this case, you can see through the object, only to see its underlying shadow. You can remove the shadow, using the method described in the section, "Drop Shadows," earlier in this chapter.

To set an opacity gradient:

1. Select an object, or select a range of text.

2. Click the object color swatch, or click the shadow color swatch.

3. Click the Beginning Opacity triangle and drag to choose an opacity value (**Figure 11.83**).

Figure 11.83 To create an opacity gradient, click the left triangle and drag to set the starting opacity level...

4. Click the Ending Opacity triangle and drag to choose an opacity value (**Figure 11.84**).

Figure 11.84 ... then click the right triangle and drag to set the ending opacity level. Choose a gradient direction as you do for a color gradient.

Figure 11.85 Click a triangle to set the direction of the opacity gradient.

Figure 11.86 Select the Eyedropper tool.

Figure 11.87 Click a color in the Title window to load an object color, or Option+click to load a shadow color.

5. Click one of the triangles around the gradient sample to set the direction of the gradient.

The object displays the opacity gradient from starting opacity to ending opacity, in the direction that you choose (**Figure 11.85**).

✔ Tip

■ The color gradient and opacity gradient must go in the same direction.

To set colors with the Eyedropper tool:

1. Select the Eyedropper tool (**Figure 11.86**).

2. *Do one of the following:*

◆ Click a color in the Title window to set the object color (**Figure 11.87**).

◆ Option+click inside the Title window to set the shadow color.

✔ Tip

■ To match an object's colors with those of another object in the Title window, select that object before you use the Eyedropper tool.

COLOR, OPACITY, AND GRADIENTS

The Color Picker

Whether you're choosing colors for title objects, backgrounds, color mattes (Chapter 3), or fill colors (Chapters 12 and 13), you use the color picker.

If you checked NTSC Safe Colors in the Title Window Options dialog box (described earlier in this chapter), Premiere warns you if you attempt to choose a color that is outside the color *gamut* (range) of NTSC video. When you click the out-of-gamut warning symbol, Premiere moves the selected color to the nearest NTSC-safe color.

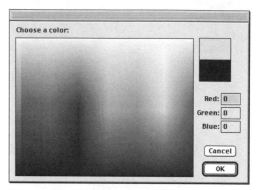

Figure 11.88 Click a color in the color picker, or type RGB values.

To use the color picker:

1. When the color picker is open, *do one of the following* (**Figure 11.88**):
   - Click a color in the color range.
   - Click a grayscale shade along the left side of the color picker.
   - Type Red, Green, and Blue values in the appropriate text boxes. You can press Tab to move from one value to the next.

Figure 11.89 If the warning icon appears, you can click it to set the color to the nearest NTSC-safe color.

2. If the out-of-gamut warning appears, click the warning icon to set the color to the nearest NTSC-safe color, or choose another color (**Figure 11.89**).

3. In the top-right side of the color picker, you can compare the color that you chose in the bottom swatch with the original color in the top color swatch.

4. Click OK to exit the color picker and apply the changes.

SUPER-
IMPOSING CLIPS

In Chapter 5, you learned that you can have as many as 99 video tracks in the timeline. Here's where you start using them—at least, some of them.

By layering clips and adjusting their opacity, you can create simple or complex blends and fades. You can also make certain parts of an image transparent. You can superimpose a title over another clip, for example, or composite a subject with another background.

The fade and transparency tools are nearly identical to those of previous versions, with just a few big differences. As you already know, higher superimpose tracks appear on higher tracks and are initially labeled Video 2 and up. Also, you can now adjust the video fade controls in increments of 1 percent, much as you can the audio fade controls.

Again, Premiere's layering and compositing tools are not as full-featured as those of a dedicated program, such as Adobe After Effects. These tools are surprisingly powerful, though, and smoothly incorporated into a solid editing program.

Like all effects, superimposed clips must be previewed (see Chapter 8). The final results depend on the image quality of the source clips as well as on the preview or output quality. As usual, there is a direct correlation between quality and processing time.

Track Hierarchy

Tracks 2 and higher are considered to be the *superimpose tracks*. If video clips are playing simultaneously in different tracks (and the monitor buttons are active), only the clip in the highest track is visible in Program view in the Monitor window, provided that you don't alter the clips' opacity levels. In other words, the superimpose tracks in Premiere work much like layers in Adobe Photoshop.

You can take advantage of track hierarchy for basic editing purposes. By placing a clip in a higher track, you can achieve an effect that looks like an overlay edit in Program view without actually recording over a clip in the timeline (**Figure 12.1**).

Superimpose tracks allow you to layer video clips to accomplish fading and keying effects. You can also apply motion settings (see Chapter 13) to layers of video to create picture-in-picture effects and complex composites.

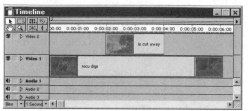

Figure 12.1 Without fading or keying (or motion) effects applied, a clip in a higher track looks much like an overlay edit.

Fading and Keying

You can superimpose clips in higher tracks over clips in lower tracks by using two methods known as fading and keying. *Fading* blends an entire clip with the clips in lower tracks (**Figure 12.2**). *Keying* combines, or *composites*, certain elements of a clip with the clips in lower tracks and *keys out* other areas, making them transparent (**Figure 12.3**). You can combine the effects of fading and keying—when you fade up a title over video, for example.

Figure 12.2 Fading a clip blends it with the clips in lower tracks.

Figure 12.3 Keying makes only certain elements transparent.

The Fade Control

You can reveal the opacity fader for clips in a superimpose track by expanding the track (see Chapter 5). By manipulating the fade line, you can blend the image of one clip with the clips in lower tracks. The video fade line controls the opacity of a clip much the same way that the audio fade line controls the audio gain levels. As you can with the audio fade line, you can use control handles to change the opacity of a clip. You can even use most of the same tools and techniques. The Fade Adjustment, Scissors, and Crossfade tools, for example, all work with the video fader.

Before you use the video fade controls, arrange clips in the timeline so that they overlap and expand the superimpose tracks.

To use a video fade handle:

1. Arrange clips in the timeline so that a clip in a superimpose track overlaps a clip in a lower track, and expand the superimpose track to reveal the fade line (**Figure 12.4**).

   The clip in the higher track acts as the foreground (higher layer of video), and clips in lower tracks act as the background (lower layers of video).

2. With the Selection tool selected, position the mouse pointer on the video fade line.

   The pointer changes to a white finger icon, indicating that you are about to create a new handle.

3. Click to create a control handle.

   A handle (red dot) appears on the video fade line (**Figure 12.5**).

4. Drag the fade handle down or up to control the opacity of the clip (**Figure 12.6**).

   The top of the fader area represents 100 percent opaque; the bottom represents 0 percent opaque.

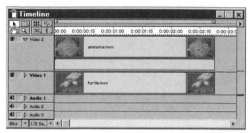

Figure 12.4 Arrange clips so that they overlap, and expand the superimpose tracks to reveal the fade line.

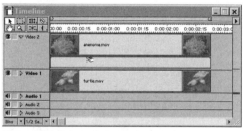

Figure 12.5 Click the fade line to create a handle.

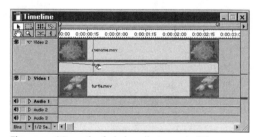

Figure 12.6 Drag the fade handle to control the opacity of the clip.

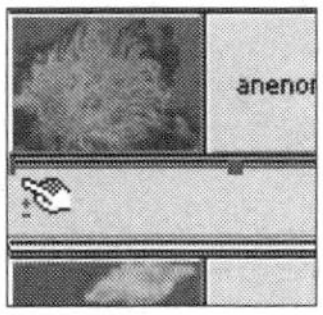

Figure 12.7 A gray finger icon indicates you can move an existing fade handle.

To delete a fade handle:

◆ Drag a fade handle all the way outside the superimpose track.

When you release the mouse button, the video fade handle disappears.

To move an existing video fade handle:

1. With the Selection tool selected, position the mouse pointer on an existing fade handle.

The pointer changes to a gray finger icon 🖑, indicating that you are about to move a handle (**Figure 12.7**). If the finger is white, you create a new handle.

2. Drag the fade handle up or down to change the opacity of the clip at that point, or side to side to change the handle's position in time.

To fade in increments of 1 percent:

1. With the Selection tool selected, position the mouse pointer on the video fade handle that you want to adjust.

The pointer changes to a gray finger icon 🖑, indicating that you are about to move a fade handle.

2. Hold down the Shift key.

The finger icon changes to the Fade Adjustment tool ⇳.

(continued on next page)

THE FADE CONTROL

3. Still holding down the Shift key, drag the handle up or down.

A numeric display appears, indicating the current opacity level. As long as you hold down the Shift key, you can drag beyond the top or bottom of the video track. This technique allows you to adjust the opacity in increments of 1 percent (**Figure 12.8**).

✔ Tip

■ You can see the current position and level value update in the Info palette as you drag a handle (**Figure 12.9**).

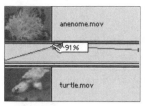

Figure 12.8 Hold down the Shift key as you drag a handle to adjust the opacity in increments of 1 percent.

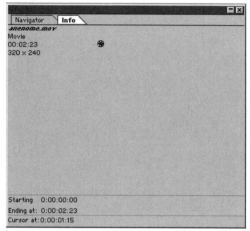

Figure 12.9 You can use the Info palette to view the position and value of a fade handle as you drag it.

Keying

In addition to fading the entire image, you can *key out* particular areas of an image, making them transparent. You can key out parts of an image based on luminance, chrominance, an alpha channel, or a separate matte image. Although Premiere provides 15 key types, they all fall into these basic categories. This chapter covers key types by category, explaining the most commonly used key types in detail and summarizing the others. You can use the fade control in combination with any key.

KEYING

Keying Controls

Every key type offers a different set of controls. If a control is unavailable, it is grayed-out. The following table summarizes the options that are available for each key type (**Table 12.1**).

To apply and preview any key type:

1. Arrange clips in the timeline so that a clip in a superimpose track overlaps a clip in a lower track.

The clip in the higher track acts as the foreground, and clips in lower tracks act as the background.

Table 12.1

Key Type Options

KEY TYPE	SIMILARITY	BLEND	THRESHOLD	CUTOFF	REVERSE KEY	DROP SHADOW	SMOOTHING
None					•		
Luminance Keys							
Luminance			•	•			
Multiply				•			
Screen				•			
Chrominance Keys							
Chroma	•	•	•	•		•	•
Blue screen			•	•			•
Green screen			•	•			•
RGB difference	•					•	•
Alpha Keys							
Alpha					•		
Black alpha matte							
White alpha matte							
Matte Keys							
Image matte					•		
Track matte					•		
Difference matte	•				•	•	•

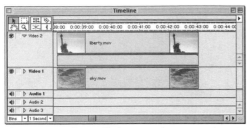

Figure 12.10 Select a clip in a superimpose track.

Figure 12.11 Choose the Transparency command.

Figure 12.12 The Transparency Settings dialog box appears for the selected clip.

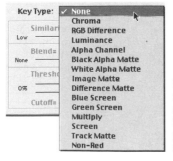

Figure 12.13 Make a selection from the Key Type pull-down menu.

2. Select a clip in a higher track to which you want to apply a transparency setting (**Figure 12.10**).

3. Choose Clip > Video > Transparency (**Figure 12.11**).

The Transparency Settings dialog box appears (**Figure 12.12**).

4. From the Key Type pull-down menu, choose a key type (**Figure 12.13**).

(See the following sections for information about individual key types.)

5. To adjust the parameters, drag any of the sliders, depending on the key type that you choose.

(continued on next page)

KEYING CONTROLS

6. Below the left side of the sample frame, click one of the three icons to view the transparency in the sample window and adjust the settings (**Figures 12.14** to **12.16**):

- Click ◪ to fill the transparent areas of a clip with black; click it again to see transparent areas as white.
- Click ▦ to fill the transparent areas of the clip with a checkerboard pattern.
- Click ◪ to fill the transparent areas of the clip with the actual background clip.

7. Below the right side of the sample frame, select any of the three icons to more closely evaluate the effectiveness of the key (**Figure 12.17**):

- Select the Zoom tool 🔍 , and click the sample frame to view an area in more detail; Option+click to zoom out.
- When you are zoomed into the sample frame, select the Hand tool 🖐 , and drag the sample frame to view different areas closely.
- If you are using the Mac OS, click the Collapse button ⬇ to preview the key effect in Program view of the Monitor window; click it again to preview the effect in the Transparency Settings window.

8. Drag the slider below the sample frame to view the effectiveness of the key type at different points in the clip.

9. Click OK to apply the settings to the clip.

Figure 12.14 Click one of the three icons below the left side of the sample frame to fill the transparent areas with black or white...

Figure 12.15 ...with a checkerboard pattern...

Figure 12.16 ...or with the lower video layers.

Figure 12.17 Use the tools below the right side of the sample frame to take a closer look at the key or to view it in Program view in the Monitor window.

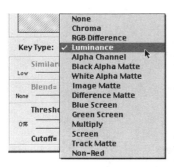

Figure 12.18 Choose Luminance from the Key Type pull-down menu, and adjust the Threshold and Cutoff sliders.

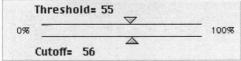

Figure 12.19 Luminance-based keys can make the brighter areas more transparent.

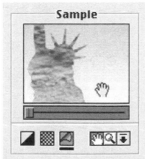

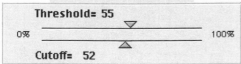

Figure 12.20 If the relative positions of the sliders are reversed, the darker areas are more transparent.

Luminance-Based Keys

Luminance-based keys use *luminance* (brightness) levels to define the transparent areas. You can choose to key out either the brightest or the darkest areas of the clip. Luminance-based key types include Luminance, Multiply, and Screen.

To use the Luminance key:

1. Select a clip in a superimpose track, and choose Clip > Video > Transparency, as described in the previous section, "To apply and preview any key type." The Transparency Settings dialog box appears.

2. From the Key Type pull-down menu of the Transparency Settings dialog box, choose Luminance (**Figure 12.18**). Drag the Threshold slider to control the range of darker values that become transparent.

3. Drag the Cutoff slider to set the transparency of the areas defined by the threshold.

4. View the effects of your adjustments in the sample frame (**Figure 12.19**).

5. When the relative positions of the threshold and cutoff are reversed, the key is reversed, and lighter areas become transparent (**Figure 12.20**).

6. When you are satisfied with your adjustments, click OK to close the Transparency Settings dialog box and apply the settings.

Multiply and Screen Keys

The Multiply and Screen keys use the underlying image to define the transparent areas of the clip. Multiply affects the opacity of the clip most in areas where the underlying image is brightest; Screen affects the opacity of the clip most in areas where the underlying image is darkest.

To use the Multiply or Screen key:

◆ Drag the cutoff slider to make the clip more opaque where the underlying clip is brightest (Multiply) or darkest (Screen).

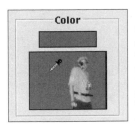

Figure 12.21 You can select the color that you want to key out by clicking the thumbnail image in the Color section of the Transparency Settings dialog box.

Chrominance Keys

Chrominance-based keys use *chrominance* (color) to define the transparent areas of a clip. Chrominance-based keys are commonly used in compositing work, in which a subject is combined with a background. Chrominance-based key types include Chroma, Blue Screen, Green Screen, RGB Difference, and Non-Red.

Chroma Key

All the chrominance-based keys work essentially the same way, although the Chroma key is the most flexible. The following sections explain in detail how to apply the Chroma key and summarize the other color-based keys.

To use the Chroma key:

1. Select a clip in a superimpose track, and choose Clip > Video > Transparency, as described in the previous section, "To apply and preview any key type."
   The Transparency Settings dialog box appears.

2. From the Key Type pull-down menu of the Transparency Settings dialog box, choose Chroma.

3. To select a key color, *do one of the following*:
   - In the Color section, click a color in the thumbnail image (**Figure 12.21**).
   - In the Color section, click the color swatch to choose a color in the color picker.

4. Drag the sliders to adjust the key:
   - Drag the Similarity slider to increase or decrease the range of colors similar to the key color that are keyed out.
   - Drag the Blend slider to blend the clip with the underlying clip.

- ◆ Drag the Threshold slider to control the amount of shadows that you keep in the range of key colors.

- ◆ Drag the Cutoff slider to darken or lighten shadows.

  Don't drag the Cutoff beyond the Threshold, or you will invert the gray and transparent pixels.

- ◆ Drag the Smoothing slider to antialias (smooth) the edges of the key.

5. View the effects of your adjustments in the sample frame (**Figure 12.22**).

6. When you are satisfied with the adjustments, click OK to close the Transparency Settings dialog box and apply the settings.

Figure 12.22 View the effect of the key in the sample box as you use the sliders to completely key out the background color

RGB Difference Key

The RGB Difference key works like a simpler version of the Chroma key. It provides only the Similarity and Smoothing sliders. You can also use t the Drop Shadow option, which adds a 50 percent gray, 50 percent opaque shadow, offset 4 pixels to the right and 4 pixels down.

Blue Screen and Green Screen Keys

The Blue Screen and Green Screen keys are optimized for use with true chroma blue and true chroma green, respectively.

Non-Red Key

The Non-Red key makes blue and green areas (non-red) transparent. This key type also provides a Blend slider.

CHROMINANCE KEYS

Figure 12.23 Use the Alpha Channel key type to key out a straight alpha channel.

Alpha Keys

Alpha-based keys use the clip's alpha channel to define transparent areas. In addition to visible red, green, and blue channels, images can contain an alpha channel. An alpha channel can be a straight alpha channel, like the one often saved in the fourth channel of a Photoshop image, or it can be premultiplied with color, like the titles that you create in Premiere (see Chapter 11). The kind of alpha channel determines the type of key that you choose.

Alpha Channel Key

Photoshop, Illustrator, and After Effects can all create images with a *straight alpha channel*—that is, the alpha channel contains all the transparency information. Use the Alpha key for images that have a straight alpha channel.

To use the Alpha Channel key:

1. Select a clip in a superimpose track, and choose Clip > Video > Transparency, as described in the previous section, "To apply and preview any key type."

   The Transparency Settings dialog box appears.

2. From the Key Type pull-down menu of the Transparency Settings dialog box, choose Alpha.

   Some areas are keyed out based on the straight alpha channel (**Figure 12.23**).

3. Preview the effects.

4. Click OK to exit the Transparency Settings dialog box.

Black and White Alpha Matte Keys

When the alpha channel is *premultiplied*, the transparency information is stored in all four channels of the image. This causes the edges of the opaque part of the image to blend into a background color. The alpha channel used by a Premiere title is premultiplied with a black or white background. Use Black Alpha Matte or White Alpha Matte with images that contain an alpha channel premultiplied with a black or white background.

To use the Black Alpha Matte and White Alpha Matte keys:

1. Select a clip in a superimpose track, and choose Clip > Video > Transparency, as described in the previous section, "To apply and preview any key type."

   The Transparency Settings dialog box appears.

2. *Do one of the following:*

   ◆ In the Transparency Settings dialog box, choose Black Alpha Matte if the clip has a black background.

   ◆ Choose White Alpha Matte if the clip has a white background.

   Some areas are keyed out based on the premultiplied alpha channel (**Figure 12.24**).

3. Preview the effects.

4. Click OK to exit the Transparency Settings dialog box.

✔ Tip

■ If you use a regular Alpha Matte key on an image with a premultiplied alpha channel, you may see a black or white fringe, or halo around the edges of the opaque image.

Figure 12.24 Use the Black Alpha Matte or White Alpha Matte key types to key out an alpha channel that is premultiplied with black or white, respectively.

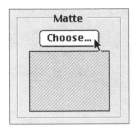

Figure 12.25 In the Matte section of the Transparency Settings dialog box, click Choose to select a file to use as a matte.

Matte Keys

Matte-based keys use an external image to define transparent areas of a clip. A typical matte is a high-contrast grayscale image (sometimes called a *high-con*). Typically, the white areas of the matte define opaque areas of the foreground clip (sometimes called the *beauty*); black areas of the matte define transparent parts of the foreground clip; and gray areas define semitransparent parts of the foreground clip.

Matte-based key types include Image Matte and Track Matte. The Difference Matte key also falls into this category, although it creates its own matte by comparing two clips.

Image Matte Key

The Image Matte key can use any high-contrast grayscale still image as the matte, including a static title that you create in Premiere. Although you choose the image in the Transparency Settings dialog box, the matte does not have to be used in the timeline or even imported into the project.

To use the Image Matte key:

1. Select a clip in a superimpose track, and choose Clip > Video > Transparency, as described in the previous section, "To apply and preview any key type."

   The Transparency Settings dialog box appears.

2. From the Key Type pull-down menu of the Transparency Settings dialog box, choose Image Matte.

   In the Matte section, click Choose (**Figure 12.25**).

   The Open File dialog box appears.

3. Locate the still image that you want to use as the matte.

4. Click Open.

A thumbnail image of the matte appears in the Matte section of the Transparency Settings dialog box. Some areas are keyed out based on the alpha channel (**Figure 12.26**).

5. To reverse the opaque and transparent areas of the key, check Reverse Key (**Figure 12.27**).

6. Preview the effects.

7. Click OK to exit the Transparency Settings dialog box.

Track Matte Key

The Track Matte key uses a moving matte, often called a *traveling matte*. The matte can be a high-contrast, grayscale video clip or an image that you animate with motion settings (Chapter 13), a filter (Chapter 10), or a text roll (Chapter 11). You can also create a matte from a clip by using the Transparency Settings dialog box. Unlike a still-image matte, a moving matte must appear in the timeline with the foreground and background clips.

To use the Track Matte key:

1. To arrange the clips in the timeline, *do the following:* (**Figure 12.28**):
   - Position the background clip in a lower track.
   - Position the foreground clip in the next-higher superimpose track.
   - Position the moving matte in the superimpose track above the foreground clip.

2. Select the foreground clip.

3. Choose Video > Clip > Transparency. The Transparency Settings dialog box appears.

4. From the Key Type pull-down menu, choose Track Matte.

Figure 12.26 The file that you choose appears as a thumbnail image in the Matte section of the Transparency Settings dialog box. The matte defines the transparent areas of the clip to which you applied the key.

Figure 12.27 Check Reverse Key to reverse the opaque and transparent areas.

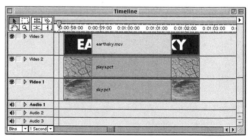

Figure 12.28 Stack the background, foreground, and matte clips in the timeline. Apply the Track Matte key to the foreground clip.

MATTE KEYS

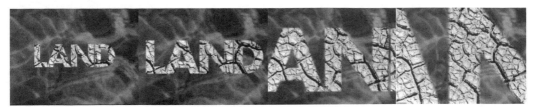

Figure 12.29 A filter applied to a title creates a moving matte for the foreground and background video.

Figure 12.30 Choose the Mask Only option to create a matte from another key type.

5. To reverse the transparent and opaque areas of the foreground image, check Reverse Key.

6. Preview the effects.

7. Click OK to exit the Transparency Settings dialog box.

When you preview or export the video, the matte effect moves (**Figure 12.29**).

Difference Matte Key

The Difference Matte key creates the transparent areas of a clip by comparing it with another still image and keying out the areas where the two clips match. The Difference Matte key is designed to remove a static background from behind a moving subject. By using a frame of a static background as the matte, you can key out the existing background and replace it with another. This key works only if the subject keeps moving and the camera remains static, however. You can also choose the drop-shadow option.

Creating Mattes

The Mask Only checkbox is available in for the None, Chroma, RGB Difference, Difference Matte, Blue Screen, Green Screen, and Non-Red key types. The Mask Only option uses the key type to create a black and white matte (**Figure 12.30**). You can use the matte that you create with the Track Matte key.

Garbage Mattes

Although it doesn't appear in the Key Type menu of the Transparency Settings dialog box, a garbage matte can be used to key out areas of a superimposed image. You can use a garbage matte in conjunction with other keys to eliminate unnecessary elements. You can also use a garbage matte alone to create a split-screen effect.

To create a garbage matte:

1. Select a clip in a superimpose track, and choose Clip > Video > Transparency, as described in the previous section, "To apply and preview any key type."

   The Transparency Settings dialog box appears.

2. In the Sample section of the Transparency Settings dialog box, drag the handles of the image to key out unwanted areas of the clip (**Figure 12.31**).

✔ Tip

- To smooth the edges of a split-screen effect, use the garbage matte in combination with the RGB Difference key. Don't select a color; simply choose Low, Medium, or High from the Smoothing pull-down menu (**Figure 12.32**).

Figure 12.31 Drag the corner handles of the sample image to create a garbage matte. Adjusting some keys (like a chroma key) are easier if you use a garbage matte to cut unnecessary portions of the image.

Figure 12.32 You can use a garbage matte to create a simple split screen. Choose the RGB Difference key to use a Smoothing option, and smooth the edge of the garbage matte.

MOTION SETTING

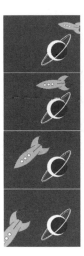

Figure 13.1 Motion settings allow you to reposition video or create two-dimensional animation.

Motion settings allow you to move, rotate, zoom, and distort an image in and through the frame in Program view (**Figure 13.1**).

Using motion settings, you can create a simple picture-in-picture effect or compose layers of video on the screen to create an elegant design. You can subtly resize and reposition the company logo or fly titles around the screen for a monster-truck-pull commercial. You can also create your own traveling mattes for Track Matte keys (see Chapter 12).

No, you can't create motion paths along Bézier curves or do sophisticated motion tracking. Look to high-end (and high-priced) dedicated motion-effects programs for those features. Nevertheless, Premiere's motion effects are impressive, especially considering the fact that they come with all the advantages of an editing program.

Motion settings are among the few unchanged features of Premiere. Now, however, you can load motion settings into the motion-effect transition (see Chapter 7).

Using Motion Settings

You apply a motion setting to an entire clip, from in point to out point. The total time of the motion equals the duration of the clip.

Motion settings affect the entire frame of the clip, not individual elements within the frame. If you want to move two title graphics in different directions, for example, create two title clips and apply motion settings to each clip.

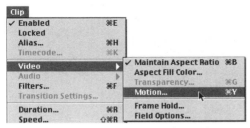

Figure 13.2 Select a clip and choose Clip > Video > Motion.

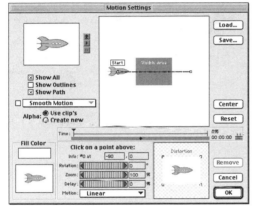

Figure 13.3 The Motion Settings dialog box appears, displaying the default motion settings.

Working with Keyframes (Again)

When you learned about filters in Chapter 10, you also learned the term *keyframes* (see the sidebar in Chapter 10). Motion settings use keyframes to define the position and other attributes of a clip at different points in time.

When you open the Motion Settings dialog box, it displays the default settings. By default, a clip is positioned offscreen left for the Start keyframe (the following section, "Setting Keyframes," explains keyframes) and offscreen right for the Finish keyframe. Therefore, the default motion setting moves the clip horizontally across the screen, from offscreen left to offscreen right. You can change the Start and End keyframes, but you cannot delete them.

To add a motion setting to a clip:

1. In the timeline, select a clip.

2. Choose Clip > Video > Motion (**Figure 13.2**).

The Motion Settings dialog box appears, displaying the default motion settings (**Figure 13.3**).

3. Set keyframes and adjust the attributes of the clip at each keyframe.

For details, see "Setting Keyframes" later in this chapter.

4. Click OK to apply the motion settings to the clip.

The clip in the timeline displays a red line, indicating that you applied motion settings to it.

To remove a motion setting:

1. Select a clip in the timeline that has motion settings.

Clips that have motion settings appear in the timeline with a red line.

2. Choose Clip > Video > Motion.

The Motion Settings dialog box appears, displaying the default motion settings.

3. Click Remove to remove motion settings from the clip.

Previewing the Motion

In the top-left corner of the Motion Settings dialog box, a sample frame previews the motion setting (**Figure 13.4**). Although the sample does not play back as smoothly as the rendered motion effect, it illustrates how the motion will look in Program view.

To preview the motion:

1. Open the Motion Settings dialog box for a clip, as explained by the task, "To add a motion setting," earlier in this section.

2. In the sample area in the upper left corner of the Motion Settings dialog box, *do any of the following:*

◆ Click the Play button 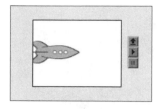 to play an animation of your motion setting in the sample area.

◆ Click the Pause button ▣ to pause the animated preview and view a static frame that represent the currently selected keyframe.

◆ Click the Collapse button ⬆ to view the preview in Program view in the Monitor window; click it again to see the preview in the sample box.

◆ Check Show All to preview the motion with clip playback, transitions, filters, transparency, and clips in lower layers visible (**Figure 13.5**).

Figure 13.4 Preview the motion setting in the top-left corner of the Motion Settings dialog box.

Figure 13.5 Choose Show All to see the selected clip play back as you preview the motion setting. Show All also shows clips in lower layers.

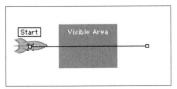

Figure 13.6 You can add and position keyframes on the motion path in the large area at the top of the Motion Settings dialog box.

Figure 13.7 You can add and position keyframes in time by adding keyframes along the timeline.

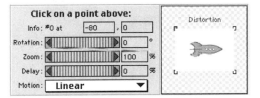

Figure 13.8 Use the controls at the bottom of the Motion Settings dialog box to control various attributes of the clip at each keyframe.

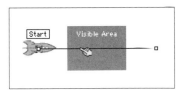

Figure 13.9 Position the mouse pointer on the motion path...

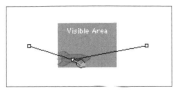

Figure 13.10 ... and click the motion path to add a keyframe. Drag the keyframe to position it in relation to the visible area of the screen.

Setting Keyframes

You can set motion keyframes in two areas of the Motion Settings dialog box. In the large box near the top of the of the dialog box, you can add and adjust points on a motion path (**Figure 13.6**). This area gives you easy control of image positioning but only rough control of timing. Elsewhere in the Motion Settings dialog box, you can add and adjust keyframes in a timeline (**Figure 13.7**). This area gives you precise control of the timing of keyframes but doesn't illustrate their positioning. The keyframes in the motion path and the timeline are the same keyframes represented in different ways.

At the bottom of the dialog box, you can control attributes of the clip at each keyframe, including position, rotation, zoom, delay, and distortion (**Figure 13.8**).

To set keyframes in the motion path:

1. Position the mouse pointer on the motion path line (**Figure 13.9**).

   The pointer turns into a pointing-finger icon ☜.

2. Click to add a point on the line.

   A thumbnail representation of the clip appears at the keyframe.

3. Drag the point to a new position (**Figure 13.10**).

   The gray Visible Area box represents the viewing area in Program view.

To set keyframes in the motion timeline:

1. Position the mouse pointer above the motion timeline (**Figure 13.11**).

2. Click to add a point to the path.

    A keyframe appears, represented by a small vertical line. When the keyframe is selected, a triangle appears above the line (**Figure 13.12**).

3. Drag the keyframe to the right or left to change its position in time.

To select a keyframe to adjust:

To select a keyframe, *do one of the following:*

  ◆ Click a point on the motion path.

  ◆ Click a keyframe in the motion timeline.

  ◆ Press Tab to select successive keyframes in order, from Start to Finish.

  ◆ Press Shift+Tab to select successive keyframes in reverse order.

To delete a keyframe:

  ◆ Select a keyframe and then press the Delete key.

To view frames and speed in the motion path:

Check the checkboxes in the top-left section of the Motion Settings dialog box to toggle the following options (**Figure 13.13**):

  ◆ Check Show Outlines to display an outline of the clip at every keyframe in the motion path (**Figure 13.14**).

  ◆ Check Show Path to display the motion path as dotted lines between keyframes (**Figure 13.14**).

Dots that are closer together represent slower speed between keyframes; dots that are farther apart represent faster speed.

Figure 13.11 Position the mouse pointer above the motion timeline…

Figure 13.12 … and click to create a keyframe in time. Drag the keyframe to reposition its position in time.

Figure 13.13 Check Show Outlines and Show Path to activate those options.

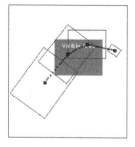

Figure 13.14 Check Show Outlines to make frames appear at each keyframe in the motion path. Check Show Path to indicate speed in the motion path.

Figure 13.15 When the arrows touch, the time display measures the location of the keyframe from the beginning of the clip.

Figure 13.16 When the arrows are separated, the time display measures the location of the keyframe from the beginning of the program.

To position a keyframe at an exact time:

◆ To the right of the motion timeline, click the small red arrows to toggle the time display:

Display the touching arrows ⬛, to measure the position of the selected keyframe from the beginning of the clip (**Figure 13.15**).

Display the separated arrows ⬛, to measure the position of the selected keyframe from the beginning of the program (**Figure 13.16**).

✔ Tip

■ When you move a keyframe in the motion timeline, look at the time display to position it exactly.

Setting Keyframe Attributes

At every keyframe, you can define the clip's position, rotation, zoom, and distortion. You can also control whether a clip accelerates, decelerates, or uses linear progression to proceed to the next keyframe.

To set the spatial position of a keyframe:

1. Select a keyframe, as described in the section "Setting Keyframes," earlier in this chapter.

2. *Do any of the following:*
    - ◆ Drag the keyframe on the motion path to change its position.
    - ◆ Use the arrow keys to nudge the position 1 pixel at a time.
    - ◆ Press Shift+any arrow key to move the position 5 pixels at a time.
    - ◆ Type *X* and *Y* coordinates for the selected keyframe in the boxes below the motion timeline (**Figure 13.17**).
    - ◆ To center the clip in the visible area (at coordinates 0,0), click the Center button.

✔ Tip

- ■ The coordinates in the Info boxes are expressed in the pixel dimensions of the sample image, which is 80x60. These numbers are scaled to your output size when the motion is rendered or exported. Therefore, a 1-pixel shift at the sample size equals a 4-pixel shift at an output size of 320x240 (4 times 80x60). To compensate for the difference, you can type fractional decimal values for the coordinates.

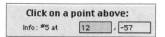

Figure 13.17 You can enter exact coordinates for the center of the clip for each keyframe.

SETTING KEYFRAME ATTRIBUTES

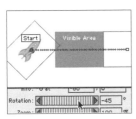

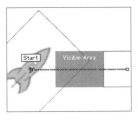

Figure 13.18 You can rotate a clip...

Figure 13.19 ...zoom it smaller and larger...

Figure 13.20 ...and pause it at a keyframe for a specified period.

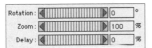

Figure 13.21 For each keyframe, enter values for a clip's Rotation, Zoom, and Delay. You can drag the sliders, click the arrow buttons, or type values in the value boxes to adjust these settings.

Rotation, Zoom, and Delay

You can think of rotation as being a rotational position or angle. The angle that you enter can range from −1440 degrees to 1440 degrees, allowing eight full rotations (**Figure 13.18**).

Zoom increases or decreases the size of the clip at the keyframe. The size can range from 0 percent to 500 percent; 100 percent equals the clip at its normal size (**Figure 13.19**).

Delay pauses the clip at a keyframe for a specified period, expressed as a percentage of the clip's total duration. When you add a delay value, a blue line appears in the timeline, representing the length of the delay (**Figure 13.20**).

To set rotation, zoom, and delay:

1. Select a keyframe.

2. Next to each attribute in the bottom section of the Motion Settings dialog box, do one of the following things to set its value for the selected keyframe (**Figure 13.21**):

   ◆ Drag the slider.

   ◆ Click the arrow buttons on either end of the slider.

   ◆ Type a value in the box next to the attribute and then press Return.

   ◆ Repeat steps 1 and 2, as needed.

   ◆ Preview your settings.

   ◆ Click OK to apply the motion to the clip.

✔ Tips

■ Remember that rotation is expressed as an angle, not as the amount of rotation from one keyframe to the next. To rotate a clip one full rotation clockwise and then remain at that angle, you make the three keyframes 0, 360, and 360. A common mistake would be making the keyframes 0, 360, and 0. These settings would cause the clip to rotate first clockwise and then counterclockwise.

■ If you zoom a clip much larger than normal size, its pixels become more noticeable and the apparent quality decreases. This effect applies even to Premiere titles and Illustrator art, because they are rasterized before the zoom is applied.

Figure 13.22 Drag a corner handle to distort the image at the current keyframe.

To distort a clip:

1. Select a motion keyframe.

2. In the Distortion section of the Motion Settings dialog box, *do any of the following*:

   ◆ Drag one of the corner handles to a new position (**Figure 13.22**).

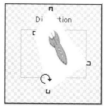

Figure 13.23 Option+drag a corner handle to spin the image around the handle.

   ◆ Option+drag a corner point to spin the image around the point (**Figure 13.23**).

   ◆ Position the mouse pointer in the center of the sample image and drag to move the entire image (**Figure 13.24**).

3. Preview your settings.

4. Click OK to apply the motion to the clip.

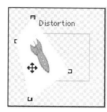

Figure 13.24 To move all four corners at the same time, position the mouse pointer in the center of the thumbnail image and drag.

To remove rotation, zoom, delay, and distortion from a keyframe:

1. In the Motion Settings dialog box, select a keyframe.

2. Click Reset to remove rotation, zoom, delay, and distortion from the keyframe.

3. Change and review your settings, as described in the previous sections.

4. Click OK to apply the motion to the clip.

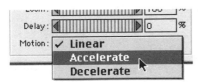

Figure 13.25 Choose an interpolation method from the Motion pull-down menu.

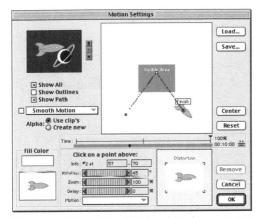

Figure 13.26 When Show Path is selected, you can see the results of the interpolation method that you choose as dots in the motion path.

To select a motion option:

1. Select a keyframe.

2. From the Motion pull-down menu at the bottom of the Motion Settings dialog box, choose one of the three interpolation options (**Figure 13.25**):

   ◆ Choose Linear to interpolate the motion to the next keyframe by using a linear progression.

   ◆ Choose Accelerate to make the clip move to the next keyframe slower and then faster.

   ◆ Choose Decelerate to make the clip move to the next keyframe faster and then slower (**Figure 13.26**).

   Motion options control the speed of motion between keyframes. The time between keyframes remains the same.

3. Preview your settings.

4. Click OK to apply the motion to the clip.

✔ Tips

■ Use the Copy and Paste keyboard shortcuts to copy the settings from one keyframe to another.

■ Because the distortion settings do not have numerical controls, it can be especially useful to copy and paste distortion settings from one keyframe to the next.

SETTING KEYFRAME ATTRIBUTES

Using Other Motion-Setting Options

In addition to keyframe attributes, you can set other important Motion Setting options. You can set the fill color behind the moving clip, add motion smoothing, and choose how to treat the alpha channel of the clip.

Fill Color

When the moving clip does not fill the visible frame, the frame is filled with a color. You can select a color for the background fill from the sample frame or from the color picker.

To set the fill color:

To set a fill color, *do one of the following:*

- ◆ Position the mouse pointer in the sample frame located in the bottom-left corner of the Motion Settings dialog box, and click to choose a color.
- ◆ The Eyedropper tool appears, and the current color appears in the swatch above the sample (**Figure 13.27**).
- ◆ Click the color swatch above the sample frame to pick a color from the color picker.

Smooth Motion

You can smooth sharp changes in direction, rotation, and distortion by selecting one of the Smooth Motion options. When you apply these options, instead of moving directly to and from a position, the clip takes a rounder, smoother course.

Figure 13.27 In the Fill Color section of the Motion Settings dialog box, click the sample frame or the color swatch to choose a fill color.

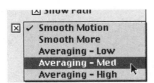

Figure 13.28 You can choose an option to smooth changes in direction.

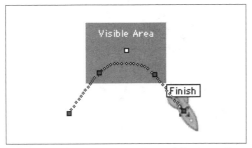

Figure 13.29 You can see the effects of the Smooth Motion option in the motion path when Show Paths is checked.

To choose smooth motion:

1. Check the box next to the Smooth Motion pull-down menu on the left side of the Motion Settings dialog box.

2. From the Smoother Motion pull-down menu, choose one of the three smoothing options (**Figure 13.28**):

◆ Smooth Motion for the smallest amount of smoothing.

◆ Averaging-Low for a moderate amount of smoothing.

◆ Averaging-High for a high amount of smoothing.

If Show Paths is checked, you can see the effects of smooth motion in the motion path (**Figure 13.29**).

Alpha Channel Options

Most often, you superimpose a clip that has motion settings over other clips in the time-line. To do so, you apply one of the Alpha Channel keys that you learned about in Chapter 12. In the Motion Settings dialog box, you must determine whether to use the clip's alpha channel or create a new one.

USING OTHER MOTION-SETTING OPTIONS

To select an alpha-channel option:

Check the appropriate Alpha radio button (**Figure 13.30**):

◆ Choose Alpha: Create new if the clip doesn't have an alpha channel or if you want to ignore the existing alpha channel.

This option creates an alpha channel in the shape of the clip as it moves, enabling you to apply the alpha key and superimpose the clip over other clips (**Figure 13.31**).

◆ Choose Alpha: Use clip's if the clip has an alpha channel.

Titles created in Premiere can have an alpha channel (see Chapter 11), as can still images from other applications, such as Photoshop and Illustrator (see Chapter 3) (**Figure 13.32**).

✔ Tip

■ If you position the clip in a superimpose track before you apply a motion setting, Premiere automatically applies an Alpha key to the clip when you add the motion setting.

Figure 13.30 Indicate whether you want to create a new alpha channel or use the clip's alpha channel.

Figure 13.31 Create a new alpha channel to key the entire frame over other layers of video.

Figure 13.32 If the clip has an alpha channel, you can use it to key out portions of the frame.

Figure 13.33 In the top-right corner of the Motion Settings dialog box, click Save to save the current settings or Load to load saved settings.

Saving and Loading Motion Settings

If you create a useful motion setting that you want to apply to other clips, you can save the motion settings as a file. Later, you can load these settings into any clip in any project. Premiere also ships with several preset motion-settings files, which are located in the Motion Settings folder inside the Premiere folder. These settings not only provide preset effects but also serve as useful examples for you to examine or modify. Don't forget that you can also use saved motion settings with the Motion transition (Chapter 7).

To save a motion setting:

1. In the Motion Settings dialog box, create a motion setting, as explained in the preceding sections.

2. In the top-right corner of the Motion Settings dialog box, click Save to save a motion-settings file (**Figure 13.33**).

3. Specify a name and location for the motion setting.

4 Click OK.

To load a motion setting:

1. In the Motion Settings dialog box, click Load (**Figure 13.33**).

2. Locate a motion-settings file (**Figure 13.34**).

3. Click OK.

   The motion settings become the current settings.

4. If you want, modify the keyframes and other settings (**Figure 13.35**).

5. Click OK to apply the motion settings to the clip.

✔ Tip

■ You can copy and paste motion settings from one clip to another by using the Paste Custom command.

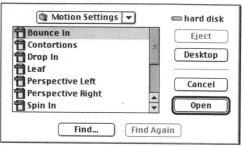

Figure 13.34 Premiere ships with several preset motion-settings files.

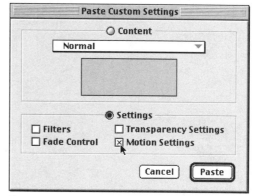

Figure 13.35 You can use the preset motion settings or modify them to suit your needs.

SAVING AND LOADING MOTION SETTINGS

14

CREATING OUTPUT

At the beginning of the editing process, you asked yourself the question, "What is my final output goal?" Now it's time to deliver.

Depending on your needs, you can output your program to videotape, as a digital file, or both. If your computer has a video capture card (or a connection to a DV recorder), you can output the program directly from the timeline to a videotape. You may also want to create a stand-alone video file. Depending on the output settings, you can also record the file to videotape or a CD-ROM or present it via the Web. The capabilities (and limitations) of your playback device help determine the characteristics of the movie.

Your edited Premiere program, of course, may not represent your completed work. The exported movie may serve as source material for other programs—including a Premiere project. You can also use Premiere to export an audio-only file, a still image, or a series of still images. If you are using Premiere as an offline editing tool (see Chapter 1), you can export an edit decision list for use with a traditional online editing suite.

Because you are already familiar with the video, audio, keyframe, and rendering from Chapter 2, this chapter concentrates on the settings that are unique to output. For details about compression, see Chapter 17.

Exporting File Types

Premiere exports various file formats for video, audio, or image sequences (**Table 14.1**). The formats that you can export depend on whether you are using the Macintosh or Windows version of Premiere. The formats that each platform opens and plays, however, depend on your particular system. You can also add formats with plug-in software modules.

Table 14.1

Exportable Formats
Video/audio formats
Animated GIF
Microsoft AVI
QuickTime
Audio-only formats
AIFF (Mac OS)
Windows Audio Waveform (Windows)
Still-image formats
Filmstrip
FLC/FLI (Windows)
GIF/GIF sequence
PICT/PICT sequence (Mac OS)
Targa/Targa sequence
TIFF/TIFF sequence
Windows bitmap (Windows)

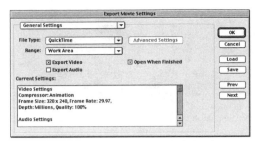

Figure 14.1 The Export Movie Settings dialog box resembles the Project Settings dialog box.

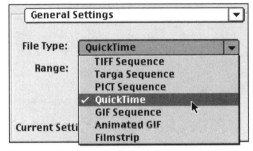

Figure 14.2 From the File Type pull-down menu, choose a file format to export.

Figure 14.3 From the Range pull-down menu, choose how much of the program you want to export.

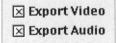

Figure 14.4 Check Export Video and Export Audio to include them in the exported movie.

Creating a Movie

You can create a single, independent file from all or part of the program in the timeline.

As you do at every step of the video process, you must specify the characteristics of the final video, such frame size, frame rate, compression, and audio quality. The settings that you choose are determined not only by your output goal, but also by the capabilities of your playback device.

To export a video file:

1. Resize the work-area bar over the part of the program window that you want to make into a movie.

2. Choose File > Export > Movie.
   The Save Export Movie dialog box appears.

3. Click the Settings button.
   The General Settings panel of the Export Movie Settings dialog box opens. It looks similar to the Project Settings dialog box but has important differences (**Figure 14.1**).

4. From the File Type pull-down menu, choose a video file format, such as QuickTime or .AVI (**Figure 14.2**).

5. To specify the range of the program that you want to export, from the Range pull-down menu (**Figure 14.3**), choose one of the following options:
   Work Area to export only the part of the program below the work-area bar.
   Entire Program to export the entire program in the timeline.

6. Check Export Video to export the video tracks or uncheck the option to exclude the video tracks from the movie (**Figure 14.4**).

(continued on next page)

7. Check Export Audio to export the audio tracks; uncheck the option to exclude the audio tracks from the movie (**Figure 14.4**).

8. From the pull-down menu at the top of the Output Settings dialog box, choose one of the following categories of settings: General, Video, Audio, Keyframe and Rendering Options, and Special Processing Options (**Figure 14.5**).

9. Click OK to exit the Output Settings dialog box.

Your choices are summarized in the Save Exported Movie dialog box.

10. In the Save Export Movie dialog box, Specify a name and destination for your file (**Figure 14.6**).

11. Click OK to begin rendering the movie.

A progress bar appears, displaying an estimate of the processing time.

✔ Tip

■ Consult your Premiere user guide to find out about batch processing, which enables you to export multiple projects or multiple files from the same project.

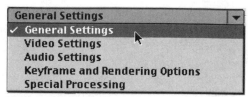

Figure 14.5 Select a category from the Export Movie Settings pulldown menu to view the panel and choose settings for that category.

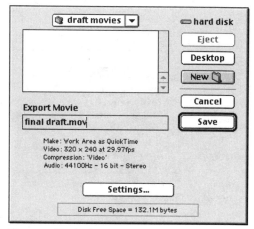

Figure 14.6 In the Save Export Movie dialog box, choose a name and destination for the exported movie.

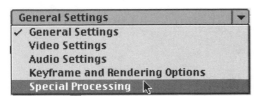

Figure 14.7 Choose Special Processing to view the special processing settings.

Figure 14.8 The Special Processing panel of the Export Movie Settings dialog box summarizes the current options.

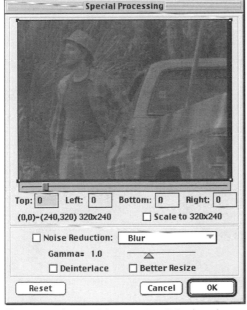

Figure 14.9 The Special Processing dialog box gives you finer control of the exported video image.

Using Special Processing Options

In the Export Movie Settings dialog box, special processing options allow you to further control the characteristics of the final movie. These options are particularly useful if you are preparing movies that require limited data rates—for CD-ROM or Web playback, for example. You can crop the movie; optimize resizing; and add noise-reduction, deinterlacing, and gamma-correction filters. Premiere dynamically previews these options, as well as the effects of any other filters and transitions.

To access special processing options:

1. Follow the steps to export a movie, as explained in the previous section. However, do not exit the Export Movie Settings dialog box.

2. From the pull-down menu of the Export Movie Settings dialog box, choose Special Processing (**Figure 14.7**).

   A summary of the special processing options appears (**Figure 14.8**).

3. Click the Modify button.

   The Special Processing dialog box appears (**Figure 14.9**).

4. Set the special processing options, as explained in the following sections.

5. Drag the slider below the sample frame to preview the effects of the options that you choose.

6. Click OK to return to the Export Movie Settings dialog box.

Resizing

If the final-output frame size is smaller than the frame size of the source clips, the Better Resize option resizes the final movie with the same interpolation method used by Adobe After Effects. Otherwise, Premiere uses a lower-quality method.

To optimize resizing:

◆ In the Special Processing dialog box, check Better Resize (**Figure 14.10**).

Cropping

Full-screen video often contains black edges. These edges are not visible when displayed on an overscanned video monitor (see Chapter 11), but they appear on a computer screen—especially when the image frame size is less than full-screen.

To crop the video:

◆ To crop unwanted edges of the image, do one of the following:

In the Special Processing dialog box, drag the corner handles of the sample frame (**Figure 14.11**).

In the boxes below the sample frame, type the number of pixels by which you want to crop the top, bottom, right, and left sides of the final movie.

Figure 14.10 Check Better Resize to activate a superior interpolation method for resizing the clip.

Figure 14.11 Drag the corner handles of the sample frame to resize the clip manually.

Figure 14.12 Check Noise Reduction and choose a noise-reduction filter.

Noise-Reduction Filter

The noise-reduction filter adds a blur to the movie, softening the image and creating the illusion of slightly higher resolution at lower data rates.

To apply the noise-reduction filter:

1. In the Special Processing dialog box, check the Noise Reduction checkbox.

2. From the Noise Reduction pull-down menu choose one of the following (**Figure 14.12**):

   Blur for the most subtle effect. Blur averages pixels next to the hard edges and shaded areas.

   Gaussian Blur to produce a hazier effect.

   Median to create the strongest blur but also preserve the hard edges.

✔ Tip

■ The noise-reduction filter especially improves the apparent image quality when you use Cinepak compression.

DeInterlace Filter

Many capture boards digitize two interlaced frames of video (see Chapter 1 for more information about interlacing). If the movie that you are compiling is smaller than full-screen, you should use the de-interlace filter. This filter removes the secondary field from each frame and doubles the dominant field. If you don't choose this option, the video is deinterlaced by means of a lower-quality method, and the movie may appear to flicker. See Chapter 17 for a complete explanation of fields, interlacing, and field dominance.

To add the deinterlace filter:

◆ In the Special Processing dialog box, check the Deinterlace box (**Figure 14.13**).

Gamma Adjustment

Brightness levels of *midtones* (middle gray levels) differ between Macintosh and Windows platforms. A movie created on a Mac appears darker on a Windows system, and vice versa. You can add the gamma filter to compensate for this difference. The gamma filter adjusts the midtones without affecting the black and white areas.

To adjust the gamma:

1. In the Special Processing dialog box, drag the Gamma slider (**Figure 14.14**).

2. Preview the changes to the midtone brightness levels in the sample frame.

✔ Tip

■ A gamma setting of 0.7 or 0.8 help a Mac-compressed clip look good on either a Mac or Windows computer.

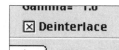

Figure 14.13 Check De-Interlace to remove the secondary field from interlaced video.

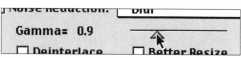

Figure 14.14 Drag the Gamma slider to compensate for the gamma differences between computer platforms.

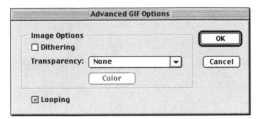

Figure 14.15 You can choose advanced options when you export animated GIFs or GIF sequences.

Working with GIF Sequences and Animated GIFs

You can export GIF sequences and animated GIFs from Premiere as you would any other image format, except that additional options are available.

To access and set advanced settings for animated GIFs and GIF sequences:

1. In the General Settings panel of the Export Movie Settings dialog box, from the File Type pull-down menu, choose Animated GIF or GIF sequence.

   The Advanced Settings button becomes available for use.

2. Click Advanced Settings.

   The Advanced GIF Options dialog box appears (**Figure 14.15**).

3. Check Dithering to simulate colors that are not available in the Web-Safe Color palette by *dithering* (or mixing) pixels of available colors.

   Although dithered colors look grainy, they can make the limited color range appear to be greater and improve the appearance of color gradients. When Dithering is unchecked, unavailable colors are replaced with the next-closest colors, often resulting in *banding*, or abrupt color transitions.

   (continued on next page)

WORKING SEQUENCES AND ANIMATED GIFS

4. From the Transparency pull-down menu, choose one of the following (**Figure 14.16**):

None, to export the animated GIF or GIF sequence as opaque.

Hard, to make one color in the image transparent; then click Color to choose the color from the color picker.

Soft, to make one color in the image transparent with soft edges; then click Color to choose the color from the color picker.

5. If you are exporting an animated GIF, check Looping to make an animated GIF play continuously; leave this option unchecked to make the animated GIF play once and then stop (**Figure 14.17**).

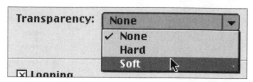

Figure 14.16 Choose a Transparency option from the pull-down menu.

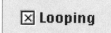

Figure 14.17 Check Looping to make an animated GIF play continuously.

Figure 14.18 Choose File > Export > Print to Video.

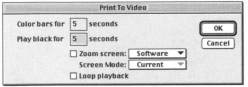

Figure 14.19 Select options in the Print To Video dialog box.

Recording to Tape

If your computer can output a video signal, you can record your program to videotape— a process called *printing to video*. You can print to video in two ways: directly from the program or from a clip.

When you record directly from the program, the settings you specify in the Project Settings dialog box (see Chapter 2) determine the characteristics of the final video, such as the frame size and image quality.

You determine the qualities of a clip, on the other hand, when you capture it (see Chapter 15) or create it from a program (as explained in the section, "Creating a Movie," earlier in this chapter).

Even if your computer isn't connected to a VCR, you can use the Print to Tape option to present the video over a blank screen.

To record to tape:

1. If you are exporting directly from the program, choose the appropriate Project Settings for final output (see Chapter 2).

2. *Do one of the following:*

   ◆ To export the program in the timeline, select the Timeline or Monitor window.

   ◆ To export a clip, open a video clip.

3. Choose File > Export > Print to Video (**Figure 14.18**).

   The Print To Video dialog box opens (**Figure 14.19**).

4. After Color bars for, type the number of seconds to play back NTSC color bars before the program begins.

5. After Play black for, type the number of seconds to play back a black video frame before the program begins (but after color bars).

(continued on next page)

6. To play the video back at double normal size, choose Zoom Screen and then from the Zoom screen pull-down menu *choose one of the following options* (**Figure 14.20**):

- ◆ Software to use software to zoom the image size.

- ◆ Hardware to use your hardware capture card to zoom the image size.

7. To play the program or clip repeatedly, check Loop Playback.

You can stop playback by pressing Command+period.

✔ Tip

- ■ If you use device-control hardware to control a deck, you can use the Print to Tape option. Consult your Adobe Premiere user guide and the documentation included with your device control and deck.

Figure 14.20 To play back the video at double its normal size, choose an option from the Zoom screen menu.

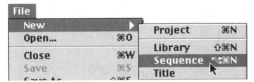

Figure 14.21 Choose File > New > Sequence to open the Sequence window.

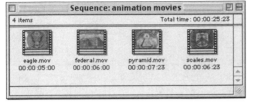

Figure 14.22 Arrange clips in the Sequence window in the order in which you want them to play.

Creating Clip Sequences

The Sequence window allows you to assemble a simple sequence of clips to export as a file or print to tape. Although you can't edit the clips in a sequence, you can use the sequence to export a quick rough cut or a series of video clips.

You can export the clips in a sequence just as you would export the program in the timeline. No additional compression is applied to a sequence, however. The clips in the sequence retain their original compression settings and play back in the order in which they were arranged.

To create a sequence:

1. Choose File > New > Sequence (**Figure 14.21**).

   The Sequence window opens.

2. Import clips into the Sequence window by *using one of the following:*

   ◆ Drag clips from a Project, Bin, or Library window into the Sequence window.

   ◆ Choose File > Import > File, Folder, or Multiple to import files into the sequence.

3. In the Sequence window, drag the clips to arrange them as you want (left to right and top to bottom) (**Figure 14.22**).

4. Choose File > Save.

5. In the Save dialog box specify a name and destination for the sequence file and click Save.

CREATING CLIP SEQUENCES

Exporting QuickTime Fast Start Movies

You can use Premiere to convert a QuickTime movie to a Fast Start movie for Internet delivery. A *Fast Start* QuickTime movie can begin playing before it has been completely downloaded by a QuickTime-enabled Web browser (**Figure 14.23**).

To export a QuickTime Fast Start movie:

1. Open a QuickTime movie file.

2. Choose File > Export > Fast Start Movie (**Figure 14.24**).

   A Save dialog box appears.

3. Specify a file name and destination.

4. Click OK.

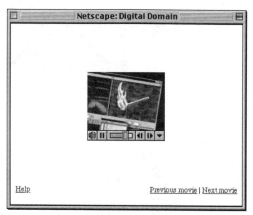

Figure 14.23 A Fast Start QuickTime movie can begin playing before the entire movie has been downloaded.

Figure 14.24 Choose File > Export >Fast Start Movie to create a Fast Start movie.

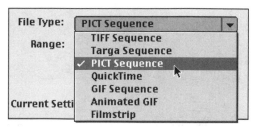

Figure 14.25 Choose a still-image-sequence format from the File Type pull-down menu.

Figure 14.26 From the Range pull-down menu, choose the portion of the clip or sequence that you want to export as a still-image sequence.

Exporting Still-Image Sequences

You can export a program or clip as a sequence of still images. Premiere numbers the frames automatically, and if you want, you can specify the starting frame number. Many animation and 3-D programs can import video images only as a numbered sequence of still-image files.

To export a still-image sequence:

1. Resize the work-area bar over the part of the program window that you want to make into a movie.

2. Choose File > Export > Movie.
   The Save Export Movie dialog box appears.

3. Click the Settings button.
   The Export Movie Settings dialog box opens.

4. From the File Type pull-down menu, choose a still-image-sequence format (**Figure 14.25**).

5. To specify the range of the program that you want to export, from the Range pull-down menu, *choose one of the following* (**Figure 14.26**)·

   ◆ Work Area, to export only the part of the program below the work-area bar.

   ◆ Entire Program, to export the entire program in the timeline.

   ◆ Entire Clip, to export an entire source clip.

   ◆ In to Out, to export a source clip from its in point to its out point.

6. Check Export Video.

7. If you are exporting a GIF sequence or animated GIF, click Advanced Settings to set these options (as explained in the section "Working with GIF Sequences and Animated GIFs," earlier in this chapter).

8. Click the Next button to switch to the Video Settings panel of the Output Settings dialog box.

9. Set or confirm the video settings, such as frame size and color bit depth.

10. Click OK to exit the Output Settings dialog box.

11. Specify a destination and file name and click OK.

   If you want, type a numbered file name.

   Make sure that you follow the numbering conventions for your computer platform, and pad the numbers with the appropriate number of zeros. You could number a sequence that has fewer than 1000 frames as seq000.bmp (a Windows format), or sequence.000 (a Mac format) (**Figure 14.27**).

Figure 14.27 If you want to set the first number of the sequence, make sure that you follow the numbering convention used by your computer platform.

Figure 14.28 You can open a filmstrip in Photoshop and paint on the frames.

Exporting Filmstrip Files

You can export a clip or any part of the program as a filmstrip file. The *filmstrip* format allows you to use Adobe Photoshop to paint directly onto the frames of video—a technique known as *rotoscoping* in traditional film postproduction (**Figure 14.28**). Unlike Premiere, however, Photoshop manipulates files directly. Be aware that the changes you make in the filmstrip file are permanent.

Appropriately enough, a filmstrip file in Photoshop looks like a filmstrip: a single still image that contains the frames of video arranged in a long column. A frame number, reel name, and timecode are displayed below each frame. If the frames of the filmstrip exceed 30,000 pixels in height, the frames continue in another column until the file reaches the maximum image dimensions for Photoshop.

After you alter the filmstrip file in Photoshop, you can import the file into Premiere and convert it back to a video file.

✔ Tips

Although you should consult your Adobe Photoshop user guide for more details on how to use filmstrip files, here are a few important guidelines:

- Don't crop or resize the filmstrip.

- You can manipulate the Red, Green, Blue, and Alpha channels of the filmstrip, but Premiere won't recognize any additional channels.

- You can paint on the gray borders between the frames of a filmstrip, but they won't appear when the filmstrip is converted back to a video file.

- Your source video should match or exceed your final output quality. Don't waste your time painstakingly rotoscoping a shot at draft quality.

To export a filmstrip:

1. *Do one of the following:*

   ◆ To export the program in the timeline, select the Timeline or Monitor window.

   ◆ To export a clip, open a video clip.

2. Choose File > Export > Movie.
   The Save Export Movie dialog box opens.

3. Click Settings.
   The Export Movie Settings dialog box appears.

4. From the File Type pull-down menu, choose Filmstrip (**Figure 14.29**).

5. If you are exporting from the program, from the Range pull-down menu choose the range of the program that you want to export:

   ◆ Work Area, to export only the part of the program below the work-area bar.

   ◆ Entire Program, to export the entire program in the timeline.

   ◆ Entire Clip, to export an entire source clip.

   ◆ In to Out, to export a source clip from its in point to its out point.

6. Check Export Video.

7. Click Next, or from the pull-down menu at the top of the Export Movie Settings dialog box, choose Video Settings.
   The Video Settings panel of the Export Movie Settings dialog box appears.

8. Change or confirm the settings, such as frame size and frame rate.

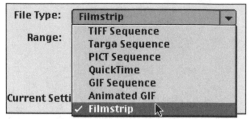

Figure 14.29 Choose Filmstrip from the File Type pull-down menu in the Export Movie Settings dialog box.

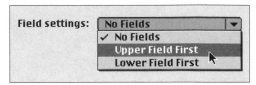

Figure 14.30 If necessary, specify the source clips' field dominance by making a choice from the Field Options pull-down menu.

9. If the video contains interlaced fields, choose Keyframe and Rendering Options from the pull-down menu at the top of the Export Movie Settings dialog box; then from the Field Options pull-down menu *choose one of the following* (**Figure 14.30**):

   ◆ Upper Field First, if the source video is field-1-dominant.

   ◆ Lower Field First, if the source video is field-2-dominant.

   See Chapter 17 for a complete explanation of fields and field dominance.

10. Click OK to exit the Export Movie Settings dialog box.

    The Save Export Movie dialog box appears.

11. Specify a file name and destination for the filmstrip file.

12. Click OK.

Exporting Still Images

You can export the current frame of video from the program or source clip as a single still-image file.

To export a single frame:

1. *Do one of the following:*

   ◆ In the program, cue the current frame to the frame that you want to export (indicated by the current frame in Program view or the edit line in the timeline).

   ◆ In a clip, cue the current frame to the frame that you want to export (**Figure 14.31**).

2. Choose File > Export > Frame (**Figure 14.32**).

   The Save Export Still Frame dialog box opens.

3. Click Settings.

   The Export Still Frame Settings dialog box opens, displaying the General Settings panel (**Figure 14.33**).

4. From the File Type pull-down menu, choose a still-image format.

   The section "Exporting File Types," earlier in this chapter, lists your options.

5. To open the still image after it's created, check Open When Finished.

6. Click Next, or choose Video Settings from the pull-down menu at the top of the Export Still Frame Settings dialog box and then set the frame size and color depth.

7. Click Next, or choose Keyframe and Rendering Options from the pull-down menu at the top of the Export Still Frame Settings dialog box to set these options.

Figure 14.31 Cue the video to the frame that you want to export as a still image.

Figure 14.32 Choose File > Export > Frame to export the current frame as a still image.

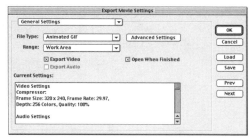

Figure 14.33 Choose options in different panels of the Export Still Frame Settings dialog box.

8. Click Next, or choose Special Processing from the pull-down menu at the top of the Export Still Frame Settings dialog box and then click Modify to set these options.

9. Click OK to close the Export Still Frame Settings dialog box and return to the Save Export Still Frame dialog box.

10. In the Save Export Still Frame dialog box, specify a name and destination for the still image.

11. Click OK.

Exporting Edit Decision Lists

As you learned in Chapter 1, the primary goal of an offline edit is to generate an edit decision list (EDL). An *EDL* describes your edited program as a list of editing events (**Figure 14.34**). Exporting an EDL enables you to transfer your offline-editing decisions to an online-editing controller. Premiere even allows you to export an EDL in a format that is compatible with several common online-edit controllers. Because these EDL formats come in the form of plug-ins, you can add other Premiere-compatible EDL formats in the future.

Most EDLs must be stored on 3-1/2-inch floppy disks formatted for MS-DOS. Fortunately for Mac users, the Mac OS includes PC Exchange, which allows you to read, format, and save to MS-DOS-format disks.

This section explains how to export a generic EDL. Creating an EDL in a specific format falls outside the scope of this section, because it requires an explanation of online editing and of how an edit controller interprets the information in the EDL. You can find a more thorough discussion of specific EDL options (such as B-rolls and wipe codes) in the Adobe Premiere user guide or through an online editor. Always keep in close contact with your online editing facility to ensure that you are properly prepared for online editing.

To export a generic EDL:

1. Choose File > Export > Generic EDL (**Figure 14.35**).

   The Save Generic EDL dialog box appears.

2. Specify a file name and destination.

3. Click Save (**Figure 14.36**).

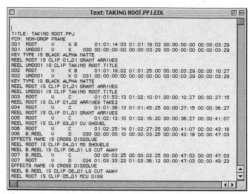

Figure 14.34 Here's an example of a edit decision list, formatted for a CMX3600.

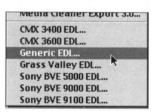

Figure 14.35 Choose File > Export > Generic EDL to create a generic edit decision list or choose a specific EDL format.

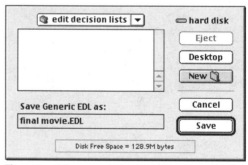

Figure 14.36 Save your EDL on a disk preformatted for the online-editing device that you will use.

15

CAPTURE

More and more, video and audio is recorded, stored, and delivered in digital formats. Image scanners, audio CDs, and digital still cameras can all transfer their media directly to a computer in digital form. Many of the newest computers are equipped with a port—commonly known as FireWire, iLink, or IEEE-1394—that enables you to transfer footage from a DV camera directly to your hard disk. These devices make it easier to acquire source material to import into your Premiere projects.

Despite the pervasiveness of digital media, video and audio are still commonly recorded, stored, and delivered via an analog signal. Common formats include VHS and Hi8 videotape and conventional audiocassette tapes.

To use analog media, most computers require a *video capture card*—add-on hardware that you can install in one of the expansion slots of your computer. The capture card enables you to *digitize* analog video and audio, which means converting it to a digital form that can be stored on your computer.

This chapter explains the digitizing process, without regard to individual capture cards. Though the overall process seldom varies, your specific choices depend on the card that you use. Chapter 17 also offers guidance on selecting and understanding capture settings.

Preparation for Capture

As you have already discovered, digital video thrives on a fast processor, speedy drives, and even additional (and often expensive) hardware.

In addition to using powerful hardware, you can take certain steps to maximize your computer's performance:

◆ Quit all other applications.

◆ Turn off file-sharing software, at least temporarily.

◆ Disable other unnecessary operating-system features.

◆ Choose a fast, large disk or disk array as your scratch disk for digitizing.

◆ Defragment hard disks with a reliable disk utility to optimize their performance.

◆ Select compression settings that do not exceed the capabilities of your system.

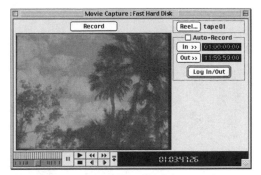

Figure 15.1 When device control hardware and software is installed properly, you can control a deck from the capture window.

The Digitizing Process

To digitize from videotape, you must configure your system with a video deck and capture card. For more professional-level editing, you may use additional options, such as device control and timecode. These options not only make automated features such as batch capture available but also make it possible to employ an offline/online editing strategy, as described in Chapter 1.

Device Control

As the name indicates, *device control* provides a means of controlling an external device—usually, a videotape deck (though it could also control a digital disk recorder or DAT player, for example). Device control consists of a cable that connects the computer to the deck and a plug-in software module that is copied into Premiere's Plug-Ins folder. When you enable device control, Premiere's Movie Capture window includes buttons that allow you to control the deck from within Premiere (**Figure 15.1**).

Timecode

If your deck can read timecode from a time-coded tape, you can encode this information into the captured clip via device control (**Figure 15.2**). Otherwise, you may be able to stamp the clip with timecode manually or use Premiere's timecode window reader feature. The timecode reference enables you to recapture exactly the same video at any time, using any compression setting. Timecode is crucial in an offline-to-online editing strategy.

Batch Capture

With device control and timecoded source tapes, you can batch-capture clips. Log a list of timecode starting and ending numbers to a batch list, and Premiere can digitize the clips in the list automatically. When you finish editing, you can recapture only the clips that you used in the final program, this time at final-output quality.

Figure 15.2 The timecoded frames of a clip can refer to exactly the same frames of the source tape.

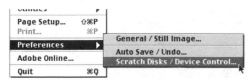

Figure 15.3 Choose File > Preferences > Scratch Disks / Device Control.

Figure 15.4 The Scratch Disks / Device Control panel of the Preferences dialog box allows you to designate scratch disks.

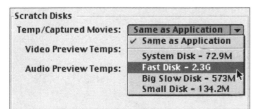

Figure 15.5 Choose a large, fast scratch disk for captured movies.

Scratch Disks

In Chapter 8, you learned to designate the disks used to save video and audio preview files. You can also designate a scratch disk for digitizing. Choose your fastest disk, because it's most capable of capturing all the frames successfully.

To set the scratch disk:

1. Choose File > Preferences > Scratch Disks/Device Control (**Figure 15.3**).

   The Scratch Disks/Device Control panel of the Preferences dialog box appears (**Figure 15.4**).

2. Choose a disk from the Temp/Captured Movies pull-down menu (**Figure 15.5**).

   To achieve the best results, choose a fast disk or disk array.

✔ Tip

■ A single QuickTime file on the Mac OS cannot exceed 2 GB. On the Windows platform, the file size limit is 1 GB to 2 GB, depending on the capture card. Finally, however, Premiere has broken the file-size barrier. It works around the file-size limitation by capturing several QuickTime movies that reference one another. A 5 GB capture, for example, would consist of three files. No file would be larger than 2 GB, but each file would reference the next one.

Capture Settings

Before you capture, you must specify the characteristics of the digitized clips. Your options will differ, according to the capture card that you use. Consult the documentation for your capture card to digitize successfully. You can also consult Chapter 17 for an explanation of many capture settings.

To choose capture settings:

1. Specify the scratch disk, as explained in "Scratch Disks" earlier in this chapter.

2. Choose Project > Settings > Capture (**Figure 15.6**).

   The Capture Settings panel of the Project Settings dialog box opens (**Figure 15.7**).

3. From the Capture Format pull-down menu, choose a video format, such as QuickTime or .AVI.

   Your choice can change the options that are available in other parts of the Capture Settings dialog box and in the dialog boxes that appear when you click the Video, Audio, and Advanced buttons:

   Check Capture Video to enable video capture; uncheck this box to disable video capture.

4. In the Size boxes (available for QuickTime), type the pixel width and height of the captured video.

   Check Constrain to constrain the numbers that you type in the Size boxes to the aspect ratio supported by your capture card (usually, 4:3).

5. From the Rate pull-down menu (available for .AVI), choose a frame rate for digitizing video.

   Choose 29.97 fps for NTSC video or 25 fps for PAL and SECAM.

Figure 15.6 Choose Project > Settings > Capture to open the capture settings.

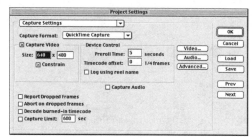

Figure 15.7 The Capture Settings panel of the Project Settings dialog box looks like this when you select QuickTime as the Capture Format.

CAPTURE SETTINGS

6. Check Capture Audio to enable audio capture; uncheck this box to disable audio capture.

7. At the bottom of the Capture Settings panel, check any of the optional settings that you want to enable.

   These settings are explained in detail in the following section, "Optional Settings."

8. Click the Video, Audio, and Advanced buttons to access options that are specific to your capture device.

9. Click OK to exit the capture settings.

   You are ready to begin digitizing clips, using the methods explained in the following sections.

Optional Settings

At the bottom of the Capture Settings panel of the Project Settings dialog box, you can choose several optional settings (**Figure 15.8**):

- ◆ **Report Dropped Frames.** Check this option if you want Premiere to alert you when at least one frame of the clip has not been digitized successfully. If frames are dropped, Premiere opens a Clip Properties window for the clip (explained in Chapter 3). This window notes the dropped frames (**Figure 15.9**). If no frames are dropped, no report appears.

- ◆ **Abort on dropped frames.** Check this option if you want Premiere to automatically stop digitizing when a frame is dropped during capture.

- ◆ **Decode burned-in timecode** (Mac OS only). Check this option if you want Premiere to read the timecode number from a timecode window dub. Consult your Adobe Premiere user guide for more information on setting up this feature.

- ◆ **Capture Limit.** Check this option to limit the number of seconds that Premiere can digitize in a single capture. This option can help prevent the error messages that result when you try to exceed the file-size limit for your system.

✔ Tip

- ■ Some capture cards seem to drop the very first frame of captured video but digitize the rest of the frames successfully. If this is the case, Abort on Dropped Frames prevents you from capturing anything. Report Dropped Frames, on the other hand, tells you how many frames were dropped. If only one frame was dropped, the capture probably was successful; if more frames were lost, you should recheck your settings and attempt to capture the clip again.

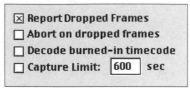

Figure 15.8 The lower left corner of the Capture Settings panel of the Project Settings dialog box contains several optional settings.

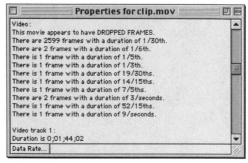

Figure 15.9 When you enable Report Dropped Frames, Premiere will open a Clip Properties window if any frames are dropped during capture.

Figure 15.10 Three buttons on the right side of the Capture panel of the Project Settings dialog box give you access to video, audio, and hardware-specific options.

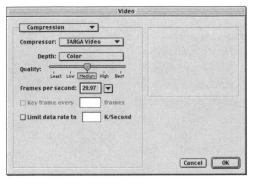

Figure 15.11 Video capture settings permit you to make selections in several categories, accessible from the top left pull-down menu.

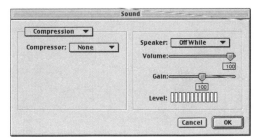

Figure 15.12 Audio capture settings also provide options in several categories.

Hardware-Specific Settings

Near the right side of the Capture Settings panel, the Video, Audio, and Advanced buttons enable you to access options that are specific to your capture device (**Figure 15.10**). Though the options can vary from one capture card to the next, the general categories are similar. Consult the documentation included with your capture card for specific instructions. See Chapter 17 for additional information on compression settings.

Video Settings

Video settings control the attributes of the captured source video. A pull-down menu in the Video Settings dialog box gives you access to four categories: Compression, Image, Source, and a hardware-specific category (**Figure 15.11**).

Audio Settings

Audio settings control the attributes of the captured audio. The pull-down menu in the Audio Settings dialog box gives you access to four categories: Compression, Image, Source, and a hardware-specific category. The audio settings also include a control for adjusting audio gain levels (**Figure 15.12**).

Advanced Settings

Advanced settings control various options that are specific to each capture card. Check the documentation included with your hardware to learn about these options.

Basic Capture

If your system is not equipped with device control, use Premiere's basic capture window and the playback controls on the videotape deck.

To capture without device control:

1. Choose File > Capture > Movie Capture (**Figure 15.13**).

2. Disable AppleTalk, if Premiere prompts you to do so (**Figure 15.14**).

    The basic Movie Capture window opens (**Figure 15.15**).

3. Using the controls of your videotape deck, play the tape several seconds before you begin digitizing, allowing the deck to reach normal speed.

4. In the Movie Capture Window, click Record.

    Premiere captures the video and audio, if they're selected.

5. Click to stop digitizing, and then stop playback on the deck.

    The captured clip appears in a Clip window. The clip is an unsaved temporary file on the scratch disk you specified.

6. With the clip window active, choose File > Save As.

7. In the Save As dialog box, specify a file-name and destination for the clip.

8. Click Save.

✔ Tip

- If no image appears in the Movie Capture window, make sure that you selected the correct Digitizer and Source in the video options of the Capture Settings panel. If the settings are correct, check the cable connections between your deck and your capture card.

Figure 15.13 Open the Movie Capture window.

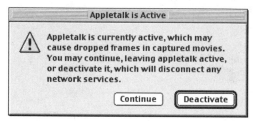

Figure 15.14 You should deactivate AppleTalk or similar functions when Premiere prompts you to do so.

Figure 15.15 The basic Movie Capture window simply displays the incoming video and a record button.

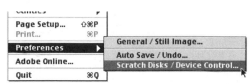

Figure 15.16 Choose Preferences > Scratch Disks / Device Control to access the Device Control settings.

Figure 15.17 The Scratch Disks / Device Control menu appears.

Figure 15.18 If your device control software is in Premiere's Plug-Ins folder, it will appear in the pull-down menu.

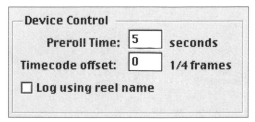

Figure 15.19 Device Control options are also available in the Capture panel of the Project Settings dialog box.

Device Control

Device control usually includes two components: a hardware cable to connect your computer to your deck and a software plug-in to put in the Premiere Plug-Ins folder. Consult the documentation that came with your device-control equipment to make sure that the equipment is set up properly.

To enable device control:

1. Choose File > Preferences > Scratch Disks/Device Control (**Figure 15.16**).

   The Scratch Disks/Device Control panel of the Preferences dialog box appears (**Figure 15.17**).

2. From the Device Control pull-down menu, choose the device controller that you are using (**Figure 15.18**).

3. To access additional options included with your device controller, click the Options button.

To set other device control options:

1. Choose Project > Settings > Capture

   The Capture Settings panel of the Project Settings dialog box opens.

2. In the Device Control area of the Capture Settings panel, enter a Preroll Time (**Figure 15.19**).

   Preroll is the amount the deck rewinds before a specified In point. Preroll allows the deck to reach normal playback speed before digitizing begins.

3. Enter a Timecode offset, according to the documentation included with your capture device and device controller.

4. Check Log using reel name, if you want Premiere to automatically enter the reel name and timecode as the name of the clips that you log to a batch list.

Capture with Device Control

You can use device control simply to control the deck from within Premiere, using the same procedures that you use with basic capture. With device control, however, you can also set the starting and ending points before you digitize, allowing Premiere to automatically capture the clip you defined. In later sections of this chapter, you learn that device control can be used to log a batch list and is required for a batch capture.

To capture using device control:

1. Set up device control, as explained in "Device Control" earlier in this chapter and according to the documentation that shipped with the device controller.

2. Choose File > Capture > Movie Capture.

3. If prompted, enter the name of the tape you will use in the Reel Name dialog box and click OK (**Figure 15.20**).

   Each tape you use should have a unique reel name. Premiere saves the reel name along with other clip information.

4. If device control is set up properly, the Movie Capture window will appear with buttons to control the deck (**Figure 15.21**).

5. Use the controls in the Movie Capture window to cue the tape to the starting point, and click In.

   The current time appears as the in point for the capture.

6. Use the controls in the Movie Capture window to cue the tape to the ending point, and click Out.

   The current time appears as the out point for the capture.

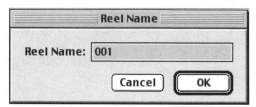

igure 15.20 Premiere prompts you to supply the name of the reel, or tape.

Figure 15.21 When device control is set up properly, the Movie Capture window includes buttons to control the tape.

Figure 15.22 After you set in and out points and check Auto-Record, click Record to capture the clip you defined.

7. Check Auto-Record to instruct Premiere to capture the clip defined by the in and out point when the Record button is pressed (**Figure 15.22**).

8. Click Record to capture the specified clip.

   Premiere automatically cues the tape for the preroll you specified, plays the tape, and digitizes the clip. The captured clip appears in a Clip window, as an unsaved temporary file on the scratch disk.

9. With the clip window active, choose File > Save As.

10. In the Save dialog box, specify a filename and destination.

11. Click Save.

✔ Tip

■ If your deck isn't reaching normal speed before the in point, the device-control software may issue an error message. Try increasing the preroll time in the device-control section of the Capture Settings panel.

Batch Lists

You can log clips to a batch list in two ways. When you use device control, you can create a batch list as you view the timecoded tape. If the tape is unavailable (or if you're using another, lesser-equipped editing system), you can log a batch list manually. To log manually, you need to have a written list of accurate timecode starting and ending numbers ready. Logging manually can help you remain productive (saving you time and money) if you do not always have access to a system that has a deck and device control.

To generate a batch list with device control:

1. Set up device control, as explained in the section "Device Control," earlier in this chapter.

2. Choose File > Capture > Movie Capture. The Movie Capture window appears.

3. Click Reel to name the tape you are using (**Figure 15.23**).

   The Reel dialog box appears.

4. Type the name of the tape and click OK (**Figure 15.24**).

   Each tape you use should have a unique reel name.

5. Use the deck controls in the Movie Capture window to cue the tape to the frame where you want to start digitizing and click In.

6. Use the deck controls in the Movie Capture window to cue the tape to the frame you want to stop digitizing and click Out.

7. Click Log In/Out (**Figure 15.25**).

8. A File Name dialog box appears (**Figure 15.26**).

Figure 15.23 When you use device control and timecode, you can use buttons in the Movie Capture window to generate a batch list.

Figure 15.24 In the Reel dialog box, type the name of the tape for which you are making a batch list.

Figure 15.25 Click Log In/Out in the Movie Capture window to save the in and out points to a batch list.

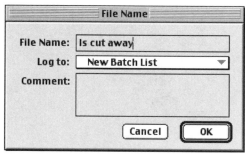
Figure 15.26 Premiere prompts you to name the file in the list.

Figure 15.27 The clip you log appears in the Batch List window.

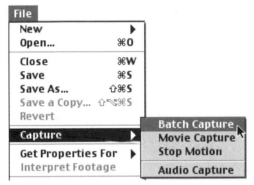

Figure 15.28 Choose File > Capture > Batch Capture.

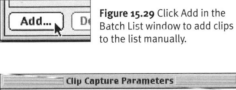

Figure 15.29 Click Add in the Batch List window to add clips to the list manually.

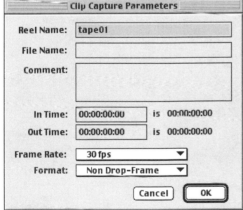

Figure 15.30 Enter information about the clip in the Clip Parameters window.

9. In the File Name dialog box, enter a name for the clip.

10. In the Log to pull-down menu, choose to log the clip to a new or already open batch list.

11. If you want, type in the Comments area of the Clip Capture Parameters window.

12. Click OK to add the clip to a batch list.
    The specified clip appears in the Batch List window (**Figure 15.27**).

13. Repeat steps 5 through 8 for every clip you want to capture from this tape.
    If you change tapes, make sure to enter a new Reel name.

14. Close the Movie Capture window.

15. With the Batch Capture window active, choose File > Save to display the Save dialog box.

16. If necessary, specify a filename and destination for the batch list and click OK.

To generate a batch list manually:

1. Choose File > Capture > Batch Capture (**Figure 15.28**).
   The Batch Capture window appears.

2. Choose File > Save As.
   The Save dialog box appears.

3. Specify a file name and destination for the batch list.

4. Click Save.

5. In the Batch List window, click Add (**Figure 15.29**).
   The Clip Capture Parameters window opens (**Figure 15.30**).

6. In the Reel Name box, type the name of the tape from which you will digitize the clip.

(continued on next page)

7. In the File Name box, type a name for the clip.

8. If you want, in the Comment section, type any comments that you want to include in the batch list.

9. In the In Time box, type the timecode in point for the clip.

10. In the Out Time box, type the timecode out point for the clip.

You don't have to type the colons between fields of the timecode number; you can substitute periods or use no punctuation. To the right of the number that you type, Premiere displays how the number will be interpreted in hours, minutes, seconds, and frames.

11. From the Frame Rate pull-down menu, choose the frame rate of the source tape (**Figure 15.31**).

Choose 30 for NTSC or 25 for PAL and SECAM, for example. Choose the frame rate of the tape, not the final frame rate of the clip. The frame rate for all NTSC video is approximately 30 fps, even if it was transferred from film.

12. From the Format pull-down menu, choose the counting method used by the timecode on the source tape (**Figure 15.32**):

◆ Non-Drop Frame if the source uses non-drop-frame timecode.

◆ Drop Frame if the source uses drop-frame timecode.

13. Click OK to close the Clip Capture Parameters window and add the clip to the Batch List window.

14. Repeat steps 5 through 13 until you have logged all the clips for your batch list.

15. Choose File > Save to save your batch list.

Figure 15.31 Choose the frame rate of the video standard you're using from the Frame Rate pull-down menu.

Figure 15.32 Choose the counting method used by your source tape from the Format pull-down menu.

Figure 15.33 Double click an item in the Batch List to make changes to it.

Figure 15.34 You can copy items from one Batch List window to another by simply dragging the items.

To change items in a batch list:

1. In a Batch List window, double-click an item (**Figure 15.33**).

   The Clip Capture Parameters window for the clip opens.

2. Change any of the parameters.

3. Click OK.

4. Choose File > Save to save the changes to the batch list.

To delete items from a batch list:

1. In a batch list, select an item.

2. Click Delete to remove the item from the list.

To copy items from one batch list to another:

1. In a Batch List window, select one or more items.

2. Drag the selected items to another Batch List window.

   The items are copied to the second Batch List window (**Figure 15.34**).

Batch-List Settings

When the Batch List window is active, a Batch List menu appears in the menu bar. The commands in this menu allow you to choose the settings applied to the items in a batch list, including Recording Settings, Video Source, and Audio Settings.

In Chapter 2, you learned to save project settings, which include the capture settings reviewed in this chapter. You can attach saved settings to selected items in a batch list. This way, clips in the batch list can use different settings from one another or from the currently selected capture settings.

Figure 15.35
After selecting items in a batch list, select Attach Settings.

To attach settings to selected items in a batch list:

1. Select one or more items in the batch list.

2. Choose Batch Capture > Attach Settings (**Figure 15.35**).

   The Open File dialog box appears.

3. Select the settings file that you want to use (**Figure 15.36**).

4. Click Open.

   Settings are typically stored in the Settings folder, which is located inside the Premiere folder. When you click Open, the settings appear in the Settings column of the Batch List window (**Figure 15.37**).

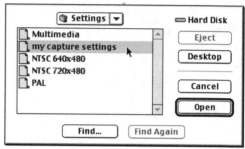

Figure 15.36 Locate the settings file you want to attach to the selected clips in the list.

To remove settings from selected items in a batch list:

1. Select one or more items in a batch list that have settings attached.

   Settings appear in the Settings column of the Batch List window.

2. Choose Batch Capture > Remove Settings.

   The settings no longer appear in the Settings column.

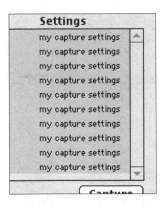

Figure 15.37 The attached settings appear in the Settings column of the Batch List window.

Figure 15.38 Click next to the clip to change the icon. A diamond icon indicates that the clip will be captured when you click the Capture button.

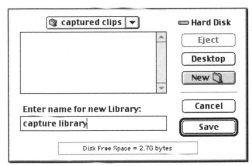

Figure 15.39 Premiere prompts you to create or add to an existing library.

Batch Capture

Before you batch-capture, check the scratch disk, available disk space, capture settings, device-control settings, and deck, if necessary. (These topics are covered earlier in this chapter.) If everything is set properly, you need to attend to the batch capture only when you are required to change source tapes.

To batch-capture clips:

1. Open a batch list.

2. If necessary, click to the left of any clip in the list to change its status (**Figure 15.38**):
   - ◆ No icon indicates that the clip will not be captured when you click Capture.
   - ◆ A diamond indicates that the clip will be captured when you click Capture.
   - ◆ A check indicates that the clip has been captured.
   - ◆ An X indicates that an error occurred during capture.

3. To arrange the list in chronological order, click Sort.

4. Click Capture to begin capturing from the list.

   Premiere prompts you to add the clips to a new or existing library (**Figure 15.39**). The clips are added to the library as they are captured.

5. Choose or name a library file and click OK.

(continued on next page)

BATCH CAPTURE

6. When prompted, supply the appropriate tape and click OK (**Figure 15.40**).

As each clip is captured, the diamond icon will change into a check (**Figure 15.41**). If an error occurs, the diamond will change into an X.

✔ Tip

■ You can attach compression settings to a batch list, as explained in the preceding section, "Batch-List Settings."

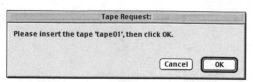

Figure 15.40 Premiere prompts you to supply the appropriate tape.

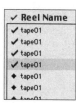

Figure 15.41 As each clip is captured, the diamond icon changes into a check icon. If an error occurs, the diamond changes to an X.

Figure 15.42 A timecode window dub has a timecode reference "burned" in to the image.

Figure 15.43 Choose Clip > Timecode to stamp the clip with timecode manually.

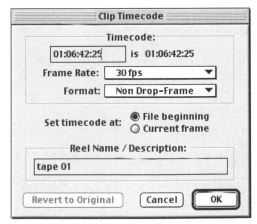

Figure 15.44 In the Clip Timecode window, enter the timecode number for the frame of the clip that matches the burned-in timecode. Also choose the frame rate and format that matches the tape.

Manual Timecode Settings

Even if your equipment doesn't support timecode, you can still add timecode to a captured clip manually.

Set the timecode manually if you are capturing from a timecode window dub. A *timecode window dub* is a copy of a timecoded tape—usually, the camera original. A window dub doesn't have actual timecode that can be read by video equipment, but it does display the timecode number in the video image, and this number can be read by humans. Because it's part of the video image, a timecode window is sometimes called *burned-in* (**Figure 15.42**).

Set the timecode of the clip to match the timecode number in the window. When you do, the frames of your clips accurately correspond to the frames of your timecoded source tape, and you can then use them in an online edit—to perform a timecode-based batch capture or to generate an EDL.

To set timecode manually:

1. Select or open a clip.

2. Choose Clip > Timecode (**Figure 15.43**). The Clip Timecode dialog box appears.

3. *Do one of the following:*
   - Type the timecode number that matches the frame that's currently visible in the clip.
   - Type the timecode number that matches the timecode number of the first frame of the clip (**Figure 15.44**).

   Refer to the timecode window (burned-in timecode) that is visible in the clip.

4. From the Frame Rate pull-down menu, choose the frame rate that matches the source tape (**Figure 15.44**).

5. From the Format pull-down menu, choose the format that matches the source tape (**Figure 15.44**).

6. In the Set timecode at section, click the appropriate radio button (**Figure 15.45**):

  ◆ File beginning to set the timecode for the first frame of the clip.

  ◆ Current frame to set the timecode for the current frame.

7. In the Reel Name/Description box, type the name of the clip's source tape.

8. Click OK to close the Clip Timecode dialog box and apply the changes.

The timecode and reel name that you specify is used by Premiere but not encoded into the source file. You can change the reel name and timecode (or revert to the clip's original reel name and timecode) at any time.

✔ Tip

■ If you are using the Mac OS, Premiere has a feature that actually recognizes the numbers in the timecode window (the burned-in timecode). Check your user guide or online help for details about the Timecode Decoder feature.

Figure 15.45 In the Clip Timecode window, choose to set the timecode for the current frame or the first frame of the clip.

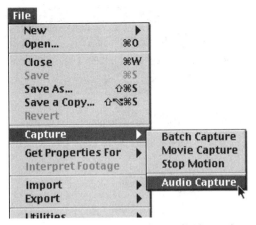

Figure 15.46 Choose Audio Capture to digitize analog audio in an audio-only format, like AIFF or WAV.

Figure 15.47 The Audio Recorder window appears.

Figure 15.48 Choose Sound Input from the Audio Capture menu.

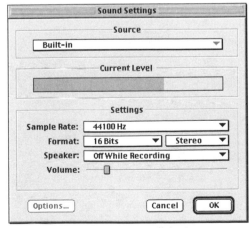

Figure 15.49 The Sound Settings dialog box appears.

Analog Audio Capture

If your computer is equipped with a sound-recording device, you can digitize audio in an audio-only format, such as .AIFF or .WAV. Unlike video capture cards, audio input is a built-in feature of most computers.

On the Mac OS, you can capture an audio-only clip directly from Premiere. On the Windows platform, you must use a separate audio capture program, such as Microsoft Windows Sound Recorder.

To capture audio using the Mac OS:

1. Choose File > Capture > Audio Capture (**Figure 15.46**).

   The Audio Recorder window appears on-screen (**Figure 15.47**), and the Audio Capture menu appears in the menu bar.

2. Choose Audio Capture > Sound Input (**Figure 15.48**).

   The Sound Settings dialog box appears (**Figure 15.49**).

3. From the Source pull-down menu, choose the audio source that you are using (such as the built-in microphone input of your computer).

4. From the Sample Rate pull-down menu, choose a sample rate.

5. From the Format pull-down menu, choose a bit depth.

6. From the pull-down menu next to the Format pull-down menu, choose stereo or mono audio.

   For more information about selecting audio settings, see Chapter 17.

(continued on next page)

ANALOG AUDIO CAPTURE

7. From the Speaker pull-down menu make a choice to specify how you want the speakers to function during digitizing (**Figure 15.50**).

Figure 15.50 In the Speaker pull-down menu, choose a speaker option.

8. Drag the Volume slider to adjust the incoming audio levels.

    The volume slider does not adjust the recording levels. Some audio hardware allows you to adjust Gain.

    Monitor the levels in the audio meter. Adjust the volume so that the meter registers a strong signal without peaking into the red too often. The audio must already be playing for you to see the levels.

Figure 15.51 In the Audio Capture window, click Record to start recording, and click again to stop recording.

9. Click Option (if available) to choose hardware-specific options.

10. Click OK to close the dialog box.

    You return to the Audio Capture window.

11. In the Audio Capture window, click Record to start recording, and click Stop to stop recording (**Figure 15.51**).

    An audio Clip window opens. The clip is an unsaved temp file on the scratch disk.

12. With the audio clip window active, choose File > Save As.

    The Save dialog box appears.

13. Specify a file name and destination.

14. Click Save.

    After you save the audio file, you can import it into a project.

✔ Tip

- After you capture audio, check the waveform display in the Audio Clip window. If the waveform looks too small, you may need to increase the audio levels. If the waveform extends beyond the top or bottom of the window, the audio levels are too loud. You should adjust the audio levels and capture the file again.

16

PREMIERE ONLINE

Chapter 1 outlined the offline/online editing process, in which you edit your program at low quality (*offline edit*) and complete it at high quality (*online edit*). Sometimes, the online edit takes place in a traditional online editing suite. This kind of online edit uses the source tapes and your Premiere-generated edit decision list (EDL) to produce a high-quality final program.

Increasingly, however, the offline and online edit are accomplished on the same system. For the offline edit, you can digitize clips at relatively low quality. When you finish editing, you simply recapture the clips—this time, at your higher, final-output quality. Fortunately, you don't have to recapture all the source clips—just the clips that you use in the final program.

As you know, using this strategy means using timecode. The clips that you use in the offline edit must have timecode that matches the timecode on the source tapes. When you recapture the clips for online edit, you need your timecoded source tapes, a deck that can read the timecode, and device control. In addition, your capture card and drives must be able to capture and play back the clips at your desired output quality.

Unused Clips

The final program rarely uses all the clips that you imported into the program. As a matter of housekeeping (and in preparation for online editing), you can remove the clips that you didn't use in the program. Although icons in the Project and Bin windows show you which clips are in the timeline, Premiere can identify these clips automatically and delete them from your project and bins.

To remove unused clips:

1. Select a Project or Bin window (**Figure 16.1**).

2. Choose Project > Remove Unused (**Figure 16.2**).

   Clips that are not used in the program are removed from the window. Unused clips in other windows and nested bins remain untouched (**Figure 16.3**).

3. Repeat steps 1 and 2 to remove unused clips from other bins and nested bins.

4. Save the file, *do one of the following:*
   - ◆ Choose File > Save to save the changes.
   - ◆ Choose File > Save As to save the project under a new name.

Figure 16.1 A bin before unused clips have been removed. In Icon and Thumbnail view, icons indicate which clips have been used in the program.

Figure 16.2 Choose Project > Remove Unused to remove clips that haven't been used in the program.

Figure 16.3 After you choose the Remove Unused command, unused clips no longer appear in the bin.

Figure 16.4 Choose Project Trimmer to create a trimmed project and a trimmed batch list.

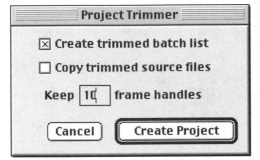

Figure 16.5 In the Project Trimmer dialog box, check Create trimmed batch list, and specify the amount of handles you want.

Trimmed Projects

The Project Trimmer feature automatically prepares your project for recapturing clips, by creating a trimmed project and a trimmed batch list.

A *trimmed project* is an exact duplicate of your project, except that it adds a number to the names of all the clips. The new name differentiates the clips of a trimmed project from those of the original project.

Created from the trimmed project, clips in the *trimmed batch list* also have a number appended to their file names. More important, a trimmed batch list includes only the portions of the clips that you used in the program. High-quality video files can be extremely large; batch-digitizing from a trimmed batch list uses your drive space efficiently by capturing only what you need to create the program.

After you capture the clips in the trimmed batch list, open the trimmed project. The project should retain all your editing decisions but refers to the new, high-quality video files. Fine-tune or export the program, as needed.

To create a trimmed project and trimmed batch list:

1. With a project open, choose File > Utilities > Project Trimmer (**Figure 16.4**).

   The Project Trimmer dialog box appears (**Figure 16.5**).

2. Check Create Trimmed Batch List.

3. Leave Copy Trimmed Source Files unchecked.

(continued on next page)

TRIMMED PROJECTS

4. For Keep Frame Handles, type the number of frames that you want to include as *handles*—frames before the in point and after the out point of each clip.

Handles give you flexibility to fine-tune the program after you recapture clips.

5. Click Create Project.

6. In the first Save dialog box, specify a file name and location for the trimmed project (**Figure 16.6**) and click Save.

7. In the next Save dialog box, specify a file name and location for the trimmed batch list (**Figure 16.7**) and click Save.

Figure 16.6 Name and save the trimmed project.

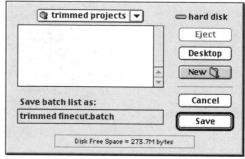

Figure 16.7 Name and save the trimmed batch list.

Figure 16.8 Choose Batch Capture to create a new batch list.

Manual Creation of Batch Lists for Recapturing Clips

Occasionally, the Project Trimmer feature doesn't function properly (yes, it's been known to happen), or you may prefer to manage your batch list yourself. In either case, you can manually create a batch list for recapturing clips.

Unlike the Project Trimmer method, this method does not rename your clips, so differentiating them from the original clips is harder. To prevent confusion, you may want to delete the original clips (if the timecode is good, you have nothing to fear). If you prefer to keep the original clips on the drive, make sure that you keep the recaptured clips in a separate, easy-to-identify folder.

Use the Re-Find command (explained in "Replacement Clip References," later in this chapter) to replace references to the low-quality clips with references to the newly captured, high-quality clips.

To create a batch list from a project or bin:

1. Remove unused clips, as explained earlier in this chapter in "Unused Clips."

   This step prevents you from recapturing clips that aren't necessary in your program.

2. Choose File > Capture > Batch Capture to create a new batch list (**Figure 16.8**).

3. In a Project or Bin window, select all the clips that you want to add to the batch list.

(continued on next page)

4. Drag the selected clips into the Batch List window.

   The clips appear in the batch list. The in and out points correspond to the in and out points used by the clips in the program (**Figure 16.9**).

5. Repeat steps 3 and 4 for other clips that you want to recapture.

6. With the Batch Capture window active, choose File > Save.

7. In the Save dialog box, specify a file name and destination for the batch list.

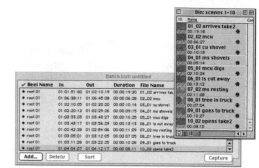

Figure 16.9 Drag clips from a Project or Bin window into the Batch List window to create a batch list manually.

MANUAL CREATION OF BATCH LISTS

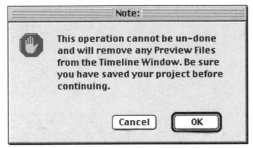

Figure 16.10 Choose Replace Files to change the files to which the clips refer.

Note:
This operation cannot be un-done and will remove any Preview Files from the Timeline Window. Be sure you have saved your project before continuing.
Cancel   OK

Figure 16.11 Premiere warns you before you proceed to replace the clip references.

Replacing Clip References

When you offline-edit in Premiere, the clips in your project refer to low-quality video files. When you recapture clips for your online version, you want the project to refer to the new, high-quality clips.

If you use the Project Trimmer before you recapture, the clips in the trimmed project and trimmed batch list are renamed. In this way, the clips in the trimmed project refer to files captured from the trimmed batch list.

If you decide not to use the Project Trimmer and opt to create a batch list manually, the clips are not renamed. Even after you recapture the clips at higher quality, the project may continue to refer to the lower-quality versions (even if they're not currently on the hard drive). You must get the project to refer to the new clips instead of the old ones.

One way to do this is to delete or move the low-quality clips and then reopen the project. When Premiere prompts you to locate the source files, simply locate the new high-quality sources.

On the other hand, you can use the Replace Files command to accomplish the same task much more easily. Replace Files allows you to change the clip references, effectively replacing one file with another. Then you can fine-tune, preview, or export the final program.

To use the Replace Files command:

1. With the Project window active, choose Project > Replace Files (**Figure 16.10**). Premiere alerts you that the command cannot be undone and will delete preview files (**Figure 16.11**).

(continued on next page)

REPLACING CLIP REFERENCES

2. In the warning box, click OK to continue to replace files.

A Locate Files dialog box appears, prompting you to locate a file (**Figure 16.12**).

3. Locate the requested files.

If you are replacing lower-quality files with higher-quality versions, make sure that you locate the correct version.

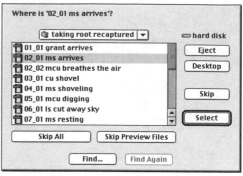

Figure 16.12 When prompted, locate the version of the files that you want to use. The clips in the project refer to the files that you choose during this step.

VIDEO AND AUDIO SETTINGS

At every major step in the editing process—capture, edit, and output—you encounter settings that control the basic attributes of the video and audio. The settings you choose for one step of the process may not be the best choices for another.

To make intelligent choices, you should have a basic understanding of topics such as frame rates, frame sizes, compression, and audio quality. You should familiarize yourself not only with how these settings relate to video displayed on computers, but also with how they relate to video displayed on televisions.

This chapter not only helps you choose settings in Premiere but also helps you understand some of the fundamental principles of all digital video. Of course, this book can only offer brief explanations. Only through further inquiry and experience can you master these concepts.

Choosing Settings

If you are using a hardware capture card, you may have already made your decisions about video and audio settings. The settings supported by your card are the most obvious choices for capture, playback, and export—especially if your goal is to produce a videotape of your final program.

Files that rely on hardware compression, however, won't play back on systems that don't have the same hardware. In fact, the files won't even open on systems that don't have a software version of the compressor. If you're editing on a different system from the one that you used for capture, you need to understand a broader range of options. Similarly, if you want to export a final movie to play back on other systems—such as another hard drive, a CD-ROM, or the Internet—you need to know which settings are most appropriate for each use.

The settings that you choose depend on your particular needs, but a few general guidelines apply:

◆ When you capture, choose settings to digitize at the highest quality possible without dropping frames.

◆ For editing, use settings that your system can process quickly and play back smoothly.

◆ When you export to tape, choose the settings that match or approach the quality of your source files, yet play back smoothly.

◆ When you create a final movie, choose settings based on the playback limitations of the least-capable target machine.

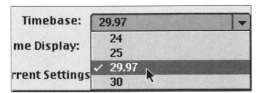

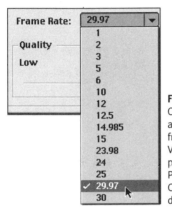

Figure 17.1 Choose the timebase of a project in the General Settings panel of the Project Settings dialog box.

Figure 17.2 Choose an appropriate frame rate in the Video Settings panel of the Project, Export, or Capture Settings dialog box.

Timebase

The *timebase* of a project determines how Premiere calculates time divisions, expressed in frames per second, or *fps* (**Figure 17.1**). The timebase shouldn't be confused with the *frame rate*—the rate at which the program displays frames. The timebase is derived from the following film and video standards:

◆ 24 fps for film.

◆ 25 fps for PAL and SECAM video (standards common in most countries outside North America).

◆ 29.97 fps for NTSC video (the standard in North America, Central America, Japan, and other countries).

◆ 30 fps for other video types.

If you're using standard video in North America, choose 29.97 as the timebase. Set the correct timebase before you start editing, and don't change it. Changing the timebase in the middle of a project affects Premiere's time calculations, causing existing edit marks and markers to shift, and changing the durations of clips.

Frame Rate

Frame rate refers to both the number of frames per second contained in a source clip and to the number of frames per second displayed by the program or exported movie. The frame rate of source video is determined when it is recorded or rendered. You determine the frame rate of a program in the Project Settings and the frame rate of an exported movie in the Export Settings (**Figure 17.2**).

Regardless of a source clip's frame rate, it is displayed in the program and timeline at the frame rate determined by the Project Settings. A 15-fps source, however, does not play back more smoothly at 30 fps; each frame of the source is simply displayed twice. Similarly, a 30-fps source in a program set for 15 fps displays only every other frame in Program view and in the timeline.

Whenever possible, you should make sure that the timebase, source frame rate, and project frame rate agree. If you choose to preview or export a movie at a lower frame rate, choose an even division of the full frame rate. A rate of 29.97 fps or 30 fps, for example, is considered to be full-motion for NTSC video. Choose 15 fps or 10 fps when you want to use a lower frame rate. Choosing a different frame rate does not affect the speed of the clip—only how smoothly (or choppily) it plays back.

Timecode

Timecode is a method of counting video frames, developed by the Society of Motion Picture and Television Engineers (SMPTE). SMPTE timecode is counted in hours, minutes, seconds, and frames. It counts 30 frames per second, up to one day.

The advantage of timecode is that it provides an *absolute address* for each frame of video—that is, each frame has a unique and unchanging number. The number acts as an address, or identity. Just as a street address helps you find a specific place, timecode helps you find a specific frame.

Timecode makes offline/online editing possible. By keeping track of timecode numbers (and the reel that they're on), you can easily re-create an offline edit.

Without timecode, frames can be counted sequentially, but they cannot be identified specifically. Without timecode, you have no way to accurately refer to a frame of video—and consequently, you have no way to create an EDL (see Chapter 14), or recapture a particular clip (see Chapter 16).

Figure 17.3 Every hour of real-time, non-drop-frame timecode has counted an extra 3 seconds and 18 frames.

Figure 17.4 Drop-frame timecode skips two frame numbers at the end of every minute, except for every 10th minute.

Consumer video equipment does not read or record timecode. Even if you are using a timecode display in your project, timecode isn't necessarily present in the source clip or the source tape.

Although the timebase of NTSC video is a constant 29.97 fps, SMPTE timecode counts it in two different ways: drop frame and non-drop frame.

Non-Drop-Frame Timecode. Even though the true timebase of NTSC video is 29.97, *non-drop-frame* (NDF) timecode counts 30 fps. Over time, however, the discrepancy results in a small but significant difference between the duration indicated by the timecode and the actual elapsed time (**Figure 17.3**). Nevertheless, NDF timecode is easy to understand and is usually used for source tapes. Video equipment displays NDF timecode with colons between the numbers.

Drop-Frame Timecode. To compensate for the discrepancy caused by the 30-fps counting scheme, SMPTE developed *drop-frame timecode* (DF). Drop-frame timecode also counts 30 fps, but it skips two frame numbers (not actual video frames) at the end of every minute, except for every 10th minute (**Figure 17.4**).

As confusing as this sounds, DF timecode displays durations that very closely match actual time. Premiere and other video equipment display drop-frame timecode with semicolons between numbers.

Time Displays

In the Monitor and Clip windows, you can choose among several time displays (**Figure 17.5**). Choose the time display that is best suited for your project. Your options are:

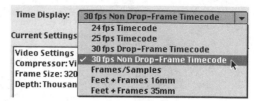

Figure 17.5 You can choose among different time displays for the source or program at any time.

◆ **24-fps timecode,** which counts for standard film frame rates.

◆ **25-fps timecode,** which counts for PAL and SECAM (common standards in most countries outside North America).

◆ **30-fps drop-frame (DF) timecode,** which counts for NTSC video (the standard in North America, Japan, and other countries) in drop-frame format. It displays with semicolons between numbers.

◆ **30-fps non-drop-frame (NDF) time-code,** which counts for NTSC video (the standard in North America, Japan, and other countries) in non-drop-frame format. It displays with colons between numbers.

◆ **Frames/Samples,** which counts video frames and audio samples.

◆ **Feet/Frames 16mm,** which counts for 16mm motion-picture film, which has 40 frames per foot.

◆ **Feet/Frames 35mm,** which counts for 35mm motion-picture film, which has 16 frames per foot.

The time display is a counting system and doesn't affect the timebase or frame rate, so you can change the time display at any time. The display represents a clip's timecode if it is present in the source or stamped manually (see Chapter 15). If no timecode is present, the display merely starts counting from zero.

Usually, 30-fps NDF timecode is a good choice, especially for sources. If the precise duration is crucial, use 30-fps DF timecode.

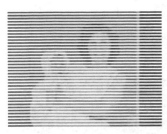

Figure 17.6
Interlaced displays present a single field that includes every other line of the image...

Figure 17.7 ...and then interlaces the opposite field to create a full frame.

Figure 17.8 Choose the correct field dominance in the Keyframe and Rendering Options panel of the Project, Export, or Capture Settings dialog box.

Interlaced and Noninterlaced Video

One important difference between television and computers lies in how they display frames of video. Television monitors display interlaced video, whereas computer monitors use a progressive scan.

In a *progressive scan*, the horizontal lines of each frame are displayed from the top of the screen to the bottom, in a single pass.

Interlaced video divides each frame into two fields. Each field includes every other horizontal line (*scan line*) in the frame. A television displays one field first, drawing alternating scan lines from the top of the image to the bottom (**Figure 17.6**). Returning to the top, it then displays the alternate field, filling in the gaps to complete the frame (**Figure 17.7**). In NTSC video, each frame displays approximately 1/30 of a second; each field displays every 1/60 of a second.

Field Dominance. The field that contains the topmost scan line is called *field 1*, the *odd field*, or the *upper field*. The other field is known as *field 2*, the *even field*, or the *lower field*. Your video equipment and the settings that you choose determine which field is the *dominant field*—the field that is displayed first (**Figure 17.8**).

Disagreement between the field dominance of a video playback device and a recording device can cause movement in the frame to appear staggered in the recorded image. Field dominance is reversed when you apply the Backwards Video filter to a clip.

Interlaced Video. You can display interlaced video on a progressive scan monitor, and vice versa. You should take into account the differences between the two displays, however, and process your clips accordingly.

CHOOSING SETTINGS

313

Only capture cards designed to work with NTSC video digitize and export interlaced video fields. Similarly, some software programs (many animation programs, for example) support *field rendering*—the capability to interlace noninterlaced source material. When you play back or export interlaced video, make sure that the field dominance you use matches the one used by your capture equipment or the target system.

If you intend to display interlaced video on a progressive-scan monitor, you should deinterlace it. *Deinterlacing* converts two fields into a single frame, either by duplicating one field or blending the two.

You should also deinterlace video when you apply a slow-motion or freeze-frame effect. When there is motion in the frame, each field captures a slightly different image. The difference becomes apparent when you freeze a frame or slow playback (**Figures 17.9** and **17.10**).

Conversely, certain graphic elements that look good on a progressive-scan monitor display poorly on a interlaced monitor. Due to interlacing, thin horizontal lines appear to flicker. Avoid using light typefaces, thin lines, and tight patterns in images that are destined for television.

The movement in a clip may appear to be stuttered if the field dominance of a clip is opposite that of your capture card or if you apply the Backwards Video filter to a clip. When this situation occurs, reverse the field dominance of the clip by selecting the clip and choosing Clip > Video > Field Options (**Figure 17.11**).

The Field Options command can process the fields of source clips. You can deinterlace your exported movie in by using the special processing options in Video Settings panel of the Project, Export, or Capture Settings dialog box.

Figure 17.9 When the subject is moving, each field captures a slightly different image, as this still frame reveals.

Figure 17.10 Deinterlacing the frame (in this case, by duplicating the lower field and eliminating the upper field) creates a more coherent image.

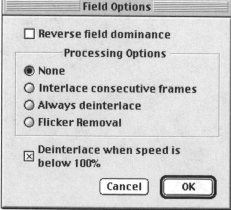

Figure 17.11 Use the Field Options command to process the fields of a clip in the timeline.

CHOOSING SETTINGS

Figure 17.12 Enter the appropriate frame size in the Video settings panel of the Project, Export, or Capture Settings dialog box.

Frame Size

Frame size refers to the number of pixels used to describe the video image. The number of pixels that equal full-screen video depends on the standard used by your capture or playback device. The most common frame sizes for full-screen video are as follows:

- ◆ **640x480:** full-screen square pixels (used for computer presentation and by some capture cards).

- ◆ **720x486:** nonsquare pixels, D-1 resolution (the standard for professional video).

- ◆ **720x480:** nonsquare pixels (DV-format video).

- ◆ **720x576:** PAL video standard.

When you use frame sizes smaller than full-screen video, choose an even fraction of the full-screen pixel size (**Figure 17.12**), such as 640x480, 320x240, 240x180, or 160x120. Uneven fractions of frame sizes are more difficult for the computer to process.

✔ Tip

- ■ In video, it's common to refer to frame size as *resolution*. The term *resolution*, however, has a slightly different meaning for video than it does for print media. Although the number of pixels in full-screen video can differ, you can think of the display size as being fixed—it's full-screen, regardless of the size of the television screen. People who are accustomed to print media are often disappointed to learn that standard-definition video always translates to a mere 72 dpi.

Aspect Ratio. *Aspect ratio* refers to the dimensions of the video frame, expressed as a ratio between the width and the height (horizontal and vertical *aspects*). Most video uses a 4:3 aspect ratio, but with the advent of new video standards, the 16:9 aspect ratio is becoming more common.

Although video frame-size formats may differ, they maintain the same 4:3 aspect ratio. A 640x480 frame size, for example, uses square pixels to form an image with a 4:3 aspect ratio (**Figure 17.13**). A 720x486 frame size (D-1 resolution) uses nonsquare pixels to achieve the same 4:3 ratio (**Figure 17.14**). The image aspect ratios are the same; the *pixel aspect ratios* are different.

Aspect Ratio, Frame Size, and Distortion. When the aspect ratio of a source clip doesn't match the aspect ratio of the program, you can maintain the original aspect ratio of the source or change it to conform to the aspect ratio of the program. As discussed in Chapter 3, changing the aspect ratio of the source results in a distorted image.

Image distortion also occurs when a source clip uses a different pixel aspect ratio from the one used by your display monitor. An animation rendered at D-1 resolution (720x486 nonsquare pixels), for example, appears distorted when you display it on a typical computer monitor, which displays square pixels (**Figure 17.15**). Conversely, a 640x480 image appears distorted when it is displayed at D-1 resolution, which uses nonsquare pixels. Some programs and software codecs (see "Codecs" later in this chapter) automatically correct for this type of distortion. Otherwise, you have to correct it by resizing the image. Better yet, prevent the problem by using a consistent image aspect ratio and pixel aspect ratio.

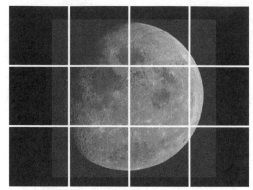

Figure 17.13 A 4:3 aspect ratio using square pixels.

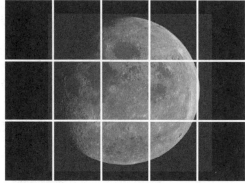

Figure 17.14 A 4:3 aspect ratio using nonsquare pixels.

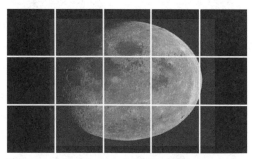

Figure 17.15 An image created with nonsquare pixels appears distorted when displayed with square pixels.

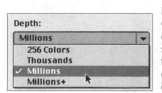

Figure 17.16 Choose a pixel bit depth in the Video settings panel of the Project, Export, or Capture Settings dialog box.

Figure 17.17 In the Video settings, click the Palette button to use or create a color palette.

Bit Depth

Computers store information in bits. *Bit depth* indicates the number of bits used to describe a single pixel. A higher bit depth produces more colors in an image and, consequently, higher picture quality. The RGB color format assigns 8 bits for each color channel—red, green, and blue—for 24-bit color. A 24-bit image contains millions of colors. If an alpha channel is present, it also uses 8 bits, for a total of 32 bits—often referred to as Millions of Colors +. Regardless of the bit depth of the source clips, Premiere always uses 32 bits to process video.

You can choose the image bit depth in the Video Settings panel of the Project, Export, or Capture Settings dialog box (**Figure 17.16**). Depending on the codec you use, you can choose any (or none) of the following bit depths:

◆ **256** (also known as 8-bit color), which produces a grainy appearance.

◆ **Thousands** (16-bit color), which is suitable for some multimedia.

◆ **Millions** (24-bit color), which produces the best image quality.

◆ **Millions+** (32-bit color), which preserves the alpha channel.

◆ **Palette.** Some older displays use a more limited bit depth, restricting the number of colors that it can display. To get the most from a limited number of colors, you can use a custom palette. You can create or use a palette that contains only the colors that appear most in the image by clicking the Palette button in the Video Settings panel of the Project or Export dialog box (**Figure 17.17**).

CHOOSING SETTINGS

Compression

Simply put, *compression* is the science of storing large amounts of data in small packages. Without compression, digital video would be impractical for all but the most powerful computer systems. A single uncompressed frame of full-screen video consumes nearly 1MB of storage. Capturing and playing back 30 uncompressed frames per second is beyond the capability of most drives and processors; the data rate is simply too high.

Fortunately, various compression schemes have been devised to reduce the file size and data rates of digital video and audio.

Codecs. *Codec* stands for *compressor/decompressor*. *Compressor* refers to encoding a file, and is synonymous with capture and rendering. *Decompressor* refers to decoding a file and is associated with playback. *Codec* denotes a particular *compression scheme*—a method of compressing and decompressing a file.

In general, you have a choice of software and hardware codecs. QuickTime and Video for Windows include several software-based codecs; others are available as software plug-ins (**Figure 17.18**).

For most high-quality video capture and playback, however, you need a hardware-assisted codec. If your hardware capture card and its software are installed properly, its codec appears in the Compressor menu of the Video Settings.

Within each codec, you usually can control how much compression is applied by using a quality slider (**Figure 17.19**), or you can define an upper limit for the data rate (see "Data Rates" later in this chapter). You may also be able to specify whether you capture two interlaced fields, or *non-interlaced video*.

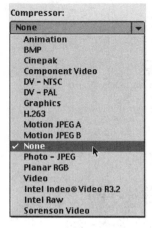

Figure 17.18 Choose one of the codecs available for your system in the Video settings.

Figure 17.19 Many codecs allow you to control the amount of compression with a quality slider.

QuickTime Video Codecs. Premiere offers the following video codecs if you choose QuickTime as your editing mode (in the Project settings) or as the file type (in the Export settings):

Animation: designed for images that contain large areas of flat color, such as cartoon animations. Lossless at its 100 percent quality setting, it's suitable for interim storage of title sequences and animations.

Cinepak: compresses 24-bit video for data rates suitable for CD-ROM playback or Internet download; can be played back on older computers.

Component Video: used for capture and as an interim storage format but not for video delivery.

DV-PAL and **DV-NTSC:** used to transfer video from a DV deck to Premiere or to transfer DV video across platforms and between computers with FireWire cards.

Graphics: intended for 8-bit images, compresses smaller than the animation codec.

H.263: used for videoconferencing at low data rates.

Video: designed for video content in thousands of colors; good for previewing edits.

Motion JPEG A and **Motion JPEG B:** used to transfer video captured with a hardware capture card.

None: serves as a pristine interim storage format, but usually are too large to be played back smoothly.

Photo-JPEG: best for still images, especially those without a lot of edges or sharp detail.

Sorenson Video: although slow to compress, yields high compression with high quality for data rates ideal for Internet download; plays back best on computers with faster processors.

Cards and Codecs

Some capture cards also offer a software-only version of the codec. Although the software codec usually can't enable you to play back the clip smoothly, it does allow you to open and process the file on computers that don't have the necessary hardware.

Codec technology changes rapidly. Visit the Web sites of codec developers to stay up to date.

Planar RGB: (a lossless codec similar to animation) best suited for images that have large areas of solid color.

Video for Windows Video Codecs. Although Video for Windows is built into Windows 95, it is no longer supported by Microsoft and is being replaced by DirectShow/ActiveMovie. The .AVI format is being replaced by .ASF (Active Streaming Format).

Premiere offers the following video codecs if you choose Video for Windows as your editing mode (in the Project settings) or Microsoft .AVI as the file type (in the Export settings):

Cinepak: compresses 24-bit video for data rates suitable for CD-ROM playback or Internet download, and for playback on older computers.

Intel Indeo 5.03: used for video distributed over the Internet for computers with fast (Pentium II) processors and designed to work with the Intel Audio Software codec.

Intel Indeo Video Interactive: similar to the Intel Indeo 5.03 codec.

Intel Indeo Video Raw R1.1: used for capturing uncompressed video with Intel video capture cards.

Intel Indeo Video R3.2: compresses 24-bit video for data rates suitable for CD-ROM playback, and comparable in quality to Cinepak.

Microsoft RLE: designed for images that contain large areas of flat color, such as cartoon animations. Lossless at its 100 percent quality setting, it's suitable for interim storage of title sequences and animations.

Microsoft Video 1: compresses analog video at 8 or 16 bits.

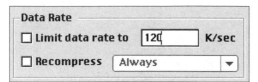

Figure 17.20 You can limit the upper data rate, according to limitations of your playback device.

Data Rates

The file size of a clip relates directly to its *data rate*—the amount of information that the computer must process each second as it plays back the clip. Most of the video and audio settings you choose influence the data rate of clips. In addition, some video codecs allow you to define the maximum data rate for the frames of the clip (**Figure 17.20**). You set a data rate according to the limitations of the playback device and the specifications of the codec.

✔ Tip

- The codec helps to determine your degree of control of the data rate, but Premiere's Data Rate Analyzer provides a powerful tool for viewing and evaluating the data rate of a clip. It's invaluable when you need to troubleshoot playback problems you may experience. See your user guide or the online help system to find out more about the Data Rate Analyzer.

Keyframes

Many codecs—especially codecs designed for low data rates —use *keyframes* to optimize compression while maintaining the highest possible image quality. Keyframes are essential to a compression technique called frame differencing

In *frame differencing*, keyframes act as reference frames, with which subsequent frames are compared. Rather than describe every frame completely, frame differencing achieves more efficient compression by describing only the changes between keyframes.

Keyframes are most effective when the image differs greatly from the preceding frame. Some codecs allow you to set the frequency of keyframes, or to insert keyframes at markers and edits in the timeline window (**Figure 17.21**). Some codecs may insert keyframes automatically when the image changes significantly. A greater number of keyframes tends to increase image quality, as well as file size. Fewer keyframes usually result in decreased file size but lower image quality.

✔ Tip

- Working with keyframes intelligently requires a strong understanding of the codec and compression, as well as a great deal of experimentation.

Audio Sample Rate

Analog signals are described by a continuous fluctuation of voltage. The analog signal is converted to a digital signal by being measured periodically, or *sampled*. If you think of the original audio as a curve, the digital audio would look like a connect-the-dots version of that curve (**Figures 17.22** and **17.23**). The more dots (or samples) you have,

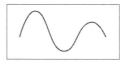

Figure 17.21 Some codecs allow you to control the frequency (and even the placement) of keyframes.

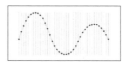

Figure 17.22 You can think of analog audio as being a continuous curve. Analog is more detailed but more difficult to copy exactly.

Figure 17.23 Sampling can closely approximate the curve. Because each sample has a defined value, digital audio can be copied exactly.

Figure 17.24 Choose a bit rate and channel options in the Format menu of the Audio settings.

the more accurately you can reproduce the original curve.

Sample rate describes the number of times audio is sampled to approximate the original analog sound. Sample rates are measured in samples per second, or *hertz* (Hz). 1000 hertz is called a *kilohertz*, or kHz. The higher the sample rate, the larger the file.

Premiere offers most standard sample rates, depending on your system. Choose the sample rate that is most appropriate for your purposes. Your options are:

◆ **48 kHz:** equivalent to DAT or Digital Betacam; not always supported by sound or video cards.

◆ **44.1 kHz:** equivalent to CD, appropriate for music.

◆ **32 kHz:** the same bit rate used by some DV cameras.

◆ **22 kHz:** a good compromise between file size and quality.

◆ **11 kHz:** adequate for narration.

◆ **8 kHz:** achieves low data rates; suitable for the Internet.

◆ **5 kHz:** achieves the lowest data rates, but the poorest quality; suitable for the Internet.

Audio Bit Depth

Audio bit depth describes the number of bits used to describe each audio sample. Bit depth affects the range of sound that the audio file can reproduce, from silence to the loudest sound. This range is known as the *signal-to-noise (s/n) ratio*, which can be measured in decibels (dB).

Premiere and many other programs express this range as bit depth and allow you to choose the one that is most appropriate for your needs (**Figure 17.24**).

(continued on next page)

Your options are:

- ◆ **8 bit:** equivalent to 48 dB; similar to FM broadcast.

- ◆ **16 bit:** equivalent to 96 dB; used by CD audio.

Stereo and Mono

You also can choose between stereophonic audio and monophonic audio. In a *stereophonic* recording, audio is mixed differently in the left channel and the right channel. When the audio is played through stereo speakers, the separate channels give the sound a sense of space. A *monophonic* recording distributes the audio evenly between the two channels, and plays back the same sounds through the left and right speakers. In Premiere, both stereo and mono audio files appear as a single clip in a track. Chapter 9 explains various ways to manipulate stereo and mono audio clips.

Audio Interleave

In the Audio Settings panel of the Project and Export Settings dialog boxes, you can specify the amount of audio interleave (**Figure 17.25**). *Audio interleave* determines how often audio information is loaded into RAM and inserted, or interleaved, among frames of video. Previous versions of Premiere referred to audio interleave as audio blocks, because blocks of audio are interleaved with blocks of video. Usually, an interleave value of one second results in smooth playback. If the audio falters during playback, however, you should adjust the interleave value. A low value needs less RAM, but requires the computer to process audio more often. A large value results in larger

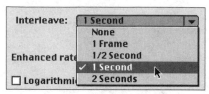

Figure 17.25 Specify the audio interleave value in the Audio Settings panel of the Project or Export Settings dialog box.

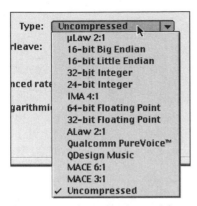

Figure 17.26 To lower file sizes and data rates, choose an audio codec in the Audio settings.

audio blocks that are processed less often, but require more RAM.

Audio Compression

If you plan to export your program to video-tape, you probably don't need to compress the audio. Audio file sizes and data rates, however, often exceed the limitations of other applications, such as CD-ROMs or Internet delivery.

Audio codecs are designed for the type of audio used in your program or clip, such as voice or music. Some codecs achieve a specific compression ratio, which is part of the codec's name (MACE 3:1, for example). Choose the codec that is best suited for your purposes (**Figure 17.26**).

QuickTime Audio Codecs. Premiere offers the following audio codecs if you choose QuickTime as your editing mode (in the Project settings) or file type (in the Export settings):

µLaw 2:1: used for digital telephony in North America and Japan; the standard audio format on some platforms, such as UNIX workstations.

16-bit Big Endian and 16-bit Little Endian: useful for hardware and software engineers to prepare processor-specific audio, but not useful for video editing.

24-bit Integer and 32-Bit Integer: useful for hardware and software engineers to prepare processor-specific audio, but not useful for video editing.

IMA 4:1: used for cross platform audio for multimedia.

32-bit Floating Point and 64-bit Floating Point: useful for hardware and software engineers to prepare processor-specific audio, but not useful for video editing.

ALaw 2:1: used primarily for digital telephony in Europe.

Qdesign Music Codec: compresses high-quality music for the Internet; capable of delivering CD-quality audio over a 28.8-Kbps connection.

Qualcomm PureVoice: designed for speech at 8 kHz.

MACE 3:1 and MACE 6:1: general-purpose audio codecs. MACE 3:1 achieves less compression and higher quality than MACE 6:1.

Video for Windows Audio Codecs. Premiere offers the following audio codecs if you choose Video for Windows as your editing mode (in the Project settings) or Microsoft .AVI as the file type (in the Export settings):

Intel Audio Software: intended to deliver music and speech over the Internet. This codec is designed to work with the Intel Video Software codec; its maximum compression ratio is 8:1.

TrueSpeech: designed for speech over the Internet at low data rates.

Microsoft GSM 6.10: used in Europe for telephony.

MS-ADPCM: a Microsoft implementation of a common format that is capable of storing CD-quality audio.

Microsoft IMA ADPCM: useful for cross-platform multimedia.

Lucent Technologies SX8300P: used for speech over the Internet at low data rates.

elemedia TM AX2400P: used for high-quality nonstreaming music files delivered over the Internet.

Voxware Audio Codecs: used for speech over the Internet at low data rates.

INDEX

Symbols and numbers
μLaw 2:1 audio codec, 325

8-bit audio, 324
8-bit color, 317
16-bit audio, 324
16-bit Big/Little Endian codecs, 325
16-bit color, 317
24-bit color, 317
24-bit Integer codec, 325
24-fps timecode, 312
25-fps timecode, 312
30-fps drop-frame (DF) timecode, 312
30-fps non-drop-frame (NDF) timecode, 312
32-bit color, 317
32-bit Floating Point codec, 325
32-bit Integer codec, 325
64-bit Floating Point codec, 325

A

A/B roll editing, 141, 142-143
Abort on dropped frames option (Capture Settings panel), 282
absolute address, 310
absolute time, 58
Accelerate motion option (Motion Settings dialog box), 247
action-safe area, 184
Add Tracks dialog box, 93
Adobe After Effects, 217
Adobe Premiere
    basics, 1-3
    commands, 42-43
    correcting mistakes in, 44
    interface, 3, 39
    keyboard shortcuts, 42
    palettes, 40-41
    starting, 6
Advanced GIF Options dialog box, 261
.AIFF file format, 24, 297
ALaw 2:1 audio codec, 325
alignment
    of objects, 209
    Snap to Edges feature for, 111-112
    of transitions, 142-143
alpha channel, 231, 232
Alpha Channel key, 231
    motion settings options, 249-250
animated GIFs
    advanced settings for, 261-262
    exporting, 262
animation
    of transition icons, 138
    video codec for, 319
anti-aliasing, 230

Anti-Aliasing button (Transition Settings dialog box), 148
Apply button (Monitor window), 66
archived projects, opening, 17
.ASF file format, 320
aspect ratios, 184, 316
    locking, 27
    pixel, 316
asterisk (*) key, 62
attributes
    setting for objects, 189
    of text objects, 194-197
audio
    bit depth, 11, 323-324
    capturing, 281, 297-298
    clips, 54-55
    codecs, 325-326
    digitization process, 275
    file formats for exporting, 254
    filters, 12, 170-172
    guidelines for choosing settings, 308
    hardware-specific capture settings, 283
    importing tracks into projects, 24-25
    interleave, 11, 324
    mixing, 159-169
    monophonic, 11, 324
    previewing, 155
    processing order and methods, 172
    ratio of tracks displayed, 91
    sample rate, 11, 172, 322-323
    settings, 11, 14, 308
    source and target tracks for, 78
    stereophonic, 11, 324
    waveform, 54-55
Audio Capture window, 298
Audio Conversion Options dialog box, 24
Audio Filters dialog box, 170
Audio Recorder window, 297
audio sweetening, 159
audio tones, 37
Auto Save feature, 17
Auto/Save Undo dialog box, 17
Auto-Record option, 287
.AVI file format, 255, 320

B

background clips
    removing, 188
    using with titles, 187-188
background color, 185
banding, 261
batch capture, 278, 293-294
Batch Capture window, 289
Batch List window, 293, 304
batch lists, 288-292
    attaching/removing settings, 292
    changing items on, 291

batch lists, *continued*
 copying items between, 291
 creating from projects or bins, 303-304
 deleting items from, 291
 generating manually, 289-290
 generating with device control, 288-289
 steps in batch-capture process, 293-294
 trimmed, 301-302
Bin window, 3
 adding clips to the program from, 80
 customizing, 31-34
bins
 batch lists from, 303-304
 creating, 29
bit depth
 audio, 11, 323-324
 video, 9, 317
Black Alpha Matte key, 232
Blend slider (Transparency Settings dialog box), 229
Block Select tool, 117, 152
block-copy function, 117
Blue Screen key, 230
Blur option, 259
Border slider (Transition Settings dialog box), 148
breaking links, 134
burned-in timecode, 295

C

Cancel Edit option, 85
capture, 275-298
 analog audio, 297-298
 batch, 278, 288-294
 device control, 277, 284, 285-287, 288-289
 preparation for, 276
 scratch disk for, 279
 settings, 280-283
 timecode reference, 278, 295-296
Capture Limit option (Capture Settings panel), 282
Capture Settings panel (Project Settings dialog box), 280-281, 282, 285
Channel Map transition, 150
Chroma key, 229
chrominance keys, 229-230
Cinepak compression, 259, 319, 320
clear objects, 214
Clip Capture Parameters window, 289-290
Clip Duration dialog box, 52
Clip Properties window, 73
Clip Timecode dialog box, 295
clips, 5, 45-73
 adding to projects, 51
 adding to the timeline, 76, 79-81, 82-87
 aligning with Snap to Edges feature, 111-112
 audio, 54-55
 background, 187-188
 batch-capturing, 293-294
 copying/pasting, 35
 cueing views, 58-59
 deleting, 35, 104
 display options, 31-34

distorting, 246
enabling/disabling, 105
filters added to, 174-175
finding, 36
frame-by-frame movement of, 108
head and tail of, 121
importing into projects, 22-23, 28
Info palette and, 72
in and out points for, 65-67, 121
inserting clips between, 80
instances of, 68
linked, 107, 108, 132, 133, 134
locking/unlocking, 106
managing, 35-36
markers used with, 60-64
master, 68
Monitor window, 46-49, 56-57
motion settings applied to, 237-252
moving, 35, 108-110
multiple, 22-25, 81, 103
opening, 51, 99
organizing, 29-30
program, 68
properties of, 73
removing, 83, 104, 300
renaming, 35, 36
replacing references to, 305-306
resizing, 258
restoring, 36, 135-136
rotating, 245
selecting, 35, 103
sequencing, 265
sizing, 245
sorting, 34
splitting, 113-114
still-image, 52-53
subclips and, 69-71
superimposing, 217-236
trimming, 119-136
using more than once in a program, 68
viewing, 50-51
codecs
 audio, 11, 325-326
 keyframes for optimizing, 322
 video, 9, 318-320
Collapse button (Monitor window), 48, 49, 226, 240
collapsed-track transitions, 141, 144-145
collapsing tracks, 97
color bars, 37
color gamut, 216
color picker, 216
colors
 background, 185
 banding of, 261
 bit depth for, 9, 317
 Chroma key, 229-230
 dithering, 261
 gradients for, 213
 NTSC-safe, 185
 for objects and shadows, 212
 setting with Eyedropper tool, 215

comma (,) key, 208
commands, using, 42-43
    See also names of specific commands
Commands Editor dialog box, 43
Commands palette, 42-43
    creating command buttons, 42
    deleting command buttons, 43
    loading command sets, 43
    saving command sets, 43
component video codec, 319
compositing. *See* keying
compression schemes, 9, 318
    See also codecs
compressor, 9, 318
concealing. *See* hiding
Convert dialog box, 24
copying
    block-copy function for, 117
    clips, 35, 115-117
    creating subclips by, 70
    items between batch lists, 291
    type styles for text objects, 195-196
correcting mistakes, 44
countdown, creating, 38
crawls (title), 200
    creating, 200-201
    previewing, 201
Create Bin dialog box, 29
cropping video images, 258
Cross-Fade tool, 165
cross-fading, 165
    audio linked to video, 166-167
Crystallize filter, 179
cueing
    the Edit Line, 102
    views, 58-59
current-time display (Monitor window), 56
customizing
    Icon view, 31-32
    List view, 31-32
    Premiere's interface, 39
    Thumbnail view, 31-32
    Transitions palette, 138
    Trim view, 130-131
Cutoff slider (Transparency Settings dialog box), 227,
    230
cutting and pasting clips, 115-117

D

data rate
    audio, 11
    video, 9-10, 321
Data Rate Analyzer, 321
Decelerate motion option (Motion Settings dialog
    box), 247
decibels (dB), 323
Decode burned-in timecode option (Capture Settings
    panel), 282
decompressor, 9, 318

Decrease Kerning button (Title window), 198
defaults
    durations, 27, 52-53, 146
    transitions, 146
deinterlace filter, 260
deinterlacing, 314
Delay controls (Motion Settings dialog box), 245
delay values, 245
deleting
    clips, 35, 104
    command buttons, 43
    fade handles, 162, 221
    in and out points, 67
    items from batch lists, 291
    keyframes, 242
    markers, 63-64
    tracks, 93
    See also removing
desktop, hiding/displaying, 39
device control, 277, 285-287
    capturing with, 286-287
    capturing without, 284
    enabling, 285
    generating batch lists with, 288-289
    options, 285
dialog boxes. *See* names of specific dialog boxes
Difference Matte key, 235
digital audio
    importing into projects, 24-25
    See also audio
digital nonlinear editing software, 1
digitizing process, 275-298
    analog audio capture, 297-298
    batch capture, 278, 288-294
    capture settings, 280-283
    device control, 277, 284, 285-287, 288-289
    preparation for, 27
    setting the scratch disk, 279
    timecode reference, 278, 295-296
Direct Show/Active Movie, 320
direction
    for moving titles, 201
    for tracks, 142
disabling clips, 105
Displace transition, 150
displaying
    clips, 31-34
    hidden transitions, 139
    palettes, 40
    tracks, 98
    See also viewing
distortion
    creating in clips, 246
    reasons for, 316
dithering, 261
docking palettes, 41
dominant field, 313
downsampling, 172
draft mode (Title window), 190
drag-and-drop editing, 79-81
    adding clips, 76, 79-80, 81

drag-and-drop editing, *continued*
    choosing source and target tracks, 77-78
    creating subclips with, 70
drawing space, 184
drop shadows, 211
    setting colors for, 212
drop-frame (DF) timecode, 311, 312
duration
    default, 27, 52-53, 146
    marking in and out points, 65-67
    setting for still images, 27, 52-53
    tips on specifying, 53
DV-PAL/DV-NTSC codecs, 319

E

Edge View option, 121, 122
edit decision lists (EDLs), 2
    exporting, 274
Edit Line
    cueing, 102
    splitting clips at, 114
editing
    drag-and-drop, 76, 79-81
    filters, 175
    four-point, 82, 84-85
    graphic objects, 204
    in and out points in, 65-67
    insert, 85-86
    markers used in, 60-64
    match-frame, 114
    monitor controls for, 76, 82-87
    nondestructive, 1
    nonlinear, 1
    offline, 2, 299
    online, 2, 299-306
    restoring synch, 135-136
    selecting text for, 194
    split edits, 132
    three-point, 76, 82, 83-84
    trimming clips, 119-136
effects, previewing, 153, 154-155
elemedia TM AX2400P audio codec, 326
ellipse, 202-203
Enable Special Timings option, 201
enabling
    clips, 105
    device control, 285
Enhanced Rate Conversion, 172
expanded-track transitions, 141, 142-143
expanding tracks, 97
Export Movie Settings dialog box, 255-256
    filmstrip options, 270
    Special Processing panel, 257
    still-image-sequence options, 267
Export Still Frame Settings dialog box, 272-273
exporting
    edit decision lists, 274
    file formats used for, 254
    filmstrip files, 270-271

GIF sequences and animated GIFs, 261-262
QuickTime Fast Start movies, 266
single video frame, 272-273
still-image sequences, 267-268
video files, 255-256
See also importing
Extract button (Monitor window), 83
Eyedropper tool, 188, 215, 248

F

Fade Adjustment tool, 221-222
fade handles
    adjacent, 164
    creating, 162
    deleting, 162, 221
    moving, 163, 221
    video, 220
fading, 162-167, 219, 220-222
    creating cross-fades, 165
    cross-fading audio linked to video, 166-167
    in increments of 1 percent, 163, 221-222
    two handles simultaneously, 164
    using video fade handles, 220
Fast Start movies, 266
Feet/Frames time display, 312
field dominance, 313
field rendering, 314
File Name dialog box, 288-289
files
    exporting, 254
    finding, 20
    missing, 20, 157-158
    offline, 19, 21
    preview, 156-158
Fill Color options, motion settings, 248
filled objects
    changing to framed objects, 206
    duplicating as framed objects, 207
    transparency settings and, 226
filmstrip files
    exporting, 270-271
    file format for, 269
filters, 173-179
    adding to clips, 174-175
    audio, 170-172
    changing the order of, 178
    editing, 175
    gamma, 260
    ignoring, 12
    image size and, 179
    keyframes and, 176-177
    removing, 175
    video, 259, 260
Filters dialog box, 174
finding
    clips, 36
    files, 20
FireWire port, 275
Fit to Fill option, 84

folders
>Goodies, 37
>Plug-Ins, 173
>Project-Archive, 17
fonts, 194
Format pull-down menu
>Clip Capture Parameters window, 290
>Clip Timecode dialog box, 295
>Sound Settings dialog box, 297
four-point editing, 82, 84-85
frame differencing, 322
frame rate, 9, 309-310
Frame Rate pull-down menu
>Clip Capture Parameters window, 290
>Clip Timecode dialog box, 295
frame size, 9, 315-316
framed objects
>changing the line weight, 205
>changing to filled objects, 206
>duplicating as filled objects, 207
frames, 53
Frames/Samples time display, 312

G

gain levels, 11, 159
>adjusting, 160
gamma filter, 260
gamut, 216
gaps between clips, 104
garbage mattes, 236
Gaussian Blur option, 259
general settings, 8
General/Still Image Preferences dialog box, 50, 53
generic EDLs, 274
GIF sequences, 261-262
>advanced settings for, 261-262
>exporting, 268
Go to Marker menu, 62
>in and out points, 67
Goodies folder, 37
Gradient Wipe transition, 150
gradients
>color, 213
>opacity, 214-215
graphic objects, 202-207
>changing the line weight, 205
>color, opacity, and gradients, 212-215
>drawing lines, 202
>drop shadows for, 211
>editing, 204
>framed vs. filled, 206-207
>polygon, 203-204
>rectangle or ellipse, 202-203
>*See also* text objects
gray finger icon, 221
grayscale images, 233
Green Screen key, 230

H

H.263 codec, 319
Hand tool, 101, 226
handles, 302
>fade, 162-164, 220, 221
>pan, 169
hardware-specific capture settings, 283
headings, rearranging, 34
Heads and Tails view, 90
Help system, Quickhelp, 42
hertz (Hz), 323
hiding
>the desktop, 39
>palettes, 40
>tracks, 98
>transitions, 139
high-contrast grayscale image, 233

I

Icon view
>arranging clips in, 81
>customizing, 31-32
>selecting options, 32
>track format and, 90
icons
>gray finger, 221
>pointing finger, 241
>selecting size of, 90
>Take Audio/Video, 78, 83
>transition, 138
identification titles, 209
IEEE-1394 port, 275
iLink port, 275
Illustrator files, 26
IMA 4:1 codec, 325
Image Mask transition, 150
Image Matte key, 233-234
Image Pan filter, 179
image quality, 9
image size
>for filters, 179
>for icons, 90
images
>cropping in videos, 258
>distortion of, 316
>importing into projects, 26-28
>*See also* still images
Import File dialog box, 22
Import Multiple dialog box, 22
importing
>clips into projects, 22-23
>color bars, 37
>digital audio tracks, 24-25
>still images, 26-28
>tones, 37
>*See also* exporting
in and out points, 65-67
>deleting, 67
>going to, 66-67

in and out points, *continued*
    marking in the Monitor window, 65-66
    specifying a range with, 86-87
    terminology used for, 121
In Time box (Clip Capture Parameters window), 290
Increase Kerning button (Title window), 198
Info palette, 72, 162, 222
inserting clips, 83, 85-86
instances, 68
Intel
    audio codecs, 326
    video codecs, 320
interlaced video, 313-314, 318
interleave, 11, 324
interpolation options, 247

J
justifying text, 196-197

K
kerning, adjusting in titles, 198
Key Type pull-down menu (Transparency Settings dialog box), 225, 227
keyboard shortcuts, 42
keyframes, 176-177
    attributes, 244-247
    audio filters and, 170
    deleting, 242
    distorting clips, 246
    interpolation options, 247
    motion settings and, 239, 241-249
    optimizing compression with, 322
    origins of term, 176
    positioning, 243, 244-245
    removing attributes from, 246
    rotation, zoom, and delay settings, 245-246
    selecting, 242
    setting options for, 12-13
keying, 219, 223-236
    alpha-based keys, 231-232
    applying and previewing key types, 224-226
    chrominance keys, 229-230
    controls used for, 224-226
    garbage mattes for, 236
    luminance-based keys, 227-228
    matte-based keys, 233-235
kilohertz (kHz), 323

L
launching Adobe Premiere, 6
layering, 217
    track hierarchy and, 218
    virtual clips used for, 151
L-cut, 132
leading, adjusting in titles, 199
libraries, creating, 30
Library window, 30
    adding clips to the program from, 80
    customizing, 31-34
Lift button (Monitor window), 83

Limit Data Rate checkbox, 9-10
Line tool, 202
Linear motion option (Motion Settings dialog box), 247
lines (graphic)
    changing the weight of, 205
    creating, 202
Link Override tool, 133
linked clips, 107, 108
    breaking and creating links, 134
    overriding links, 108, 132, 167
    restoring synch between, 135-136
    trimming with Link Override, 133
List view
    customizing, 31-32
    rearranging headings in, 34
    selecting options in, 33-34
    sorting items in, 34
Load Project Settings dialog box, 14
loading
    command sets, 43
    motion settings, 252
    selected settings, 14
    transition sets, 140
Locate Files dialog box, 306
locking
    aspect ratios, 27
    clips, 106
    tracks, 96, 106
Logarithmic Audio Fade options, 11, 172
Looping option, 262
Lucent Technologies SX8300P audio codec, 326
Luminance key, 227
luminance-based keys, 227-228

M
MACE 3:1/6:1 codecs, 326
Macintosh platform
    analog audio capture, 297-298
    exportable formats, 254
    gamma adjustment, 260
    importing audio CD tracks, 24-25
    importing multiple clips, 22-23
    maximum size of QuickTime files, 279
    Timecode Decoder feature, 296
Make Subclip dialog box, 70
managing
    batch lists, 291
    clips, 35-36
Mark In/Out buttons (Monitor window), 65
markers, 60-64
    adding, 60-61, 62-63
    deleting, 63-64
    going to, 62-63
    making visible in the Timeline, 64
    shifting during editing, 64
    tips for using, 62
Mask Only option (Transparency Settings dialog box), 235

master clips, 68
    subclips from, 69-71
match-frame edit, 114
matte-based keys, 233-235
mattes
    creating, 234, 235
    garbage, 236
    traveling, 234
Median (blur) option, 259
Microsoft codecs
    audio, 326
    video, 320
Mirror filter, 178
missing files
    opening projects with, 20
    preview files, 157-158
mistakes, correcting, 44
mixing audio, 159-169
    adjusting gain levels, 160
    audio linked to video, 166-167
    controlling audio quality, 160
    creating cross-fades, 165-167
    fade controls, 161, 162-164
    pan controls, 161, 168-169
    stereo channels, 169
    subtractive mixing, 162
monitor controls, 82-87
    adding clips to the timeline, 76, 82-87
    choosing source and target tracks, 77-78
    removing clips from the timeline, 83
Monitor window, 3, 46-49
    controllers in, 56-57
    editing controls in, 82-87
    marking in and out points, 65-66
    modifying, 48-49
Monitor Window Options dialog box, 57, 130
monitoring tracks, 95
monophonic audio, 11, 324
Motion JPEG codecs, 319
motion path, 241
motion settings, 237-252
    adding to clips, 239
    alpha channel options, 249-250
    distorting clips, 246
    fill color option, 248
    interpolation options, 247
    loading, 252
    positioning keyframes, 244
    previewing, 240
    removing from clips, 239-240
    rotation, zoom, and delay settings, 245-246
    saving, 251
    setting keyframes, 241-243
    smooth motion option, 248-249
    for transitions, 150
    using, 238
Motion Settings dialog box, 239-240, 241, 242
motion timeline, 242
Movie Capture window, 284, 286, 288

moving
    clips, 35, 108-110
    fade handles, 163, 221
    objects, 208
    palettes, 40
Multiply key, 228
Multirazor tool, 113
Multitrack tool, 110

N

Name Only view, 90
naming
    clips, 35, 36
    tracks, 94
navigating the timeline, 100-102
Navigator palette, 100, 101, 102
Navigator window, 89
nesting virtual clips, 151
noise-reduction filter, 259
nondestructive editing, 1
non-drop-frame (NDF) timecode, 311, 312
noninterlaced video, 313-314, 318
nonlinear editing, 1
Non-Red key, 230
NTSC-safe colors, 185

O

object-oriented graphics, 181
objects, 208-209
    aligning, 209
    changing the stacking order, 210
    color, opacity, and gradients, 212-215
    drop shadows for, 211
    moving, 208
    selecting, 208
    setting attributes, 189
    transparent, 214
    See also graphic objects; text objects
offline clips, 19
offline editing, 2, 299
offline files, 19
    creating, 21
    replacing, 20, 21
online editing, 2, 299-306
    creating a trimmed project and batch list, 301-302
    manual creation of batch lists, 303-304
    removing unused clips, 300
    replacing clip references, 305-306
opacity, 185, 214
    setting gradient for, 214-215
Open File dialog box, 292
opening
    clips, 51, 54, 99
    projects, 18-20
    Transitions palette, 138
organizing clips, 29-30
out points. *See* in and out points
Out Time box (Clip Capture Parameters window), 290
out-of-gamut warning, 216

output options, 253-274
    converting QuickTime to Fast Start movies, 266
    creating clip sequences, 265
    exporting, 254, 255-256, 261-262, 267-268, 269-271, 272-273, 274
    recording videos to tape, 263-264
    special processing options, 257-260
overlaying clips, 83
overscan, 184

P

palettes, 3, 40-41
    custom, 317
    displaying/hiding, 40
    docking, 41
    moving, 40
    selecting, 9
    separating docked, 41
    See also names of specific palettes
panning, 168-169
    an audio clip, 168
    filters for, 172
    in increments of 1 percent, 168-169
    moving two pan handles simultaneously, 169
    using stereo channels, 169
Paste Custom command, 116-117
    for motion settings, 252
    for pan and fade adjustments, 161
Paste to Fit command, 115
pasting
    clips, 35, 115-117
    type styles into text objects, 195-196
Pause button (Motion Settings dialog box), 240
period (.) key, 208
Photo-JPEG codec, 319
Photoshop files, 26
pixels
    aspect ratio, 316
    height/width, 9, 22
placeholders, inserting, 19
Planar RGB codec, 320
Play button (Motion Settings dialog box), 240
playback line, 55
Plug-Ins folder, 173
pointing finger icon, 241
points, 82
    marking, 65-67
    zero point setting, 92
    See also in and out points
Polygon tool, 203
polygons
    creating, 203
    smoothing, 204
positioning keyframes, 243, 244-245
Preferences dialog box. *See* specific settings and options
Premiere. *See* Adobe Premiere
premultiplied alpha channel, 232
preroll setting, 285

preview files, 156-158
    choosing a scratch disk for, 157
    missing, 157-158
previewing
    audio, 155
    effects, 153, 154-155
    files created by, 156-158
    key types, 224-226
    motion settings, 240
    to RAM, 155
    title rolls and crawls, 201
    trimmed edits, 130
    the work area, 154
Print To Video dialog box, 263-264
printing to video, 263-264
program clips, 68
Program view (Monitor window), 46, 153
programs, 75-87
    adding clips to the timeline, 76-78, 79-81, 82-87
    adding markers to, 61
    block-copying a range in, 117
    choosing source and target tracks, 77-78
    deleting markers from, 63-64
    extracting segments from, 87
    insert editing in, 85-86
    lifting a range from, 86
    multiple use of clips in, 68
    removing clips from the timeline, 83
    restoring synch in, 135-136
    trimming, 119-136
    viewing, 100-101
progressive scan, 313
Project Settings dialog box, 280-281, 282, 285
Project Trimmer dialog box, 301-302
Project Trimmer feature, 303, 305
Project window, 3
    adding clips to the program from, 80
    customizing, 31-34
Project-Archive folder, 17
projects, 5
    archived, 17
    creating batch lists from, 303-304
    importing elements, 22-23, 24-25, 26-29, 37
    leaders for, 37-38
    opening, 17, 18-20
    organizing clips for, 29-30, 31-34
    saving, 16-17
    settings for, 7, 8, 9-10, 11, 12-13, 14, 15
    starting, 6
    titles added to, 182-183
    trimmed, 301-302
    viewing properties of clips in, 73
properties of clips, 73

Q

Qdesign Music Codec, 326
Qualcomm Pure Voice codec, 326
Quality slider, 9
Quickhelp, 42

QuickTime files
    audio codecs for, 325
    exporting video files as, 255-256
    maximum size of, 279
    video codecs for, 319-320
QuickTime movies
    converting to Fast Start movies, 266
    exporting, 255-256
QuickTime transition, 150

R

RAM, previewing effects to, 155
range
    block-copying, 117
    lifting from a program, 86
    moving in the timeline, 109
Range Select tool, 103, 104, 109, 174
Razor tool, 113
Recompress option, 10
recording to tape, 263-264
rectangles, creating, 202-203
Redo feature, 44
Reel Name dialog box, 286, 288
Re-Find command, 303
relative time, 58, 59
removing
    attributes from keyframes, 246
    audio filters, 171
    background clips, 188
    clips from the timeline, 83
    drop shadows, 211
    filters from clips, 175
    motion settings, 239-240
    settings from batch list items, 292
    unused clips, 300
    See also deleting
renaming clips, 35
    and restoring original file names, 36
rendering options, 12-13
Replace Files command, 305-306
Report Dropped Frames option (Capture Settings
    panel), 282
resampling, 172
resizing
    the bounding box for text objects, 192
    video clips, 258
    See also sizing
resolution, 315
revealing. *See* displaying
Reverse Key option (Transparency Settings dialog
    box), 234
RGB Difference key, 230
Ripple Delete command, 104
Ripple Edit tool, 123-124
ripple edits
    in the timeline, 123-124
    in Trim view, 127-128
Rolling Edit tool, 124

rolling edits
    in the timeline, 123, 124
    in Trim view, 129
Rolling Title Options dialog box, 201
Rolling Title tool, 200
rolls (title), 200
    creating, 200-201
    previewing, 201
rotating clips, 245
Rotation controls (Motion Settings dialog box), 245
rotoscoping, 269
round-cornered rectangle, 202-203

S

sample rate, 11, 172, 322-323
Sample Rate pull-down menu (Sound Settings dialog
    box), 297
Save Export Movie dialog box, 255, 256, 267
Save Export Still Frame dialog box, 272, 273
Save Generic EDL dialog box, 274
saving
    Auto Save feature for, 17
    command sets, 43
    motion settings, 251
    projects, 16-17
    properties as a text file, 73
    and reverting to last saved version, 16
    selected settings, 14
    titles, 182
    transition sets, 140
scan line, 313
scratch disk
    for digitizing process, 279
    for preview files, 156, 157
Screen key, 228
scrolling through the timeline, 101
scrubbing the time ruler, 154
Search window, 36
segments, extracting, 87
selecting
    clips, 35, 103
    keyframes, 242
    objects, 208
    palettes, 9
    text for editing, 194
Selection tool, 121, 133, 192, 193, 194
Sequence window, 265
sequencing clips, 265
settings
    guidelines for choosing, 308
    project, 7-15
Settings dialog box (Filters), 174
Settings pull-down menu, 7, 8
Settings window, 8
Shadow Offset control (Title window), 211
shadows, 211
    setting colors for, 212
shape tools, 202-203
Show Audio Waveforms checkbox (Timeline Window
    Options dialog box), 90

Show Outlines checkbox (Motion Settings dialog box), 242
Show Path checkbox (Motion Settings dialog box), 242, 247
shy tracks, 98
signal-to-noise (s/n) ratio, 160, 323
Similarity slider (Transparency Settings dialog box), 229
single-track transitions, 141, 144-145
sizing
    clips, 245
    filters, 179
    icons, 90
    text objects, 194
    transitions and overlaps, 144
    See also resizing
Skip All option, 158
Skip All Preview Files option, 158
Slash Slide transition, 149
slide edits, 125, 126
Slide tool, 126
slip edits, 125
Slip tool, 125
Smooth Motion options, 248-249
smoothing polygons, 204
Smoothing slider (Transparency Settings dialog box), 227, 230
Snap to Edges feature, 111-112
    tips for using, 112
    toggling on and off, 111
    trimming and, 122
Snap to Grid feature, 32
Society of Motion Picture and Television Engineers (SMPTE), 310
Soft Link tool, 134
soft links, 107, 134
soloing tracks, 95
Sorenson Video codec, 319
sorting
    clips, 34
    transitions, 138
Sound Settings dialog box, 297-298
source clips, adding to the timeline, 79-80
Source Count pull-down menu (Monitor Window Options dialog box), 57
source tracks, 77
    selecting, 78
Source view (Monitor window), 46
    adding markers in, 61
    drag-and-drop editing in, 79
    opening clips in, 50, 54
Source View pull-down menu, 50, 68
spatial positioning, 244
Speaker pull-down menu (Sound Settings dialog box), 298
Special Processing dialog box, 257-260
special processing options, 257-260
    accessing, 257
    cropping, 258

deinterlace filter, 260
gamma adjustment, 260
noise-reduction filter, 259
resizing, 258
special transitions, 150
split edits, 132
splitting clips, 113-114
split-window bar, 91
stacking order, 210
starting Adobe Premiere, 6
stereophonic audio, 11, 324
still images
    exportable formats for, 254
    exporting, 267-268, 272-273
    importing into projects, 26-28
    locking aspect ratios of, 27
    setting duration for, 27, 52-53
storyboard arrangement, 81
Stretch tool, 193
stretching type, 193
styles, type, 194
subclips, 69-71
    creating, 69-70
    extending the start and end of, 71
subtractive mixing, 162
superimpose tracks, 218
superimposing clips, 217-236
    fading, 219, 220-222
    keying, 219, 223-236
    track hierarchy, 218
synch, restoring, 135

T

Take Audio icon, 78, 83
Take Video icon, 78, 79, 83
target tracks, 77
    insert edits and, 85-86
    selecting, 78
text
    changing the text orientation, 197
    justifying, 196-197
    selecting for editing, 194
    setting font, style, and size, 194
text files, saving properties as, 73
text objects, 191-197
    changing text orientation in, 197
    color, opacity, and gradients, 212-215
    copying/pasting type styles into, 195-196
    creating, 191-192
    drop shadows for, 211
    font, style, and size settings, 194
    justifying text in, 196-197
    resizing the bounding box for, 192
    selecting text for editing, 194
    stretching type in, 193
    See also graphic objects
three-point editing, 76, 82, 83-84
threshold, duration, 53
Threshold slider (Transparency Settings dialog box), 227, 230

Thumbnail view
    customizing, 31-32
    selecting options in, 33
    sorting items in, 34
time count, 92
time displays, 312
time measurements, 56
time ruler
    options, 92
    scrubbing, 154
Time Unit pull-down menu, 100, 101
timebase, 309
timecode, 278, 285, 310-311
    decoder feature, 296
    drop-frame, 311
    non-drop-frame, 311
    setting manually, 295-296
timecode window dub, 295
timeline, 3, 89-117
    adding clips, 76, 79-81, 82-87
    copying and cutting clips in, 115-117
    cueing the edit line, 102
    customizing the appearance of, 90-91
    deleting clips from, 104
    enabling/disabling clips in, 105
    keyframes on, 176-177
    linking clips in, 107
    locking/unlocking clips in, 106
    making markers visible in, 64
    moving clips in, 108-110
    navigating, 100-102
    opening clips in, 99
    pasting clips in, 115-117
    removing a portion of programs from, 83
    scrolling through, 101
    selecting clips in, 103
    Snap to Edges feature, 111-112
    splitting clips in, 113-114
    time ruler options, 92
    track options, 93-98
    trimming in, 120, 121-126
    zero point setting, 92
Timeline Window Options dialog box, 64, 90
Title window, 181
    draft mode, 190
    options, 184-186
Title Window Options dialog box, 185
titles, 181-215
    adding to projects, 182-183
    background clips with, 187-188
    color, opacity, and gradients for, 212-215, 216
    creating, 182
    drop shadows for, 211
    identification, 209
    kerning adjustments for, 198
    leading adjustments for, 199
    objects as, 189, 191-197, 202-207, 208-209, 210
    opening, 183
    rolling and crawling, 200-201
    saving, 182, 183

title-safe area, 184
tones, importing, 37
Tools palette
    Block Select tool, 117, 152
    Cross-Fade tool, 165
    Eyedropper tool, 188, 215
    Hand tool, 101, 226
    Line tool, 202
    Link Override tool, 133
    Multirazor tool, 113
    Multitrack tool, 110
    Polygon tool, 203
    Range Select tool, 103, 104, 109, 174
    Razor tool, 113
    Ripple Edit tool, 123-124
    Rolling Edit tool, 124
    Rolling Title tool, 200
    Selection tool, 121, 133, 192, 193, 194
    Slide tool, 126
    Slip tool, 125
    Soft Link tool, 134
    Track tool, 109, 110
    Type tool, 191, 194
    Virtual Clip tool, 152
    Zoom tool, 100, 101, 226
Track Matte key, 234-235
Track Options dialog box, 93, 94
Track tool, 109, 110
tracks
    adding, 93
    choosing a track format, 90
    deleting, 93
    direction of, 142
    expanding and collapsing, 97
    locking/unlocking, 96
    monitoring, 95
    moving all clips in, 109, 110
    naming, 94
    ratio of video to audio, 91
    revealing/concealing, 98
    source, 77-78
    splitting clips in, 113
    superimpose, 218
    target, 77-78, 85-86
Transition Factory, 150
Transition Settings dialog box, 148
transitions, 137-158
    alignment of, 142-143
    changing the settings for, 147-149
    collapsed-track, 141, 144-145
    color, 261
    default, 146
    expanded-track, 141, 142-143
    special, 150
    track direction and, 142
    virtual clips and, 151-152
Transitions palette, 138-140
    customizing, 138
    hiding/displaying transitions in, 139
    loading transition sets in, 140

opening, 138
reordering transitions in, 139
saving transition sets in, 140
transparency
control options, 224-226
fill settings, 226
keying out image areas for, 223
luminance-based keys and, 227-228
Transparency Settings dialog box, 225
Key Type pull-down menu, 225, 227
transparent objects, 214
traveling matte, 234
Trim Source option, 84-85
Trim tool, 121
Trim view, 120, 127-131
activating/deactivating, 127
applying trimmed edits, 130
canceling trim edits, 130
customizing, 130-131
exiting, 130
previewing trimmed edits, 130
ripple edits in, 127-128
rolling edits in, 129
trimmed batch list, 301-302
trimmed project, 301-302
trimming clips, 119, 120
Link Override for, 132, 133
ripple edits, 123-124, 127-128
rolling edits, 123, 124, 129
slide edits, 125, 126
slip edits, 125
in the timeline, 120, 121-126
Trim view for, 120, 127-131
TrueSpeech audio codec, 326
type styles, 194
Type tool, 191, 194

U

Undo feature, 44
Universal Countdown Leader Setup window, 38
unlinking clips, 134
unlocking
clips, 106
tracks, 96
upsampling, 172

V

video
bit depth, 317
codecs, 318-320
cropping images, 258
cross-fading audio linked to, 166-167
data rates, 321
digitizing, 275-298
exporting video files, 255-256
fade handles for, 220
file formats for exporting, 254
filters, 12, 259, 260
frame rate, 309-310
frame size, 315-316

gamma adjustment, 260
hardware-specific settings, 283
interlaced and noninterlaced, 313-314, 318
keyframes, 12-13, 322
ratio of tracks displayed, 91
recording to tape, 263-264
rendering options, 12-13
resizing clips, 258
settings, 9-10, 14, 308
single frames, 272-273
source and target tracks for, 78
time displays, 312
timebase, 309
timecode, 310-311
video capture cards, 275
Video for Windows
audio codecs, 326
video codecs, 320
viewing
clips, 50-51
keyboard shortcuts, 42
properties of clips, 73
See also displaying; previewing
views
changing, 31
cueing, 58-59
customizing, 31-32
Monitor window, 46, 48-49
selecting view options, 32-34
Virtual Clip tool, 152
virtual clips, 151-152
Visible Area box (Motion Settings dialog box), 241
Volume slider (Sound Settings dialog box), 298
Voxware Audio Codecs, 326

W

.WAV file format, 297
waveform, 54-55
Waveform button, 54
White Alpha Matte key, 232
windows (desktop)
displaying/hiding, 40
separate, for clips, 50-51, 54, 79-80
See also names of specific windows
Windows platform
exportable formats, 254
gamma adjustment for, 260
importing multiple clips in, 23
maximum size of QuickTime files on, 279
video codecs, 320
work-area band, 154
work-area bar, 154

Z

zero point, 92
Zoom controls (Motion Settings dialog box), 245, 246
Zoom Screen option (Print To Video dialog box), 264
Zoom tool, 100, 101, 226